GET 'EM ALL! KILL 'EM!

GET 'EM ALL!
KILL 'EM!

Genocide, Terrorism, Righteous Communities

Bruce Wilshire

LEXINGTON BOOKS

A division of
Rowman & Littlefield Publishers, Inc.

Lanham • Boulder • New York • Toronto • Oxford

LEXINGTON BOOKS

A division of Rowman & Littlefield Publishers, Inc.
A wholly owned subsidiary of The Rowman & Littlefield Publishing Group, Inc.
4501 Forbes Boulevard, Suite 200
Lanham, MD 20706

PO Box 317
Oxford
OX2 9RU, UK

British Library Cataloguing in Publication Information Available

The hardcover edition was previously catalogued by the Library of Congress as follows:

Wilshire, Bruce W.
    Get 'em all! kill 'em! : genocide, terrorism, righteous communities / Bruce Wilshire.
        p. cm.
    Includes bibliographical references and index.
    ISBN: 0-7391-0873-5 (cloth : alk. paper)
    1. Genocide. 2. Genocide—History—20th century. 3. Genocide—Prevention.
4. Terrorism.
I. Title. II. Title: Get them all! kill them!.
HV6322.7.W55 2005
304.6'63—dc22   2004016986

Printed in the United States of America

∞™ The paper used in this publication meets the minimum requirements of
American National Standard for Information Sciences—Permanence of Paper
for Printed Library Materials, ANSI/NISO Z39.48–1992.

There is nothing more fantastic than reality itself.

—F. M. Dostoyevsky

It was no man that you wanted, believe me, you wanted a world.

—Friedrich Hölderlin

Once you make contact [with the remote tribes], you begin the process of destroying their universe.

—Sydney Possuelo

CONTENTS

FOREWORD

To think about genocide and terrorism is to accept an invitation from hell. In fact, hell may be too tame a term, for that word makes a kind of sense. At least it does within a view of the world in which a supreme Master prepares a place of punishment for those who disobey Him.

But what sense does it make to kill or disable all members of an other group just because they are that other group: men, women, children? That group needn't be belligerent, just other. What sense can we make of genocide? The very meaning of "sense" threatens to disintegrate.

Well over a century ago, R. W. Emerson experienced this sudden unraveling of mind, this falling into the nonsensical or the unthinkable. In his essay, "History," he claims that we do understand the past, and that we do so because we identify with those who created past events. We share their motivations: to escape oppression, to achieve and be glorified, to eat and sleep, to make merry, to exact revenge, to understand, etc. He feels at home in the centers of Western civilization: Athens, Rome, Constantinople, Paris, from which centers we inherit the very idea of understanding, of finding reasons, of making sense.

Then in the last page of the essay, a terrible second thought stops him in his tracks. It's as if an evil wind strikes him in the face.

Is there somewhat overweening in this claim? Then I reject all I have written, for what is the use of pretending to know what we know not? But it is the fault of our rhetoric that we cannot strongly state one fact without seeming to be-lie some other. I hold our actual knowledge very cheap. Hear the rats in the wall, see the lizard on the fence. . . . As old as Caucasian man—perhaps older—these creatures have kept their counsel beside him, and there is no record of any word or sign that has passed from one to the other. . . . What a shallow village tale our so-called History is. How many times we must say Rome and Paris and Constantinople? What does Rome know of rat and lizard? What are Olympiads and Consulates to these neighboring systems of being?

Emerson confronts an hitherto unsuspected vista. He sees that our in-herited idea of making sense, of understanding, is undermined, is not fun-damental. That we are not enclosed and at home in "the family of man," but that we are neighbors to, in fact kin to, the rats in the wall, the lizard on the fence, primitive forms of scurrying, anxious life.

New sense must be made of "sense" itself. If we would grasp what hu-mans sometimes do, we must grasp how anxiety ridden we are in our being. In other words: that all the ideas, symbols of civilization, understandings, imaginings that do distinguish us, rest upon and conceal a primitive level of common or shared life that we ourselves hardly dare to imagine. It is there, we sometimes glimpse, but not hardly thinkable.

As we will uncover, the deepest root of the genocidal urge appears to be disgust and dread in the face of abounding, fecund, life itself—swarming, creeping, scurrying, unboundable, uncontrollable. If this is so, genocide and terrorism are the ultimate anti-ecology. It is this tremulous hell that in-vites us in. The incentive to enter? The excitement of adventure and the de-sire to survive.

ACKNOWLEDGMENTS

This book has exacted much of the last five years of my life, and owes—extraordinarily—to stimulation from others. My wife of forty-five years, Donna, provides an ever-present matrix that seeds and nourishes ideas. The threat of his immanent death to which Glen Mazis responded in such an exemplary way goaded me into reflection. Merrill Skaggs soldiered through an earlier draft and helped in many ways, one of which was coaching me in modulating scatological aspects of my pollution theory of genocide so that it would be more acceptable to the general reader. A very busy Edward Casey somehow always finds time to help with my work—a seemingly inexplicable gift. Likewise, Calvin Schrag's lengthy, sage comments on this manuscript helped in times of my bafflement and discouragement. Perceptive comments from our son and daughter-in-law, Gilbert and Regina, prompted the foreword. They also suggested an afterword that would point the relevance of this book to explaining the American humiliation and degradation of Iraqi prisoners, but I've concluded that our stress-born actions, ignorance, and hauteur are disgustingly and alarmingly clear enough.

I thank these publishers for permission to quote from the following works: *The Terrible But Unfinished Story of Norodom Sihanouk, King of Cambodia*, by Hélène Cixous, translated by Juliet Flower MacCannell, Judith Pike, and Lollie Groth, reprinted by permission of the University of Nebraska Press. Copyright © 1994 by the University of Nebraska Press. Copyright © Théâtre du Soleil 1985, Tours; "Brief Excerpts," from *Nausea*, by Jean-Paul Sartre, translated by Lloyd Alexander, copyright © 1964 by New Directions Publishing Corp. Used by permission of New Directions Publishing Corporation; pages 256, 257, and 268 from *War and Peace* by Leo Tolstoy, edited and translated by Louise & Aylmer Maude. Copyright © 1991. By permission of Oxford University Press.

INTRODUCTION

Happy shall he be, that taketh, that dasheth thy little ones against the stones.

—Psalm 137

On top of Solomon's Temple, to which they had climbed in fleeing, many were shot to death with arrows and cast down headlong from the roof. Within the Temple about ten thousand were beheaded. If you had been there, your feet would have been stained up to the ankles with the blood of the slain. What more shall I tell? Not one of them was allowed to live. They did not spare the women and children.

—Fulcher of Chartres on the First Christian Crusade to Jerusalem, 1099

Both genocide and conventional warfare are acts of aggression committed by groups against groups. But in conventional warfare, the objective is typically gained when one group disables the other's armed forces. Genocide must be sharply distinguished from war in the usual sense. For its objective is to destroy or disable all members of an alien group—even sometimes fetuses have been dug out of newly dead pregnant women and destroyed.

Now why? A clue lies in the fact that *all* members of the alien group must be killed or disabled. There is something about that group as such and as a whole that is absolutely repugnant to the home group. Their alien way of being in the world is inassimilable, choking. This focuses on how groups constitute or "construct" a meaningful world for themselves through their ingrained rites, customs, interpretations, perceptual stances, attitudes and beliefs.

In other words, a group's habitual and unquestioned ways of experiencing things form for it a world in their experience. It is typically unquestioned because that "is just the way things are." Though it is a bit awkward to put it this way, let us call it the group's world-experienced. For most members of the group, it is equivalent to the world itself.

Could it be that in eruptive times of shock and stress for the home group the possibility of questioning their world-experienced gapes open for them? An alien group and its members constitute a world-experienced that the home group dimly but profoundly suspects might upset their own? On a level of awareness not easily thought or spoken—the possibility is only a churning in the stomach—the home group feels psycho-physical earthquake and terror? Since every member of the alien group carries the bacillus of the alien world-experienced, the siren call of genocide sounds: Get 'em all, kill 'em. I will develop this clue.

*   *   *

The radical excesses and apparent irrationalities of genocide call out for a radical hypothesis to explain them. Revealingly, genocide has often been called unthinkable. We shouldn't limit the meaning of unthinkable to the morally out of bounds or outrageous only, but take it also in the most literal sense. That is, we who look on and who share the basic assumptions of the group to be genocided cannot think the genocide, cannot find reasons for it. What possible reasons could there be for killing or disabling all the alien persons—women, children, fetuses, doddering old men?

We know that genocide happens all right, but it's as if it happens outside the world. That is, outside the world as we are able to "construct" it, think it. Outside the world as we are able to grasp the very meaning of world and of what happens in it, that is, outside the domain for which we can find reasons—outside our own world-experienced. Genocide happens in a nightmare of non-sense.

When events appear to be unthinkable, they don't clearly appear to be occurring in the world at all. They are "impossible." Yet, in shock, if we attain an instant's reflection, we can't deny that they are occurring. They occur in a glittering and hellishly lit netherworld.

We hold the clue fast. All members of the alien group must be killed or incapacitated because each carries the germ of the alien world-experienced: each threatens to poison and undermine the only world in which the home group has learned to live. They are the rats in the wall.

The clue suggests that the genociding home group is as terrorized in its own way as the group to be genocided is in its. To avoid the hellish world in which no reasons can be found for anything—to avoid an experienced world turned to chaos, to diarrhea—all the aliens must be killed or incapacitated. That is the reason for genocide.

*   *   *

This book develops this clue and tries to confirm it. We will focus on five cases of genocidal activity: Nazis' in Europe, Serbs' in Bosnia, Pol Pot's group's in Cambodia, Hutus' in Rwanda, whites' in California. In each case we see how weirdly excessive the activity was, and how radical the hypothesis must be that would try to explain it.

We have referred to the key fact that all those others must be killed or incapacitated. We will also note the explosiveness and suddenness of genocidal activity. For example, tens of thousands of "ordinary" Germans were enlisted emotionally through Hitler's mass rallies in a single day; practically overnight Serbs in Bosnia turned against their Muslim neighbors with whom they had lived peaceably for generations; in the batting of an eye, over a million of the "corrupt city dwellers" of the Cambodian capital were emptied out into the forests and jungles by Pol Pot's genociders (or tortured to death in the city's prisons); California saw irruptive holidays in which "Digger" Indians were hunted down and shot for sport.

It's as if a group's whole "mental set" would suddenly shift, as if a particle were to be dropped into a supersaturated solution and a crystal lattice abruptly formed. But I will not speak of "mental set," for that suggests a division of mind from body. Needed to explain outbursts of genocidal activity is a unified view of minding bodies caught up mimetically and hysterically in the twists and turns of the corporate body, the group.

Seldom if ever is there a single reason why anything happens. Things that actually get done, either by individuals or groups, get done for a number of reasons: they are overdetermined. So conventional reasons drawn from the conventional social sciences may throw some light on genocide—I mean economics, history, political science, demography, for example. Much contributes to a genocidal eruption. (See Momdani, Sources, on the political background of the genocide of Tutsis by Hutus in Rwanda; for globalization's politico-economic inequities inciting genocide, see Chua.)

But almost inevitably the strange excesses of genocide create problems for the conventional social sciences. This is understandable, since before these sciences begin their specialized inquiries they take the everyday

workaday world-experienced for granted. This is a world of relative calm
and detachment in which reasons for events are sought, in which events are
construed as effects of causes.

But it is precisely this relative calm and detachment that goes out the win-
dow in genocidal rampages. If Pol Pot, for example, had been thinking along
the lines of conventional economics, say, he would not have exterminated
the scientifically and technologically educated urbanites of Phnom Penh. He
had spent years in France. How could Cambodia compete in a highly tech-
nologized world without these people? What could he have been thinking?

I hypothesize that he was not thinking at all in any of the conventional
senses of thinking. I believe that he was erupting in terror and rage. I hypothesize that the causes of genocide reach sufficiency when the everyday culture's
world-experienced gives way beneath its leaders' and its members' feet.

Since the conventional social sciences take the everyday world of reasons
and of causes and effects for granted, they are in no position to explain what
happens when this world itself is threatened and falls apart. From the point
of view of these sciences, I am exploring an "X factor."

I propose to explore systematically a prereflective domain of terror and
hysteria. It's not as if nobody had ever before suggested my hypothesis. In
Group Psychology and Analysis of the Ego, Sigmund Freud writes that a
group is extraordinarily credulous and open to influence; Stanley Milgram
experimented famously on how susceptible people are to influence by authorities, even when they are instructed to act against their own affections
and contrary to their own moral principles (see sources); Dr. Robert Jay
Lifton conducted extensive psychiatric-like interviews with Nazi medical
doctors and disclosed that they behaved like clay in the hands of the group's
leaders (see sources and chapter 2 below). Lifton even suggests that the
Nazi corporate body, the Volkskörper, believed itself to be infected by alien
elements, "germs." I think that this is fundamentally true and important.

But in none of these important thinkers have the conceptual problems
of genocide been worked out systematically: for example, the task of explaining just how the identity of the individual is enmeshed with the identity of the group. Or, more specifically, of explaining how the perceptual
life of individual members is tied into the perceptual life of the stratified—
and at times precariously balanced—corporate body. What is required is a
phenomenology of we members' prereflective and highly emotional immediate engagement in the group's world-experienced. Indeed, the difficult question must be clearly posed and pursued: How is a culture's world-
experienced built up over time through consensual validation by its
members and leaders?

*   *   *

Yes, we are after an "X factor." We are after a reason for activity that erupts when ordinary reasons fail us and fail our group—genocide. We are after a primal or primitive level of human being that scientific and logical modes of reflection and analysis typically gloss over and conceal. We are after something that appears to be nonsensical.

All conventional science requires that things or events be objectified so that they can be measured; then they can be related to causes or reasons that can likewise be measured. But before they can be objectified and measured, they are already known to some extent on a prescientific or primal level. I mean things as we engage with them immediately in everyday life—things that are venerated, used, discussed, joined, propitiated, feared, avoided. This is a culture's primally experienced world, and I am hypothesizing that it can be profoundly disturbed by another culture's primally experienced world abrading and grinding against its own. I think that conclusive reasons for genocide that account for its excesses, its differences from ordinary war, elude containment by conventional natural and social sciences. The latter simply assume that the world is already objectified, set to be measured and related to measurable causes or reasons. But these sciences presuppose and overlook cultures' prescientific, primally experienced worlds in which members blur, so to speak, with their experienced environments.

William James spoke of "the circumpressure" of "the whole residual cosmos" that works on us members of cultures primally, pervasively, moodily, and also unconsciously. Things, persons, events, the meaning of "our own" and "other," are initially "squeezed into shape" and formed some way within this circumpressure. Basal meaning emerges within the molten cauldron of immediate involvements with things, persons, and others that determines survival or extinction in that culture. It is prescientific meaning presupposed tacitly by all conventional science, and typically hidden from it.

Whole bodily persons engage with the whole surround. This is that fundamental erotic engagement in which we members of groups appropriate a surround as our own, our own world-experienced—in which we mate entrancedly with that surround. This domain has not yet been diced up into discrete objects to be measured, experimented with, predicted by any of the conventional sciences. This, our domain, is the deposit of the culture's multiform traditions of living, interpreting, perceiving, working, playing, celebrating, praying, dreaming, surviving. Cultures modify their members' neural structures.

True, the basal erotic engagement to which I refer typically generates the wildest-sounding ideas about things that cannot be seen or touched. But we are still held in the grip of the surround-experienced and appropriated as ours—our gut sense of space, time, body, group, primal rightness and wrongness—wriggle, scream, cry, pray as we might.

Indeed, the surround can get through to us whether it is experienced or not. But the primary point remains: without this prescientific level of meaning, laid down in the very beginning of experiencing, the relatively detached scientific treatment of things as objects to be measured could never happen.

On the primal level of this immediate involvement, this unique lived cohesiveness, things just look the way they look, sound the way they sound, and feel the way they feel. All this regardless of how logic or reason says they ought to be experienced, and regardless of what science says they are. For example, if people who normally drive on the right side of the road are suddenly dropped into a place where it is done on the left, this will seem immediately, viscerally *wrong*. This is the level of experiencing on which genocide occurs. Those others are simply wrong—wrong and dangerous. Our group is righteous, theirs is evil. Reflecting and thinking Jews and Christians, for example, would recall Isaiah 64:6: "But we are all as an unclean thing, and all our righteousness is as filthy rags." But thinking and reflecting are not happening.

I am hypothesizing that in times of great stress, another group's way of constituting a world-experienced may threaten the very sanity of the home group. There is psycho-physical earthquake and terror. The door is open to genocide. Get 'em all, kill 'em.

Nobody can be experiencing another's experiencing just as he or she is living through it each instant. For what each individual immediately senses (I don't say perceives) are electrochemical events in each of their brains and skulls. Nobody can live another person's body just as that person lives it.

But, these events within particular brains occur within whole bodies that have been profoundly conditioned from birth by others around them to notice what the group takes to be essential, and to deny or ignore as the group dictates or insinuates. In all things, to move, work, play, manipulate, perceive, deploy themselves in space and time in the time-proven ways of the group. Each normal individual is a body that imitates others undeliberately and more or less successfully. I call this mimetic engulfment (see my *Role Playing and Identity*, Sources).

In times of stress another group's ways of moving, working, playing, deploying themselves in space and time are experienced as simply wrong by the home group. Imagine this scene: A home group encounters an alien one that brings with it, of course, its own alien world-experienced. It has "constructed" this through its own funded traditions of intercorporeal and intersubjective activities. I mean its two-legged, dexterously handed, sign- and symbol-using ways of knowing and living. The home group is stressed in this encounter: because the alien group is not experienced in a scientific and detached way as "out there," as a demarcated corporate object out there in the colossal container of space.

The home group dreads the aliens' ways of constructing their world-experienced, for it dreads that these may cut across and disable their own ways of constructing their own world-experienced. "There must be one world, right, and what could it be but our world-experienced?"—that is the tacit assumption. The home group is not engaged in philosophical speculation about the limits of any world-experienced or about the limits of imagination. Terrorized, the members of the home group experience disorientation and destruction.

Note well: the home group's members are experiencing beings only because they are experiencing bodies immediately caught up actively and sensuously in their surround. Their bodies are porous membranes; they absorb the vibratory reality of the alien group. The aliens' activities are not experienced as just "out there," but as a churning reality within the home group's members' bodies. Nauseating revulsion tends to result. Given the right circumstances, any human group can fall into this defensive-aggressive stance, this hyperstressed, dizzying revulsion. The antidote that all too easily presents itself—Get 'em all, kill 'em.

In the foreword I alluded to Emerson's sudden and shocking insight that we are intimately related to lizard and rat, but there are no records of signs having passed between us. Bodily beings as are they, we share their vulnerability and their fear (signs of fear do communicate, and we must learn to think and acknowledge them). But biology and scientific ecology teach us that their initiatives and responses are pretty well set instinctively: prey fear all manner of predators, but differential responses among different forms of nonhuman life are pretty well set by what has proved adaptive for a species over long periods of time.

Though likewise bodily in our corporeal being, our human situation is immeasurably more complex and strange, because our bodies are deeply affected by processes of enculturation far beyond what is true for even our nearest primate relatives. A difference between cultures that evolves over time in speaking of a Supreme Being, say, may prove odious and terrifying in certain situations—psychophysical earthquake. It is a fact, for example, that Jews, Christians, and Muslims are all "children of Abraham." But this makes little or no difference in their actual group behaviors, for these have been set by very different histories in which the groups have been conditioned by very different complexes of concrete circumstances. We are the most precariously balanced of animals.

I wish not simply to supplant scientific studies, but to use them in a context larger than what is usual for them. Trying to grasp and to think "the unthinkable," we need all the help we can get (see note at end of the introduction).

*   *   *

The book before you systematically questions all taken-for-granted naive realisms: "The world is just out there, isn't it? We experience the real world. You don't deny that, do you?"

Of course, the world does exist, and would exist whether any sentient beings were around to experience and know it. But as best it can, each of our cultures must constitute or "construct" the meaning of world, and the meaning of its constituents. And we, looking on and hypothesizing about causes of genocide, must "construct" how this "construction" itself takes place.

*   *   *

At the risk of sounding like Voltaire's insufferably cheery Dr. Pangloss, we can speak of a silver lining on the cloud of suffering and devastation caused by the terrorist attacks on the United States of September 11, 2001. These were clearly genocidal in intent.[1]

Our habitual, prescientific, utterly taken-for-granted point of view on the world was so violently confronted and contradicted that we perhaps became aware of it as not the, but a, point of view. Instead of too often bullying the world (we have not always been blessings to other nations or peoples), we experience being bullied.

In psychotherapy this is called role reversal: it conduces to self-insight. We feel our way into how the others experience us. Realizing, finally, how we are actually experienced by members of some other cultures (not only by fundamentalist Islam, but by Native Americans, say), we are open to a greater reach of the world's reality—of our own reality and of the rest of the world's. We are ventilated, given fresh air. We may escape suffocation by our own unexamined assumptions. For whether or not we are aware of other cultures' points of view on us, these points of view fundamentally affect our reality. They may determine whether we live or die.

The whole circumpressing background world primally experienced moulds our perceiving of foreground objects and events in the world; it also masks-out what is not perceived at all, what is not even suspected. I think that many young and middle-aged people in North Atlantic culture absorb themselves in particular events here and now or in microhistories (such as the evolution of rock bands or the so-called corporate cultures of businesses). They do so because they live in a world—or live a world—devoid of a future that they can count on. They lack rituals whose point is to make persons feel at home day by day, year by year, generation by generation in their experienced world. They are fundamentally insecure. But most, I think, are incapable of saying this.

Lived reality involves the belief in continuity in space and time. Though we know that particular events may surprise us, we believe that the general sorts of events that structure our world will continue. In stable, time-proven, and ritualized cultures, people believe that there is more to come of the sorts of things they have now, just as what they have now has emerged from the past.

Exacerbated now by the sensationalism of the electronic media, the continuity of world for many people in North Atlantic culture begins to shatter into bright glassy bits: for example, myriads of "snapshots" from the Second Gulf War just as it was happening—or very nearly as it was happening so far away. Bodily beings' cohesive experiencing of a present and actual world-experienced attenuates; along with this, a reliable future flakes away and vanishes. I think that many people live in what Soren Kierkegaard called despair unconscious of itself.

The strangely toned silver lining of September 11 is the possibility that despair may become conscious of itself: that the current probability of the destruction of human life on this planet will provoke a wave of what Karl Jaspers calls passionate reason that rolls through the relatively thoughtful populations of the world and holds off perdition.

*   *   *

Moreover, we may gain some compassion for all human beings. We may discover how very vulnerable and panic-prone are we human animals in various cultures who strive to construct a world-experienced in which members can protect themselves, survive, and perhaps flourish.

As the colossal World Trade Center towers sank down from the sky and into themselves, they spewed out their burned guts in an impossible fountain of horror. Impossible and unthinkable, yet it was happening all right.

But it also appeared to be occurring outside the everyday ordered, experienced world in which things make sense.

We might try to understand how North Atlantic and/or North American secularism, commercialism, militarism, science, and technology strike a fundamentalist Muslim in Saudi Arabia, Afghanistan, say, or in Iran, Pakistan, or Indonesia. For example, merely by pushing a few buttons a child with a computer can flash hard-core pornography onto the screen. This in addition to the everyday TV, video, and movie fare of sex and violence, infidelity and assorted aberrations, sensationally and grippingly presented to the masses. For the fundamentalist and militant Muslim, this is literally the work of demons, literally and absolutely evil.

North Atlantic secularism is undermining the religious foundations of their states and groups, their very lives, they are convinced. We ought to be stopped. The bacillus of our way of experiencing and constructing a world-experienced will fatally poison them, they believe. As the Nazis thought that Jews' ways of constituting a world-experienced infected the body of the folk, the Volkskörper, so terrorist Muslims believe this about us.

No matter how small and feeble a single germ may appear, it can reproduce, spread, and fell a vast organism. The metaphor has great immediacy and power: Each of us is a germ, an infectious way of experiencing world. Thus each of us must be exterminated or incapacitated, so the terrorists believe. Our secular Western corporate body ingrains in each of us its members perceptual stances and prideful, acquisitive, and profane attitudes corrosive to the abject worship of God—Allah—that sustains them, so fundamentalist Muslims live fervently convinced. All of us must go, and all electronically communicated images of us must go too.

The X factor in genocide is any home group's dread of pollution by the other group: the infectious smearing and disintegration of its world-experienced, and the consequent annihilation of themselves. Extremist Islamists see us as contaminator-destroyers. Dominantly secularist education in the North Atlantic world leaves us unknowing of what could possibly motivate them.

The silver lining on the cloud of destruction and carnage surrounding the events of September 11 exhibits a greatly strange patina or toning. The lining's promise is that the destruction may jolt us out of naive realism, might, just possibly, jolt us from the belief that our point of view on things is the only reliable one: that our point of view reveals the way the world is. But the jolt threatens to be painful and we tend to recoil and blink. I think that we don't want to see ourselves from the point of view of an attacked group. We don't want to think that Cornel West may have a point: the events of September 11 are "the Niggerization of the United States."

*   *   *

Recall that I mentioned above that the primal surround can affect us whether it is experienced or not. Most specifically, other groups' points of view on us—which we cannot acknowledge or understand—can determine whether we live or die.

At rare moments, we may dimly and disturbingly suspect that all our efforts to understand the world—to classify and categorize things, to plot causes and reasons within the world—leaves some unknown range of things left out of our account, a range in excess of all our efforts to disclose. We cannot, of course, know *what* is left out of the account, but in these moments we suspect that there is something—a *that*, a something.

Under conditions of stress, members of a culture can find this suspicion profoundly disturbing. For it suggests that their culture's world-experienced does not simply coincide with the world as it is. Perhaps, just perhaps, what is left out of the account is essential for the members' survival? Perhaps another culture, abrading against the home culture, is better able to survive? The home culture can experience psychophysical earthquake.

With one fell swoop we seem to have opened a clear path to thinking the unthinkable, to finding reasons for genocide and terrorism. On the primal level of experiencing, distinctions easily made in times of reflective calm are not easily made in times of stress—or cannot be made at all. I mean, in this case, that the excess, the something left over, can be construed as waste. And this waste—call it great waste—is not easily distinguished from the wastes of the human body. Particularly is this so in times of great stress, when persons try, crazily, to escape their bodies—the vulnerable contents of which can be smashed out of them. So the apparent pathway to genocide opens: "They are subhuman, their world-experienced does not count, waste them before they waste us!"

This pathway is particularly enticing when we survey actual cases of genocide in this century. What we can call the anality of most genocidal cultures fits right into this general view. It's the purification mania that stands out. For but two examples: Hitler and Pol Pot were obsessed with ridding corporate and individual bodies of impurities, contaminants, filth. Anything irregular or messy or in excess was anathema. I think that the overflowing fecundity of the Earth itself appalls them.

It is so easy to apply Freudian terms to the sweeping philosophical analysis. The fear of messing, of anal expulsion, excites a reaction formation: anal retention, the pulling in tightly of the boundaries of the corporate body, the exclusion of those contaminating others.

In fact, I happen to think that this is true. As a card-carrying member of the Western rationalist tradition, I am tempted to develop this general viewpoint, allied with Freudian analysis, right off the bat in this book. After all, doesn't the most general view of things disclose what is most basic about these things? What applies to everything—everything in any way experienceable—mustn't that be what's most basic about things?

But I am profoundly suspicious of this sweeping point of view. I believe that it covers over and conceals concrete particularities of the human condition that make all the difference in how and why terrorism and genocide occur. I mean particularities of time, place, body, eruptive states of immediate awareness, etc. I think that to assert a truth prematurely, that is, before we have gotten straight on the concrete meaning of the terms involved, is, ironically, to block the road of inquiry. I think that grand theorizing, prematurely launched, can be unwittingly and profoundly blind or evasive.

I will try to exhibit the concrete reality of what is experienced immediately, sensuously, intensely. Especially what is experienced as other, as overflowing our catalogues, as encroaching on us, as intolerable excess (for but one example, anything alive that alights on our skin unexpectedly is instinctively swatted away in an instant's panic).

I mean things like this: Gypsies "breeding in the woods like rabbits," "Digger Indians grubbing and eating like animals"—or, actually, any excessive activity in matter. A boar in spasm emits jets of sperm from a corkscrew penis; insects hatch off a stream and swarm; salmons' pods of eggs bulge glistening scarlet, only a few become fish; countless amoebic proliferations, some sorts undiscovered; a kicked-over stone, and sow bugs and tiny centipedes—and what else?—scurry away. The examples are endless, unboundable, always an excess, which is the point.

*   *   *

A note about the general plan of this book: Most books in our fast-lane culture today are linear, progressive, "forward-marching reading experiences," "page-turners." No matter the particular genre or format—science, history, suspense thriller—they are all linear. So we discover a fact, which enables us to discover another fact, and on and on. Then at the end it's usually all added up neatly.

This book is not linear. In the typical crude sense of "empirical fact," I have discovered no new facts about genocide and terror. Instead, I have relied on facts already published. What I want to discover is new meaning in the facts already discovered. I want to discover what could possibly motivate people to do the apparently irrational and horrendous things that they do in genocide. Even if we conclude that genocidal acts are irrational, there must be *some* reason why people do them: we must suppose this if we are to seriously inquire into why people do them. Moreover, we must suppose that these acts have some meaning for the people who commit them: for, again, we must suppose this if we are to seriously inquire into why people do them.

"Meaning" has at least two meanings. First, the meaning that any prosaic statement or belief must have if it is to be either verified or falsified (say a statement about how most people behave when lost or abandoned, or when they fear they can find no reasons for why things happen, or no reasons to do anything). If such a statement is found to be true, it is added to our store of what William James calls knowledge by description. We inquirers typically remain detached and "objective."

But there is another kind of knowledge, what James calls knowledge by acquaintance, and this involves us with a second sense of meaning: for example, Was that a meaningful experience for you? That is, does it stand out from the ruck of experiences, stick with you, change your ways of being and behaving, happily or not? Is it visceral knowing, affective and effective knowing? People who commit genocidal acts vibrate, tremble, overflow, sweat with meaning in this sense. They know in their bones and viscera that the acts must be done.[2]

I want to discover more meaning in both senses of the term. I want to discover the sorts of reasons people do apparently irrational things. And I want to discover ever more visceral meaning for ourselves, so that we know in our viscera and bones that we must not do genocidal acts. So that the statistics of genocide aren't merely "astronomical" numbers that we gasp over for a moment and then forget (Hitler with his six million killed, Stalin with his twenty-plus million, Mao with his sixty—estimated). Meaning in this sense: that it sticks close to us and becomes means for living in new ways that make genocide less likely.

John Dewey has his version of James's knowledge by acquaintance. He calls it "the realizing sense" of things. That is, the sense in which things are experienced all through our bodily selves as real. In the same vein, the writer of Deuteronomy refers to "astonishment of heart" (28:28). For these thinkers, belief is the feeling of reality. I want to turn up, discover, more of that feeling.

As noted, the book before you is more cyclical than linear. It is a progression in intensity, not extensity. What I hope to progressively intensify is the meaning of the facts, in both senses of that term. To achieve this I must follow out the initial clue. That is, I need to be more deeply, feelingly, aware of the corporate individual, the group. I need to become aware of just how vulnerable each of us individuals is, and how, in times of great stress, we tend to hole up and to try to protect ourselves in the tormented group.

Homeless, exposed, battered by storms, Shakespeare's King Lear curses life itself: Spill all the seeds! Finally he sees ordinary mortals: larval, swarming, scurrying, frightened. He learns compassion—

Poor forked creatures.

NOTES

1. As far as I know, all genocides involve terrorism. But not all cases of terrorism need be genocidal in intent. A group might terrorize intruders into their land, but with no intention to incapacitate or exterminate whole intruding groups. The home group may be too weak to reasonably expect to accomplish that, even if they wanted to do so, and the groups involved may settle for a standoff. Relevant demographic factors are discussed in endnote 4 of chapter 5. (See also Margolis and Trotsky, Sources)

2. All conventional sciences, natural or social, require measurement. An account of a twenty-seven-year-old woman, a Palestinian attorney, who served as a suicide bomber, exemplifies the relevance, yet the insufficiency, of scientific explanations (reported in *The Denver Post*, for example, October 5, 2003, via the *New York Times*). Many of the deficiencies of the Palestinians' situations may be measurable ones of food, shelter, clothing, mobility, and other matters. But an ingredient in this woman's motivations is a sense of a deficiency of justice. To speak of a deficiency of justice, however, is only a manner of speaking, and an awkward one at that. No definite numbers can be placed on this deficiency, nor on how its felt sense or meaning impacts her whole spiritual-mental-physical life at a particular moment. Who could possibly predict when a sense of injustice will, in any individual case, break the threshold and become "acting-out behavior"? There is no way to exactly judge how inflamed and agonized is a person's primal sense of right and wrong, those basal felt meanings in one's troubled world-experienced. As we will see in later chapters, Dostoevsky, for example, marvels at the indeterminacy and unpredictability of situations in which "the self calls to itself," in which one hears the call of conscience.

1

GENOCIDE AND TERRORISM

And they stripped him, and put on him a scarlet robe. . . . And when they had platted a crown of thorns, they put it upon his head . . . and they bowed the knee before him, and mocked him saying, Hail, King of the Jews! . . . And they spit upon him, and . . . smote him on the head. . . . And when they were come to a place called Golgotha, that is to say, a place of a skull. . . . And they crucified him, and parted his garments . . . and sitting down they watched him there. . . . Now from the sixth hour there was darkness over all the land unto the ninth hour . . . And about the ninth hour Jesus cried with a loud voice, saying, Eli, Eli, lama sabachthani? My God, my God, why hast thou forsaken me?. . . Jesus, when he had cried again with a loud voice, yielded up the ghost.

—Mathew, 27:28–50

The crucifixion of Jesus on the cross is the central symbol of Christianity. Symbols are powerful because they draw masses of people into speeding white-hot orbits around them. Moments of individual lives are fused together over time. Individuals are fused with each other. Lives take on a radiant identity, endurance, apparent solidity. We participate in a corporate identity, carry a common glittering insignia.

A tangled bolus of theological and metaphysical issues and interpretations trail from the event of the crucifixion and its symbol, the cross. As intriguing as these may be, they distance us from the crucifixion event in its immediacy. We tend not to feel the deepest bite of it. Which is, I think, that we see a person tortured to death—and an innocent one in addition.

Why should so many humans have so deeply identified with the person on the cross over the centuries? Once the question is asked, the answer begins to appear. It is that we see ourselves in the crucified one, at a level of direct acquaintance and knowing in which no articulation or explanation is needed.

For each of us is born, is thrown into the world without our knowledge and consent. We are helpless for years in the face of what happens to befall us. All our behaviors bear the blind impress of events. Though some lives are much more protected, honored, fostered than are others, many of us feel ourselves in moments at least to be blasted, befuddled, abandoned, innocent sufferers. We are like lost children, only more dangerous.

These moments of present suffering form a marginal, haunting, and sickening sense of the ever present possibility of more suffering. Those who have been most protected may feel least confident and competent to face their woeful aloneness and vulnerability. "Poor little rich girls and boys" are often miserable addicts.

Now perhaps we better see why the heavy bolus of institutional interpretations and disputes—voluminous commentaries and theologies—has grown up around the event of the crucifixion. It is not only that the interpretations have a coherence and continuity of their own that help carry us through the black holes, the eruptive exhilarations and agonies, of our moments. And it is not only that they have a certain charm. They quite literally charm and benumb and carry us along when all else fails. The crucifixion carries a message of final overcoming of suffering in resurrection.

It is also that we need to be kept at a certain distance. Yes, we need to be focused on the crucifixion event, and the overcoming of death in resurrection. And yes, we can't get too close. For if we saw the event too clearly, we might not be able to believe that anybody—not even a being believed to incarnate God himself—could ever overcome aloneness, suffering, death. We need the distance and the gauzy wrapping around the event.

*   *   *

I agree with the United Nations' "Convention on the Prevention and Punishment of the Crime of Genocide," 1948 (Sources). Genocidal acts needn't involve the intention to kill outright all members of an alien group. Simply to harm them and incapacitate them as a group is sufficient. So understood, the use of terror can amount to genocide.

We cannot be on this planet without having bodies, and because our bodies are incredibly vulnerable, we deeply dread bodily harm and violation. This dread has been used famously at times as a means of crushing persons' urge to independent movement and autonomous life, to incapacitate whole peoples. The *Pax Romana*—Roman Peace—was achieved in many instances through the use of terror. Torturing to death through crucifixion was the favored form of terror. With victims lifted high up on a cross in open areas, crucifixion had the advantage of exhibiting for all to see the agonies of those being executed. When, for example, the Romans forcibly subjugated the Jews in A. D. 66–70, mass crucifixions were staged on the hills surrounding Jerusalem. "Let this be a warning to anyone who dreams of deviating from the guidelines!" Much of the remaining Jewish populace was subjugated, their rebellious ways stifled, at least for a time, through their own dread.

*   *   *

Philosopher Susanne Langer puts it succinctly for most of us: death is intolerable. Humans have invented countless ways of seeming to acknowledge it, only to deflect attention from direct encounter with it, or to deface it. Buddhism alone in its purest and most uncompromising form takes suffering to be the essential fact of life, and our laboring to detach ourselves from it the chief labor of our lives.

I will try to show that the denial of death is not only deliberate, as we see in most of the world's religious systems. But, beyond this, I will try to show that there is something about human consciousness itself that tends to occlude and deny our individual vulnerability and mortality. An illusion of immortality springs up in most persons' lives, and is maintained naturally.

The illusion arises prereflectively, undeliberately, unacknowledgeably. For the vast majority of persons, the illusion is tidal, inevitable. The enduring group's dominant symbols, institutions, and habitual ways of experiencing their world feed the illusion. We find ways of protecting and cherishing it. For lurking on the margins of each person's consciousness is a fear of suffering, indeed ultimate suffering. In moments, as we will see, the fear is focal in consciousness and acknowledgeable. It's not for nothing that so many people so deeply identify with the person on the cross.

* * *

Jesus and his group of followers were profoundly *other* both with respect to the Romans and to the Jews. They deeply disturbed these ruling groups, and punishment was meted out to them.

> And when they were come to the place, which is called Calvary, there they crucified him. . . . Then said Jesus, Father forgive them; for they know not what they do. And they parted his raiment, and cast lots.
>
> —Luke, 23:33–34

* * *

Let us begin to unpack the illusion of immortality, exhibit it in the light of day. In general, it is the illusion in which we deny the reality of death. In a crucial way, as we will see, this involves the denial that our own group will perish at some time, and also the denial that the world-experienced or "constructed" by the group will perish. I will proceed slowly and carefully, for we are dealing with our own dauntingly complex identity, our individual and our communal reality.

First, we must make a distinction. We must distinguish an individual's experiencing from what is experienced by that individual. Very often, what is experienced—at least as a bare fact—is something that somebody else does or could be experiencing. For example, the sun coming up on a cold winter morning, the dog running in the yard, etc. Or the commonly held facts may be more conceptual, like the earth more nearly resembling a ball than a plate. In any case, we automatically agree on these matters experienced.

But all the while each of us is experiencing these common facts experienced in our very own individual way. For example, you are experiencing happily the dog running in the yard on the cold winter morning, for you like the dog and know that he has been very sick. But even though I too know that the dog has been sick, I am in fact experiencing indifferently the dog's running.

Here is the first indication of how easy it is to pave over and ignore one's own individual way of experiencing the world—the world experienced by all of us to be there for each of us to be experiencing in some individual way—also how easy it is to pave over one's own individual existence as an experiencer. For if I should notice the contrast between my friend's happy experiencing of the dog and my indifferent way, I can do so only because of the bare fact jointly and automatically believed by both of us: the dog is running in the yard.

And here's the point: the commonly assumed simple fact experienced has its meaning determined in advance by the cultural group into which each of us has been born. We take this utterly for granted. So completely is it taken for granted that each of our modes of experiencing it is easily eclipsed by it. And, ironically, this is so either because we all automatically agree on how we should be experiencing some fact, or, because—as in this case— I don't want my indifferent and deviant way of experiencing to be noticed. By systematically hiding my deviant ways of experiencing things from others, I may be impeding or obscuring even my own recognition of them.

The payoff, the first light on the illusion of immortality: My own passing, ephemeral experiencing of things tends to be eclipsed by the ongoing group's cemented ways of making the commonly experienced world meaningful. So my very own vulnerable, passing existence as an individual person, an individual experiencer, tends to be systematically eclipsed. We tend to be absorbed by our group. And because we believe unquestioningly that our group will endure, we slide into the blurry illusion that our own existence will go on, and on, and on.

Thus exposed is the taproot of the everyday illusion of immortality. Within its sap and endurance we find sanctuary automatically, without thinking about it. But again, my own fleeting, flitting perceiving and experiencing can cease at any moment, and I along with it.

*   *   *

As we will see, the illusion of immortality can be shattered at times for any of us. When we are nearly knocked unconscious, say, I the victim know: That happened to me, to me. Or when I am very ill, and see others going about their business around me, or trying to comfort me. I see another world out there, the world of the well and the fit. Such experiences single me out.

Still, after we regain composure and health, we typically slip back quickly into the ongoing group: we submerge ourselves in its apparent durability or even invulnerability. We slip into the illusion of enduring existence, the illusion of immortality.

*   *   *

Now, it is terrifying enough for any of us to have our illusion of individual immortality shattered. But we must try to imagine something beyond this if we would imagine how the so-called unthinkable, genocide, can and does happen. Given our utterly taken-for-granted reliance on the shared cultural world of commonly accepted facts and meanings, what could be more terrifying than every person's illusion of immortality shattering at once? The group is shaken to its foundations.

Nobody in one's group finds sanctuary in the illusion. Nobody can lose themselves in the group. Nobody perceives a stable and determinate world-experienced. Everybody thrashes around in terror trying to stay upright and find their way, trying to survive. This is psychophysical earthquake.

But how could this happen? It's the task of this book to explain how, for on this hinges the explanation of genocide as a defensive-aggressive mass action.

As I have already sketched, this can happen if our own group is shaky for whatever reason, and it believes that another group's habitual patterned way of experiencing the world cuts across and undermines our group's way. The alien group is experienced as infecting and weakening us, as polluting and destroying the home group, and our previously secure way of perceiving and experiencing the world-experienced. Inexorably, shockingly, and sickeningly, our experienced world is felt to give way beneath us.

Now, if we can exterminate or disable every member of that alien group, and do it in time, may we save ourselves? Every member—since every member is a carrier of the infecting way of perceiving or experiencing things. There can be only one world, and what could it be but the one we know, our own world-experienced? We can expect and imagine no other world. The alien group is experienced to be demons, to be unnatural beings. Genocide them!

But, I remind myself, what I have just written is my reflecting thought trying to render a sketchy explanation of genocidal frenzy. I have put words in genociders' heads. Transported in the ecstasy of slaughter, nobody is thinking through an explanation, sketchily or at length. In the orgiastic drama of ritual mayhem and murder, nobody is thinking. Not so the thinking could acknowledge itself and critically review itself.

We must strive to penetrate to a primal level of experiencing that is opaque to itself. People who engage in genocide have trouble recalling just what they did. Perhaps during the frenzy of killing they regress to the level of infancy? A baby sometimes looks to be enraged, but what is she or he actually feeling? The baby cannot tell us, and how could we, looking on, ever know enough to classify it in the categories we as adults devise? Babies' cries often bring aid from the parents—as if by magic, as if by omnipotence, we might say. But when the cries do not avail, dread and rage is the plausible response, is it not? None of us can remember—not so that we can say—

just what we felt. I think regression to an infantile state is a plausible explanation of why people who engaged in genocide have difficulty recalling
what they did.

As one reduces living humans to a mess of flesh, bones, and blood at one's
feet, who could believe that he himself is also fragile, mortal? One finds
oneself at those moments playing the role of a god. Caught up in the fascination, terror, and delight of group frenzy, one seems to oneself and to others in the group to be a supernatural being. The illusion of immortality on
all levels is pumped up yet again.

* * *

Some deeply believe that any attempt to explain genocide is a tacit exoner-
ation of it. One thinks: "To explain it is to adduce causes such that those
caught up in them cannot do otherwise. So they are not responsible. So they
cannot be blamed. No, genocide is absolute evil, the work of weird demonic
forces beyond natural understanding."

But I believe this is an inverted form of dogmatism, group mystification,
a version of tacit supernaturalism. It is to claim to know we cannot know
evil, and without even trying to know it. It cannot face the actual facts of our
weird emotionality, our ephemeralness and vulnerability, our limited point
of view, and the devious ways of denying these painful actualities.

If we begin to explain evil acts it will not be to deny that they are evil. It
will deepen our sense of what evil is, of how wretched, pathetic, horrible,
and deplorable it is. Evil is an ever-present possibility of the human condition, I believe.[1] We must try to stop it. Without understanding its reasons
and causes, we cannot hope to stop it.

No escape into tacit supernaturalism and dogmatism! Let the supernatural
be what it may be. There are perplexities and mysterious depths all around
and through us all the time: twinings and intertwinings, mysteries and perplexities of Nature and culture, wheels within wheels, and manifold illusions,
that we must try to open up and understand.

* * *

As emphasized in the introduction, there is an X factor in the explanation
of genocide. It lies deeper than all conventional categories of explanation.
All these categories unwittingly presuppose this factor. They all presuppose
the world in which the events they purport to explain occur. Particular objects or events in the world singled out by the sciences presuppose a visceral

and moody background level of primal meaning, the world-experienced in which they occur.

In *The Varieties of Religious Experience*, William James writes of the experience of "the whole residual cosmos, intimate or alien, that everyone possesses." A clue appears in the Nazis finding the Gypsies dirty and disorderly (for not only Jews were genocided). The Gypsies were unhindered; they propagated irresponsibly—more like rabbits than humans. Nazis felt their presence to be a sickening disordering and polluting of "good Germans'" ways, the right ways of experiencing the whole residual world-experienced. Gypsies sickened their world.

As infants and then as toddlers growing up we simply absorb unwittingly, by osmosis as it were, the sense of world that the authorities all around us have themselves brought with them to every situation. That is, we absorb our culture, and its taken-for-granted background sense of world, involuntarily and, so to speak, mindlessly. We directly, moodily, assume it to be the domain in which we can do A, B, C. We directly and moodily feel it to be a friendly "place," say, or an obdurate and hostile one; or a clean and orderly "place," or an infected and disintegrating one. The world is the "place" of all places in the literal sense: all the places that we can pin down, objectify, and precisely locate through the sciences.

I think that the monstrousness of genocide cannot be explained without referring to a home group's immediately engulfing world-experienced being radically upset by an alien group's.

* * *

It is understandable that most members of a culture are naive realists: the world is "out there," and it just is as our culture "constructs," interprets, invests it with meaning. Then, in times of great stress, other groups that construct the world differently are weird or evil, wrong. Perhaps they should be genocided.

As long as we remain naive realists, we can never understand what's going on, never understand genocide. How do the basic structures of world—space, time, things, our actions—get their being for us, their primal meaning in experience? Always there is the immediate, residual meaning of world—the ultimate context in which everything first gets the meaning it has for a culture. As noted in the introduction, without this primal meaning, we cannot begin to objectify things and to deal with them mathematically and scientifically. How is this ultimate or primal meaning generated?

The abiding task of this book is to repeatedly pose and to try to answer that question. It must be repeatedly posed, because we ever tend to slip back insensibly into naive realism. The reason is that we are habituated bodily beings who must constantly adapt to the experienced-world as "constructed" by our culture or we will be ostracized or we will perish. Slipping back into naive realism might be called a meta-addiction, for it dominates most people's lives most of the time: each of us must be confirmed by the world as experienced by our culture. If we don't, we collapse, or lose our minds. Naive realism might be compared to alcoholism. If the alcoholic does not attend Alcoholics Anonymous meetings, say, with a kind of religious punctuality and dedication, he or she may relapse.

Of course the world would exist whether or not any human beings were around to experience it. But we must mainly experience it in culturally determined ways. Of course space and time would be real whether or not any human beings were around to experience them. But we do and must experience them—and in the right way—if we would retain our identities, our very reality as persons. We must do so in a way that leads us, guides and navigates us, rather than misleads us. We must do this even if it means at times that we go out of touch with our own very individual ways of experiencing things.

We are taking the first steps in understanding how another culture's way of structuring their world-experienced may so profoundly upset us. For notice again: though each of us is an individual body with an individual brain, each of us as infants must imitate the authorities first around us, and we must do this before we can consciously intend to do so. We must notice the things they notice, and how they notice them. To be sane, we must be mimetically engulfed in the group.

In her great book, *Purity and Danger*, Mary Douglas digs to the roots of a culture's profoundest prescientific ways of "constructing" an experienced world, and its profoundest aversions and taboos. She is particularly attentive to ancient Hebrew dietary laws, the prohibition against eating pork, for example, or eels. Reasons easily available may apply to some extent, but they are insufficient, she finds, to account for the intensity and durability of the aversion. For example, it may be true that pork easily spoils without refrigeration, and consumers may contract trichinosis. But eating eels doesn't entail such a dire disease, yet they too are heavily proscribed.

What pigs and eels share, she finds, is most revealing. They both move improperly in space and time. According to Hebrew law, proper movement of water creatures is supplied by their fins; eels have no fins. According to Hebrew law, swine are also unclean and forbidden to be eaten, because their feet and their whole mode of locomotion on land are also improper for such creatures. Consuming these beings disrupts the Hebrews' gut sense of their ordered and meaningful world-experienced. It is so disruptive that it is almost literally unthinkable.

Now we begin to see why another culture's way of forming a world-experienced can be so deeply disturbing. The other culture rides roughshod over, is oblivious of, the very structure of the home culture's lived reality. Since these others "get away with it," the home group may begin to doubt its own experienced-world's reality. If more than a passing qualm, this is psychophysical earthquake.

And the clinching reason? It has been touched on in the introduction. Disordered and disordering movement isn't just happening in a colossal spatiotemporal container "out there." As immediately experienced, immediately impacting, it is happening in the bodies of any of those experiencing the movement as disordered. Disowned it may be, intellectually, "That is not our way." But on the primal level of experiencing there is disturbance. If conjoined with other disturbing factors, a genocidal impulse may be excited. No naive realism, no facile objectification of the world and of ourselves, no matter how sophisticated in some of its aspects, can grasp this.[2]

Note: It's not just movement in itself that is considered unnatural, but movement experienced within the whole experienced world generated intercorporeally and intersubjectively by a culture. More specifically, in the case of the Hebrews, it is eels and pigs experienced within a particular patriarchal culture that are proscribed. Such a culture has sought to define and individuate itself by contrasting itself as dramatically as possible with much earlier cultures. We are who we are because we are not them.

These earlier cultures were ones grounded in all probability in a matristic way of experiencing, goddess cultures, that understood Nature as voluminously fecund, as female. (See Sources, Donna Wilshire, *Virgin Mother Crone*.) Both eels (and other snakelike beings) and swine figured in these cultures as sacredly fecund and regenerative, as representative of the great goddess. Snakes lived in holes in the ground: they were familiar with the body of Mother Earth. The value of these goddess-revered and goddess-revering beings was inverted and reversed, demonized, by patriarchal cultures intent upon individuating themselves. Paradigmatic instances of patriarchal cultures are the three great Western religions: Judaism, Christianity, and Islam.

*   *   *

We have a leg up on thinking the so-called unthinkable. Take another particularly vivid and apt case: the genocide of witches in the fifteenth through the seventeenth centuries in Europe and America. No exact numbers are available, but it is estimated that several hundred thousand women were killed for witchcraft, and most of the rest terrorized to the point of incapacitation. The massacres meet the definition of genocide we have formulated.

Armed with a more developed and intensified hypothesis, we can begin to grasp the causes of this reign of terror. The witches, most of whom were female, moved improperly and unnaturally in space and time. Inscrutably, they rode on broomsticks through the air, say, and alighted abruptly and unpredictably on their perches. Hags (from Hagazussa), were liminal beings—neither precisely here nor precisely there (see Duerr, Sources). They haunted the world. A man might awake at night and find one perched on his sexual organs—a succubus, so it was believed. The underlying, typically unacknowledgeable fact: we are highly vulnerable organisms with highly permeable membranes in the world-experienced. In many stressful situations, we are wildly labile and emotional.

Add to all this, the witches' "familiars," the various subhuman animals that assist them in their shadowy tasks. It is no great wonder that the witch hunters were, almost always, males in positions of power in a patriarchal society. They clung to these positions. Witches were unwelcome reminders of very ancient matristically oriented cultures and their swarming abundance of life. The slippery and shifting residues of these cultures threatened the home group. The structure of its experienced world threatened to disintegrate in a poisonous mess. Speaking of the witches, Macbeth says,

> Infected be the air whereon they ride,
> And damned all those that trust them!

*   *   *

The terrible events of September 11, we see, present themselves with a sinister alteration of signature. We can no longer speak of shaky home groups as if they were home groups other than ours, just matters of fact "out there." For now our own corporate body has been broken into, troubled, violated. Our own experienced world has been shaken. Many feel haunted by sleeper terrorist cells, somewhere, anywhere.

Shouldn't we try to change our way of thinking? For I believe that humans are beset on all sides by illusions. The ultimate illusion is that our own group cannot suffer from illusions, and that it goes on and on.

Thinking of any number of unprecedented acts or "impossibles and unthinkables" may not be as impossible as we fear, now that we are in the process of enduring an impossible and an unthinkable that has happened to us. For to face the human condition, to face fear, suffering, vulnerability, ignorance, illusion, and death, may defuse some of their power to paralyze us, or to wall us up in tunnel vision. Our gut sense of world may dilate and become steadier.

More than an individual's illusion of his or her own immortality may collapse. What happens when our group's corporate illusion of its ever-ongoing reality collapses? What happens when our group's experienced world quakes beneath all our feet in a kind of intolerable nausea?

* * *

I have noted the irrational excesses of genocide. Irrational, or so they certainly appear. We can find no ready reasons for them. They appear to be unthinkable.

The excesses take at least two forms. First, that all the alien group's members must be killed or incapacitated. Second, that the genocidal onslaught erupts so suddenly, and hence swiftly pursues its goal. I will argue that group identity is extraordinarily unstable and labile, in times of great stress particularly, when threatened by incursion from another culture's alien world-experienced.

We will find that the group must maintain an illusion of its immortality, and that it pumps it up frenziedly when its integrity is threatened. Hitler trumpeted his thousand-year Third Reich. Whites who genocided tribes of indigenous Californians blithely rationalized their actions with the slogan of Manifest Destiny: from the foundations of civilization itself, the destiny of Europe and the West is to conquer, civilize, and humanize the globe. Pol Pot believed that he served the destiny of the Khmer people—the real Cambodians—to restore themselves to their native purity and to establish permanently their beneficent rule of that region. It was Nature's law—the timeless wisdom of the folk. Parallel reasoning occurred among the Hutus of Rwanda. And so on.

As noted, the most plausible explanation for genocidal totalizing is the belief that all members of the alien culture carry the infecting bacillus of their alien, disrupting world-experienced; so all must be killed or incapacitated. As for the eruptive suddenness of the genocidal onslaught, I think the most plausible explanation is this. At times of threat, the sneaking suspicion leaks into the home group's awareness that their group is not immortal, omniscient, all-sufficing. This triggers a panicked reaction: the alien group must be obliterated now before the home group is itself obliterated.

As if one were to rigidly stare at some thing, afraid to turn the gaze for an instant, for the thing might not be there when the gaze returns to it. And if not there, then perhaps behind us? So vulnerable are we.

"As ifs"—along with metaphorical renderings of situations—approach them from unexpected angles and place them in unexpected contexts. This disrupts the trance of everyday life and refreshes the meaning of the facts.

I will be particularly concerned with developing the metaphor of the corporate body: the helmeted head ordering its executives, its right arms, to battle, and these in turn ordering the minions and untouchables below them. When overwhelmed with fear, the corporate body can go to pieces.

*   *   *

We are embarking on a difficult journey—difficult in every way, conceptually and emotionally. It is best to acknowledge this. To avoid naive realisms and simplistic solutions, it is best to acknowledge how profoundly we need ready and easy answers, such as "We're righteous, they're evil—to be rid of them!" The most insidious danger is to slide into despair or hopelessness unaware of itself. For, after all, we are vulnerable, and genocide frequent, horrendous, and difficult to grasp. It does no good, really, to exhort ourselves to be compassionate, concentrated, patient. For as Herman Melville pointed out in "Bartleby," a subliminal conviction of hopelessness can trigger unwittingly and furtively a self-defensive numbing, a turning off and turning away from the thought or sight of misery:

> So true it is, and so terrible too, that up to a certain point the thought or sight of misery enlists our best affections; but, in certain special cases, beyond that point it does not. They err who would assert that invariably this is owing to the inherent selfishness of the human heart. It rather proceeds from a certain hopelessness of remedying excessive and organic ill. To a sensitive being, pity is not seldom pain. And when at last it is perceived that such pity cannot lead to effectual succor, common sense bids the soul be rid of it. (Sources, 121–22)

NOTES

1. The ever-present possibility of genocidal evil is exemplified at the roots of Judaism and Christianity. The Hebrew Bible or "Old Testament" (for but one example, *Joshua* 10:40) records, "So Joshua smote all the country of the hills, and of the south and of the vale, and of the springs . . . he left none remaining, but utterly destroyed

all that breathed, as the Lord God of Israel commanded." The Israelites were surrounded by enemies: we will emphasize the perilous state of genociding groups. I will not enter at any length into the controversies surrounding the interpretation of such passages (for instance, "The Canaanites were terrible people, engaging in child sacrifice"). Even Regina Schwartz, greatly alarmed at tendencies to intolerance and aggression inherent in Hebrew monotheism, writes, "Conquering the Canaanites was the fantasy of an exiled people" (Sources, x). It wouldn't follow from this that conquering them was never more than a fantasy, but her statement might suggest that it was only that. At the very least, such fearful and aggressive sentiments, powerfully voiced—as in this verse from *Joshua*—favored genocidal propensities.

2. The Internet's "Science Daily" (11-4-03) offers an example of how a culture automatically fits matters into its presupposed matrix of primal meanings. Scientists had located the brain correlates of the "funneling illusion": when two fingers are touched simultaneously the person reports that the stimulating source lies between the fingers (*Science*, 10-31-03). The Internet headline reads, "Brain Maps Perceptions, Not Reality." This conforms to our primal-sclerotic cultural presuppositions that (a) Perceptions are "in the mind" and reality is "out there," and (b) That if reality itself—pure of interpretation—is ever to be revealed it must be so (probably) by science. Our culture's appropriation of scientific findings conceals the fact that perceiving is always interpreting, sometimes in a verifiably reliable way, other times in a deceiving way. That there must be a pure reality that requires no interpretive experiencing is a rampant delusion (naive realism) that afflicts, at various points, all cultures. The researchers try to defuse "illusion." "Illusions are not unusual or strange—they are how we interpret the world. We think we know what's out there in the physical world, but it's all interpreted by our brains. Everything we sense is an illusion to a degree." At least this effort is commendable, although it risks demoralizing many people, lodged as they are in utterly uncritical mind/body dualisms. The whole vexed affair reignites interest in Dostoevsky's "There is nothing more fantastic than reality itself."

2

SPECIFIC CASES OF GENOCIDE:
NAZI GERMANY, CALIFORNIA INDIANS

Albert Speer would confess to everything except to knowledge of the extermination of the Jews.

—Gitta Sereny

No doubt, human organisms are individual ones, at least in the sense that one can usually be separated from another fairly easily—at least if force is applied. We are also essentially social and cultural organisms, beings who bond. From our genetics and biology we inherit the potentiality to become human, rather than simian or bovine, say. But to actualize this we must co-exist in the most intimate and intricate reciprocity with human organisms that have already become developed humans—parents and caregivers, then larger human groups. We become human only by learning to interact within corporate bodies of humans, and for this we must learn the perceptual attitudes as well as the symbolic meanings and codes of the culture. True, we must remain organisms that are individual and unique: something unclassifiable, personal, and private always remains over, an excess. But we must fit into the corporate body of the culture to some fundamental extent; otherwise we are insane and must be incarcerated.

What characterizes a group in genocidal fusion and rampage is the extraordinarily viscous or entangled coherence of the group—its remarkably rigid and monolithic character. The fiery fusion produces a group that resembles a glassy igneous rock. There is no room for the free play of individuals within it reacting to things as they happen. As the head of the corporate body inclines, so inclines the group—a mindless automatism and loss of individuals' sense of their reality and responsibility as individuals. Responsibility implies responsiveness. It is just the hysterical rigidity and loss of responsiveness to what actually happens moment by moment that characterizes the genocidal group. As in a dream or a compelling fantasy, they execute their bloody business.

Such groups are usually guided and incited by patriarchal heads. These fanatical and canny characters realize that any strong dissident voice may shatter the glassy rigidity of the group. So dissidents are summarily dispatched or hidden away in jails. The heads realize intuitively what psychologists of mobs and gangs have established through empirical research: that most persons desperately need to belong in groups. Even those who are bullied by other members of the group may stick around and take it, because they so dread being alone.

Why this rigidity and terrible coherence of the genocidally inclined group? The most plausible answer in most cases is that the corporate body has reacted violently to the threat of its own disintegration. This does not rule out the motive of retaliation for past grievances. Should the aggrieved group not take the opportunity to retaliate when the possibility arises, self-loathing would itself be a disintegrative factor. The group reacts against this threat.

Thus the mindless "allness" of the genocidal group, and the equally mindless allness attributed by it to the group felt to be unassimilable, the one to be exterminated, or at least to be incapacitated. There is hysterical loss of discrimination in all battles, the famous "fog of battle." But in anything like conventional warfare, does it reach the point at which combatants can't distinguish an enemy soldier from an infant or a pregnant woman near term? Norbert Elias, a student of warrior societies in the middle ages, quotes a knight's diary from that time:

I tell you that neither eating, drinking, nor sleep has as much savor for me as to hear the cry "Forwards!" from all sides, and horses without riders shying and whinnying, and the cry "Help! Help!", and to see the small and the great fall to the grass at the ditches and the dead pierced by the wood of the lances decked with banners. . . . War is a joyous thing. We love each other so much in war . . . a sweet joy rises in our hearts, in the feeling of our honest loyalty to each other; and seeing our friend so bravely exposing his body to danger in order to keep and fulfill the commandment of our Creator, we resolve to go forward and die or live with him and never leave him on account of love. This brings such delight that anyone who has not felt it cannot say how wonderful it is. Do you think that someone who feels this is afraid of death? Not in the least! He is so strengthened, so delighted, he does not know where he is. (*The Civilizing Process*, Sources, 193, 197)

Anyone who cannot discern and acknowledge this level of experiencing—this fiery and bloody fusion and ecstatic transport—should not speak at all about human beings. But the question must be pressed: At any time in anything like conventional war are combatants so fogged that they cannot tell the difference between an enemy soldier and an infant or a pregnant woman close to term? I doubt it.

But left at this point the question is academic, because not only do genociders lump all of *them* together, but, as I have noted, sometimes make a special point of identifying the alien group's pregnant women, disembowelling them, and inspecting to see that the fetus is also dead.

There is a special level of horror, loathing, and disgust that we encounter in genocide: a cringing recoiling at the very possibility of them being in the same world as are we, the genociders. The only explanation that approaches adequacy, I believe, is that any of them, actual or possible, is felt immediately to embody and project an experienced-world that threatens to infect and disintegrate one's culture's own experienced-world, thus reducing it—and ourselves in it—to a flood of diarrhea. "There can only be one world. And it must have a determinate structure. What could that structure be but the one that our experience finds in it? Smell the stench of rot and death. This infection must be eliminated." So the thinking would go if it could speak.

Thus we see again the special aptness of the pollution model for grasping genocide. As any single germ, no matter how apparently inconsequential, may spread in a contagion of infection that fells a great body, so every one of them must be exterminated or incapacitated. In the next chapter, I will try to build a theoretical framework in which identities of individual members are seen perspicuously to be tied to the identity of the corporate body, particularly in the hysterical fusion of genocide.

To anticipate: I will try to work out why corporate bodies, especially genocidal ones, must have a head. That is, I will try to establish a necessary parallelism between the head of the individual body and that of the corporate one, and, moreover, how the parallelism exists at every level of bodies, from heads down through the eliminative and procreative organs to the feet.

How do corporate bodies pick the individual who becomes their head? Roughly, when the corporate body's needs and disturbances match the needs and disturbances of an aggressive and charismatic individual, things click into place—there's a match. The head is found. This, I think, most plausibly explains why so many maimed, deformed, wretched, borderline or outright insane people become heads of violent, angry, humiliated nations. No individuals in the corporate body are in a position to lock them up.

Hence Hitler was not promoted beyond corporal in World War I because his superiors—austere officers of the regular army—judged he lacked leadership potential. He did lack it, in a more or less normal world. In a disturbed, fearful, demonically resentful and driven world, he was perfect.

If the theoretical project of this book is successful, we will not just have peculiarly vivid and apt metaphors, or pungent historical records, to gain purchase on genocide. But we will see how the metaphors and records form an integral part of the pollution hypothesis concerning the phenomenon. The hypothesis will account for the facts that the metaphors and records show or expand, and for other facts as well.

*   *   *

The Nazi-perpetrated horror has become, for many, the paradigm case of genocide. This has an up and a down side. The up is that this one has been the subject of countless studies, many of them very good. Probably it is the most studied genocide in history. There are several reasons. This was the work of dramatic fanatics of most questionable sanity who seized and developed tremendous power and who nearly realized their goal: to rule the world in a pan-Aryan empire and to exterminate or incapacitate every "undesirable" and "defective" on earth.

Particularly were Jews regarded as poisonous to the corporate body. If Hitler had thought that Jews were in outer space, would he have pursued them there, had he been able? The man lived a fantasy that wove itself through ever-ramifying actuality.

Another reason Hitler's work has been so thoroughly studied and exposed, is that so many Jews are highly educated and knowledgeable, hence able to broadcast their views, and are obviously so concerned.

The down side is that we may conclude that somehow this is the most important genocide, the only truly paradigmatic one. This would be disastrous for understanding genocide. We might conclude that it owes to something uniquely defective in the German "character," and that it is not—what I believe it is—a weakness in the human condition itself. It is an ever-present possibility for humanity, particularly under certain conditions. Would that the Nazi genocide were unique. Hideous as it is, it is not unique. We all must stand in scrutinizing light.

Among the many good books about Nazi terrorism and genocide is Robert J. Lifton's *The Nazi Doctors*. As noted, he painstakingly gathers many facts about the large number of German doctors of medicine who were caught up in Hitler's campaign of cleansing the Volkskörper of undesirables, germs. An undesirable was anybody who didn't fit the mold of true Aryan physical and mental identity as defined by the head of the corporate body, Hitler—together with his minions, particularly Heinrich Himmler.

The Aryan model emerged full-blown from the brow of a concocted myth. Hitler employed malleable and imaginative folklorists who pieced together and fabricated an origin myth for his state. To wit: the roots of fully human culture are Nordic, the blue-eyed, typically blond humans who formed the only true culture-creating culture, as opposed to various dark-eyed, dark-skinned peoples who never attained fully human status.

Note well: light-skinned is equated with light, which is equated with enlightenment and mind, the distinctly human; while dark is equated with darkness and ignorance, the inferior human or subhuman. If the human race is ever to progress, the Nordic or Aryan stock must be purged of degrading and infecting elements; it must be cleanly pruned of them, so it was thought. The purified, reinvigorated stock would then spread its progeny as a "master race" over the planet.

Lifton's book is especially valuable because it helps us grasp how presumably well-educated doctors devoted to fostering health could be sucked into Hitler's murderous, megalomaniacal projects. He preyed on their interest in health by presenting his various projects as essential to the health of the truly human corporate body—the corporate body of humanity. At least as he and his forceful and unabashed propagandists, scientists, and pseudoscientists defined that body.

Before his preoccupation with Jews became obviously paranoid—obvious at least to persons with a modicum of disinterestedness and intelligence—he concentrated on ferreting out genetic disorders: for example, hemophilia or congenital blindness. These disorders exist, of course: and with them "the camel got his nose under the tent," and a significant number of people, otherwise not malicious or paranoid or hugely anti-Semitic, got caught up increment by increment in his vast murder machine.

A diabolically clever rationalization for genocide was promulgated. Those others, just because they are those others, must be eliminated, all of them. Indeed it is our duty as conscientious physicians—as well as conscientious educators, statesmen, whatever—to do this admittedly unpleasant and difficult task. It is a remarkable fact that no researcher has, to my knowledge, discovered instances of Germans actually punished for unwillingness to participate in genocidal plans and deeds. Those who flagged were considered not up to the heavy task laid upon them. Or they were thought to be temperamentally unsuited to the challenge, and were transferred to other positions in the Reich.

Reichsführer Himmler was, next to Hitler, the chief physician in this monstrous ministration to the corporate body. He appeared to be—and was in a twisted sense—very concerned about those entrusted with this taxing but necessary duty. He realized, for example, that men in the death squads—their emblazoned insignia the skull—were very apt to need significant time for R & R, rest and recreation. He was willing and able to supply it when needed.

Lifton's book is important because it helps us to see and accept key facts that are difficult to believe. And he himself at several points suggests the pollution hypothesis to explain genocide. Nevertheless, he does not develop the hypothesis systematically. More is required for this than sedulously recording facts concerning particular events, beliefs, behaviors. We are required to change the way we think about individuals and corporate individuals or groups, any individual, any group. Indeed, we are required to change the way we think about world—experienced world.

We are required to reconceptualize and reimagine what it means to be a human being. We are required to find new possibilities for thinking about ourselves, new possibilities that lie outside the orbit of our habitual culture-bound ways of experiencing: about why we do very strange things. We need to be startled, jolted out of the same old stale presence of things as we habitually perceive them, and into an awareness of new possibilities for the way things might be. If we should get these—new horizons of expectation—and if we could tolerate this abundance, we might be able to assemble accountings, retrodictions, and perhaps make predictions, all of which have hitherto been impossible. Lifton does not provide this fresh conceptual and imaginative reorientation.

Now a brief word about some of the other paradigmatic features of genocidal programs. The Nazi case has been so thoroughly documented that we can be brief. Was the corporate body stressed and disturbed during Hitler's rise to power during the twenties and early thirties? The answer is clearly affirmative. The nation was humiliated and demoralized after their defeat in the First World War. In part because of war reparations payments exacted by the Allies on Germany, its economy was in a shambles, inflation accelerating at an unnerving pace. The Weimar Republic, an experiment in democracy, was notably ineffectual.

The masses wanted scapegoats, and Hitler's overwhelming hatreds, fears, and histrionic powers quickly identified some. Along with his odious and pathetic disciples—notably the architect, Albert Speer—Hitler presented genocide as a kind of unstayed, unpent theatre: Redemption Through Extermination.

Did Hitler present an individual head that the corporate body could easily find atop itself as leader? Again, clearly yes. His fears, hatreds, resentments paralleled those of the larger body, and his unrestrained and probably unrestrainable need to project these found ample resonance in the larger body. His cries became the nation's. He was the perfect man to state and to seem to meet the immediate needs of the time. Elected Chancellor in 1933, he rapidly and systematically dismantled the Weimar Republic.[1]

But the tide of hysterical reality flows at a level difficult to describe. Hitler's experienced world was metastable, tormented, forged into a kind of unity by main strength, "the triumph of the will." Of course, this matched the nation's torment, and that was his source of strength and his chief resource. Both the individual and the corporate individual were contorted in wretched pain, to the point that consensual reality, the structure of the communally experienced world, was on the point of disintegration. Hitler posed as the savior.

If they—the Jews, gypsies, handicapped, and so on—were subhuman, then their cross-cutting, differently structured experienced worlds could be dismissed; they posed no threat to continued mainstream life. These deviant peoples could be described as living filthy, degenerate, disordered, that is, subhuman lives. No, Hitler seemed to communicate, it is not our experienced world that is crumbling in a tide of diarrhea, it is theirs. (Hitler's disgust with "unclean, irregular gypsies" nearly equaled his disgust with the Jews. As I've mentioned, Gypsies were unhindered: they propagated indiscriminately; they "bred like rabbits." As for the Jews, it was their "love of money, filthy lucre." He shares with Pol Pot, say, an obsessive anality, a fear of being soiled.) All such subhumans, non-Aryans, must go. "All life unworthy of life" must go.

Hitler could propound an alleged cure that was convincing to many, because very probably he so intensely felt in himself humiliation, grotesque inadequacy, exclusion from the normal—wretchedness. He apparently was monotesticular, and perhaps impotent. Some psychiatrists have concluded that he was preoccupied with coprophilia—habitually employing anal practices and fetishes in obsessive sexual arrangements. (Of course, conventional heterosexual activity is no guarantee against genocide. "Get the perverts!")

It is at least very interesting that so many of the leaders of genocidal or genocidally inclined nations were physically maimed as well as morally disturbed: not only monotesticular Hitler, but the German Kaiser of World

War I with his withered arm; Stalin likewise with a withered arm, usually carefully hidden; apparently Mao with his various venereal diseases. Only intellectuals chronically dissociated from their own bodily reality neatly distinguish moral and psychological distortions from physical ones.

Some so-called skinheads, neo-Nazis, claim to deny that Nazis' genocides actually occurred—these, some of the best-documented events in history. When a neo-Nazi is convicted of some outright crime, I suggest that he (are there women neo-Nazis?) be required to visit Auschwitz I, II, and III—then sent back to his homeland to complete his sentence.

*   *   *

For the next paradigm case of genocide, I have chosen the persecution, and in some cases the outright extinction, of certain groups, tribes, nations of so-called Digger Indians in California.

This genocide brings the whole matter home to us, and not just in a geographical sense. For it is our own immediate reaction to profound otherness close at hand that must be tracked, caught, and acknowledged before it flits by without leaving a trace—at least not one we can clearly remember or talk about.

Unlike war, which is usually gussied up and trotted out with a wrapping of rationality—or rationalization—genocide incubates and breaks forth on a different level. True, genocide too is typically wrapped in various rationalizations. But more basically and centrally than is the case with war, genocide is literally a gut reaction that besets us without warning: a turning of the stomach, a cringing in the genitals, a sudden wave of tremulous nausea and revulsion that sweeps through the body. The reaction is huge and disturbing, and we clutch for some reason for it. What we sometimes find is this: they are multiplying and poisoning and polluting us and our world.

I recall this aversion felt immediately one day driving for the first time through Plainfield, New Jersey. This is a city with a large black population. I am white. The sickening feeling was just there in the pit of my stomach, there immediately for no reason I could have given.

Now that we have lived in Plainfield for more than twenty years, with black neighbors on both sides of us, the feeling is typically supplanted by feelings of friendliness and respect. The initial reaction has been almost totally deactivated by an accumulating body of experience, and inferences drawn intuitively from this data. We neighbors have good reason to trust each other. But that initial reaction, immediate in the face of the alien and overabounding, left its mark.

Why? To account for reactions so eruptive, radical, and strange, we need radical, strange, and eruptive hypotheses. I am supposing that when for some reason we are stressed and thrown off balance, alien ways of being in the world and experiencing it so cut across and disturb our own, that we are shaken through our cores. We lose our way, suffer psychical earthquake and primal abandonment terror. I am supposing that the aversive response to the alien had—and still has in some instances—survival value. For what is alien is unknown and untried, and may be dangerous. So the aversive response is extraordinarily difficult to root out when it occurs inappropriately.

In the next chapter I will dwell at length on how a group builds up its world-experienced through habitual, tacit, primitive, and typically unacknowledgeable consensuality. This is a coded network that establishes the nature of things for the group. Differently put, it establishes the conditions of identity of the corporate individual itself, the group. If I am successful, we will see how disturbance in this corporate individual runs in ramifying fractures throughout its members.

The task is extremely difficult, for our inherited bias in the West is to take individual members as primary, and to try, in thought, to build up the group from these "simples." Seduced by what can easily be pointed to, we overlook the communal and mimetic nature of us individual organisms: how we experiencing beings are engulfed in the corporate individual's ways and means of experiencing.

The only hope of resisting this seduction is to employ all our resources of understanding—that is, conceptualization, metaphorization, and, above all, concrete examples of genocides themselves. We need both knowledge by description and knowledge by acquaintance.

We Westerners in particular tend automatically to sort out the world analytically, to array it as objects that instantiate prescribed sorts. We tend to take this detached and analytical attitude toward everything, including our own selves. This third-person point of view has values. But its grievous cost is that we lose touch with our immediate first-person experiencing, our primal reactions and feelings as enculturated bodies.

We don't experience immediate terror at the alien for no reason. But we can't typically give the reason, which adds to the uncanniness and the terror.

The most plausible reason for the hysteria, however momentary it may be on occasion, is that our experienced world disintegrates in the face of the alien, it gives way, and we body-selves fall. We gasp or lurch, the heart thuds, the chest is oppressed, the stomach churns. The ecstasy of the intact, smoothly functioning body deserts us. It is replaced immediately by a horrendous malaise, the absolute opposite of humming vitality and the honeying

savoring of wellbeing. It is what abruptly intrudes and violates: it can be infinitely disturbing, noxious, disgusting. The whole experienced world gives
way.

Hence the metaphor I use for the disintegration of the experienced
world—a flood of diarrhea overtaking us. We are thrown into the eliminative regions of the personal and corporate bodies. Another metaphor that
helps us to intensify and grasp our immediate reactions, those genocidal
triggers: In the face of the alien we experience a visceral recoiling—like
throwing back bedcovers in a luxury hotel to find seething bedbugs.

*   *   *

Now let us delve within the fairly recent history of what I take to be the corporate body of most of my readers. It is my own home group: the gross European incursion into this continent, the Western Hemisphere, the New
World (all of course locutions generated by ethnic prejudice). If there has
ever been a corporate body more aggressively expansive than our own, we
would, I suppose, have to go back to Genghis Khan to find it (and, at that,
he was more interested in pillaging and magnificently subduing than in taking and holding land).

Focus on the famous—for Native Americans, infamous—doctrine of
Manifest Destiny: Since Europe is God's gift to the planet, and since our
civilization is manifestly superior to any other, it is perfectly clear that we
are destined to subdue all semblances of civilizations already here. Moreover, our version of European civilization is the newest, most vital, most lib-
erated from ancient prejudices—so we believe. This epitomizes the propul-
sive, booming attitude of self-righteous expansion.

Hence, as the Eastern or Atlantic coast is a natural boundary—established
as it were by Providence, "in God we trust"—so the Pacific is manifestly the
Western. The well-formed and vital corporate body must have a vital and
comely geographical shape. It will have it! The triumph of the will.

Among the most avid and irrepressible proponents of Manifest Destiny
in the mid-nineteenth century United States was the powerful senator from
Missouri, the Gateway to the West, Thomas Hart Benton. Numbered
among his fellows was the Secretary of State at the time—later President—
James Buchanan.

Was there a helmeted head to mount atop the advancing front of Western
expansion? Indeed—Benton's son-in-law, John C. Fremont, nicknamed the
Pathfinder. In him a man was at hand who completely embodied the Biblical injunction to never turn back once resolved, to "set one's face like a flint."

In years to come he would push himself and his men beyond any reasonable limit of endurance, and many died under his leadership. In his fourth expedition he tried to survey a railroad route that his master, Senator Benton, thought should follow a certain parallel of latitude. Trying to follow this in winter through the San Juan mountains of Colorado, his group lost their way. Bogged down in deep snow and completely disoriented, the men endured unmentionable sufferings, then mental derangements and deaths, with the suggestion of cannibalism at the end. Fremont himself, in a kind of mania, recovered and left the region before knowing the fate of some of his band. Without the compassion of one of his injured subordinates, who went back in search of the incapacitated, a few who survived would not have.

Thomas Jefferson had sent the intrepid Lewis and Clark and their men (and woman) to explore all the way across the incredibly vast Louisiana Purchase, all the way to the Pacific. They had survived (barely), returned and lived to tell the tale. The goal that would suck us violently into expansion was contacted, the alluring Pacific, but the land in between was touched, scratched, in only the smallest degree of its vastness.

It must be mapped, area by area, subdued and populated, subjected to the marvels of technology, and to the laws of a complete republic. Missionaries would then bring all the inhabitants the saving message of Jesus Christ. Enter Fremont and his five expeditions of exploration, terrible suffering and loss in the fourth, and conquest. The Indians of the Plains, great warrior and also trading nations, had adopted the horse from the Spanish in the sixteenth century. That animal was quickly ordered into their way and vision of life—rapidly ritualized as the Earth's gift to them.

These Indians radiated a kind of terrifying romance, along with their generally disgusting "primitiveness" in the eyes of many white settlers, traders, trappers, miners. And they not only appeared daunting, they were so for many years. But they had little idea of what had overtaken them, leaking in, infiltrating, rushing in noxiously from all sides to destabilize and finally to destroy the world as they could experience it—the only one they could imagine to live in.

After Fremont and his band in one of his earlier expeditions had forced their way across the snowbound California Sierras in winter, they found shelter at Sutter's Fort. This was the site of the imminent discovery of gold, and of the soon-to-begin rush from all quarters to dig, hose, hack, coax it from the ground.

The Indians of the California regions had not adopted the horse. They appeared utterly lowly and filthy, of the earth, digging roots out of the ground "as if they were dogs," subhuman. They appeared to lack a full complement of mind, of rationality, and they were promptly overwhelmed by immigrants who experienced the earth and all life completely differently from the indigenous ways. For whites they were all things to be conquered, subjugated, used, turned into commodities; and these immigrants had the mind and the equipment to do this. When the indigenous populations weren't enslaved, de facto or de jure, they were taken on as "the White Man's burden" to civilize and humanize. Or they were categorized as, for instance, cattle-rustling thieves, and killed. Unpent, unstayed, children of Nature were not to be abided.

One gets the distinct impression reading histories of California written by people of European extraction that the Indians there were barely visible, except when they could be used. When they couldn't help but be seen, they were perceived as predatory animal-like beings. If there hadn't been a world for whites to conquer, the ruling or semi-ruling Mexicans to outwit, and gold to be extracted from the ground—if there hadn't been glittering and challenging distractions—the disgust at the sight of these Indians might have disturbed, perhaps unhinged, many of the whites.

A perceptive settler from Virginia jotted this vignette in 1845:

> The Captain [Sutter] keeps from 600 to 800 Indians in a perfect state of slavery. I had the mortification of seeing them dine. A lot of troughs, three or four feet long, were brought out of the cook room and set out in the broiling sun. All the laborers, great and small, ran to the troughs like so many pigs and fed themselves with their hands as long as the troughs contained the least bit of moisture. There was no need of cleaning up after them. (David Roberts, *A Newer World: Kit Carson, John C. Fremont, and the Claiming of the American West*, Sources, 148)

To say the corporate body of white America was disturbed at this time and place is worse than understatement. Was there a corporate body at all? We should say that particular corporate bodies of white Americans were profoundly disturbed and distracted, fired by a destiny they couldn't really understand, living by their wits. They were on the ragged edge most of the time, wondering if they would survive. Would the Mexicans drive them out? Would the British invade California? Was their leader, Fremont, under secret orders from Senator Benton and Secretary Buchanan, orders the regular U.S. Army knew nothing about? (Fremont was in fact brought east and tried and convicted of insubordination in an Army court-martial.) Might the Russians reassert themselves in California?

In any case, corporate European-American bodies—Fremont's group was one of them—could see of the Indians only what they were willing and able to see. What they saw were Diggers. Other nearby tribes were not seen at all. Those who subsisted on the acorns of the Blue Oak, for example: the acorns ground to flour in mortars worn on tables of vast stone, the flour leached in special ways in basins of liquids to remove its bitterness. The oak was revered and adored as the tree of life, woven into tales and rituals that guided and sustained the people. Or their tales of creation of the world by Spider: creation as a webbing of sustaining connections.

Everything indigenous seen at all was registered as childish nonsense at best, a predatory threat at worst. A bounty was placed on the heads of Indians, as if they were coyotes, wolves, or mountain lions: so and so much money per scalp. Parties of whites made holiday of shooting expeditions into the upper canyons where Indians tried to hide away. As the Californian, philosopher, and part-time historian Josiah Royce noted in his history of California, Indians "were used as target practice" (see Sources, 286–87). Terror drove the survivors into the high mountains where they tried to live out of sight.

After a few decades of this, some hereditary indigenous groups were extinguished entirely, others so disordered in their mental, ritual, economic lives that their cultures collapsed. Dispirited, some of the groups dragged on, no longer the vital humans they once were. Many, many died of infectious diseases to which they had no immunity.

Finally, in 1911, the Oroville, California newspaper could print news of "the last wild Indian." He was the lone survivor of his band, which had subsisted by hiding itself in the upper canyons for years and foraging secretively. Nearly starved to death, he stumbled out of a canyon. Miraculously, he fell into the hands of two anthropologists, T. T. Waterman and Alfred J. Kroeber.

Kroeber in particular was a kind of linguistic genius who could, with some learning from both sides, communicate in the indigenous man's understandably strange dialect. This was a branch, now nearly extinguished, of the Yana language community in which the anthropologists were conversant. The "last wild Indian" was protected, his marvelous paleolithic arts, skills, and knowledge fostered, photos of him taken, and the man given certain tasks in the archaeological museum.

But what was to be his name? This paleolithic man never used his own name. (See Theodora Kroeber, *Ishi in Two Worlds*, Sources, 1961.) Was it because we humans are named by our community—the name is bestowed upon us as a gift—and since his community had vanished, his name could no longer be used, neither by the namers, of course, nor by him, the named? (Which recalls Royce's phrase, "the blessed community.") And/or is this a paleolithic and indigenous practice that manifests a great wisdom about personal names: that they do not merely refer to us as do common names? Those can be used by anyone to refer to anything in a world objectified, analyzed, laid out before us impersonally. But rather, we persons' names signal our very being-in-community, our essence and wholeness. They are sacred, and can be used only with great care in the proper setting.

In any case, the man had to have a name. The best Kroeber and Waterman could do was to call him Ishi, which simply means "man" in the Yana language community. Theodora Kroeber writes,

> He accepted the new name, answering to it unreluctantly. But once it was bestowed it took on enough of his true name's mystic identification with himself, his soul, whatever inner essence of a man it is which a name shares, that he was never again heard to pronounce it. (128)

*   *   *

Alfred Kroeber's life might serve as a model through which we could better understand our own. He was a person of great learning, intelligence, and compassion. But there was a certain disconnect in his experiencing that helps us grasp a typical disconnect in our own.

Kroeber exhibits considerable ambivalence in his relationship to Ishi. On the one hand, he admires his personal qualities and his knowledge and skills. But on the other, he has a greatly difficult time making sense of all this within the confines of what he considers to be scientific anthropology: the world reliably, analytically, scientifically "constructed." Ishi died when Kroeber was on sabbatical leave at the Museum of Natural History in New York City. He had left instructions with his physiologist associate not to anatomize Ishi's body, for it had been anathema to Ishi and his people to thus mutilate the body—the body and the spirit were for them so intimately interfused. The physiologist does it anyway. By the time the train brings Kroeber back across the country, Ishi's brain is capped in a bottle of formaldehyde.

Kroeber accepts the fact, and the brain now resides in the Smithsonian Museum in Washington, D.C. Indigenous people of California are, as I write, trying to have it returned to California. (Indigenous populations generally have their identity in their place and over their time—their place and time both as individuals and as corporate bodies. Western science and philosophy are said to begin triumphantly in the transcendence of local place and local time: the basic elements out of which everything is composed are what they are at any place or time. But we need both the possibility of abstract thought and a rooted sense of our particular place and time, don't we?—See Edward Casey, *Getting Back into Place* and *Representing Place*, Sources.)

It is said that Kroeber underwent prolonged psychoanalysis after Ishi's death. When he emerged he published his chief work, *Handbook of the Indians of California*, 1925, with 419 illustrations and 40 maps, 995 pages. It is a model of the naked positivist-scientific. One searches in vain for an account of the genocide of the Indians of California, and the multiple cultural, human, psychological, spiritual aspects of this (though something is written about the imported diseases that felled so many.) One learns exactly how many shells of a certain type are owed to a Yurok husband by a man caught cuckolding him—demonstrable and measurable facts like that.

Perhaps Kroeber believed that his task was to describe what the Indian cultures had been, not what caused them to cease to be? That has a certain myopic and deformed logic. It's as if Kroeber cannot allow his science and his human perceptiveness to mix, as if one would pollute the other. All this is happening in one man.

I think it's safe to say that Kroeber the scientist doesn't want to see certain things. He will not and does not see them. Yet he is also a human, a compassionate and perceptive one. This white man's dilemma—so sharply if inarticulately felt by so many—is the greatest lesson Kroeber's life can teach us now.

It is this that is marvelously conveyed in the HBO movie "Ishi," starring Jon Voight as Kroeber, and other fine actors. Here are the climactic scenes: Ishi tells Kroeber that since he alone survives of his group, there is nobody left to sing him into the afterlife. He asks Kroeber to do the singing. Kroeber is shown sniffing at this, gently scoffing and apologizing that, as a scientist, it would not be quite right for him to do such a thing.

Then we see Kroeber back from New York in California, Ishi is dead, and Kroeber remembers his request. In an unforgetable enactment, Voight gives us a brilliant interpretation of Kroeber: he gazes at Ishi's back as the paleolithic man walks away from him forever into the mist, and singing in a cracking, pathetic little up and down voice, tears streaming down his face, Kroeber belatedly sings Ishi into the afterlife.

Whether or not completely accurate historically, the film helps us face the reality of our own confused and ambivalent responses, our half-hidden infantile matrix that stays with us. These responses are something more important

than historical facts—truths "out there." As we will see in the fourth chapter:
In the same way the TV picture of Serbs pouring shells into the Sarajevo hospital remains with us, this does. In the same way the scene of the drowned
Rwandan woman with the four children tied to her extremities remains with
us, this does. It feeds our ruminations: that slow spading up and over in our
bodies and souls. The tilling that might just change us and be really educational. Not the incredibly superficial business we currently call education in
North Atlantic culture.

For us today, understanding means mainly the scientific sort, and knowledge means mainly the descriptive sort. But this doesn't give us enough to
live by, not in the face of overwhelming human vulnerability, fear, and eruptive distortions, limitations, and illusions at the heart of consciousness.
More than empathy and intelligence—as both are commonly understood—
is needed in the face of genocides. What could it be?

Writing from a perspective of half a century, Kroeber's wife, Theodora,
relates,

> In contrast to the Forty-niners whom [historian J. G.] Bruff describes, whose
> morality and morale had crumbled, Ishi and his band remained incorrupt, hu-
> mane, compassionate, and with their faith intact even unto starvation, pain,
> and death. The questions then are: What makes for stability? For psychic
> strength? For endurance, courage, faith? (98)

I believe that genocide is a possibility of the human condition itself, particularly under certain circumstances. But we can at least ask, Might paleolithic humans, hunter-gatherers, have had more stability, endurance, authenticity, than do we?[2] With all our apparent power, why are we still so
disturbed by otherness? Why are so many of us afflicted with addictions and
with mental illness?

We have lost the power of Paleolithic myth to connect us to the sustaining and nurturing presences of the universe, the world's regenerative cycles
of all sorts, its weavings and reweavings of human life. We in the secular
West rattle around now in merely linear history, rootless.

*   *   *

In the introduction I described this book as a progression in intensity: it has
an ineluctable cyclical dimension. What is intensified is not just the piling
up of empirical facts about genocide, but the intensification of the meaning
of the facts. The next chapter intensifies meaning in both key senses of

"meaning." The sense that is central in knowledge by description, and then also the sense that is central in knowledge by acquaintance—visceral and personal knowledge.

The key concept in explaining genocide theoretically and intellectually, knowledge by description, is the corporate body, the mega-individual we call the group, the identity of that through time. As mentioned earlier in the present chapter, a bias emphasizing the member of the group, the individual simpliciter, runs through all Western thinking. It must be counteracted. Just how is it that habitual consensus—automatic, preconscious, subconscious—builds up the group's world-experienced? So engulfing and "natural" does this become that most individual members act out their roles in the whole automatically and subconsciously. They do what is *right*. Any suspicion that the home group is not omniscient and all-sufficing is countered by ever stronger assertions of the group's dominance and endurance, even its immortality.

The second sense of meaning is that which is central to knowledge by acquaintance. What does genocide mean to us personally? How deeply do we believe—that is, feel—its reality? As James put it, the sting of belief, which can awaken us from our everyday trance in the group, and might deter us from contributing to a genocidal rampage. For, as I said, I believe that the potential for genocide is inherent in the human condition, and can be activated in certain conditions of great stress.[3]

NOTES

1. Laconic and phlegmatic though he typically was, yet Admiral Günther Lütjens, commander of the doomed battleship Bismarck, delivered himself of this ejaculation in a final transmission to Hitler: "We will fight to the last, believing in you my Führer, and with unshakable faith in Germany's victory." Hitler responded, "All of Germany is with you. . . . Your performance of your duty will strengthen our Folk in its belief in our struggle for existence." Note reification of the German people as a corporate body, the Folk (Volkskörper), as if this were a quasi divinity. Also the belief that the corporate body had been attacked, "our struggle for existence." Note that the corporate body has a head, "my Führer." (Sources, Bercuson and Herwig, 284)

2. Vine Deloria Jr. (Sources) quotes William Carlos Williams, "The land! Don't you feel it? Doesn't it make you want to go out and lift dead Indians tenderly from their graves, to steal from them—as if it must be clinging even to their corpses—some authenticity." (53) Deloria writes in his own voice: "At worst, the end of one form of colonialism means the beginning of a movement to feudalize political systems around the globe so as to stabilize the economic conditions of the more af-

fluent nations. Either approach means that the ecological problem is not dealt with, the problem of technological dehumanization is not reduced, and the breakdown of individual and community identity is not reversed." (64) These themes recur below.

3. Nazis' genocides differed from whites' in that their efforts were highly articulated and organized, while the whites' may appear to be haphazard. But in California, white groups placed bounties on the heads of "Digger" Indians. When members of a population tacitly or explicitly assent to practices that they should know will probably result in the extermination or incapacitation of another group, that population should be charged with genocide. I don't think that highly articulated, Nazi-like organization is a necessary condition for genocide, the motivations for which occur on a miasmic level of primal meaning-making—a fetid, misty level, a wave of foul air. Any group that excites revulsion and pollution in an ascendant group that labels it "subhuman" can be targeted for genocide. (Some indigenous groups in the Americas were genocided with Nazi-like organization. For instance, Charles Darwin noted from his voyage on The Beagle that General Rosas was hired by the Argentinian government to exterminate the Indians.) The California case is not unique. For example, the North Carolina delegation to the Continental Congress proclaimed it Christian duty "to extinguish the very race of them [Cherokees] and scarce to leave enough of their existence to be a vestige in proof that the Cherokee nation once was." See Gallately, sources, 378.

3

THE EVERYDAY ILLUSION OF
IMMORTALITY AND ITS DISRUPTION

One of the functions of consciousness is to limit itself. The most obvious form of this is more or less voluntary. I mean, for example, how persons distract themselves by enclosing themselves in nearly constant noise: Muzak, a TV running with nobody watching, a radio with nobody "really listening," people talking just to be talking, just to be warding off the engulfing silence with their own sounds.

Routinized movements or mannerisms perform the same limiting function. Part of the allure of smoking is that we know what to do with our hands. Otherwise we might be flabbergasted in the face of countless possibilities, at a loss, dumbfounded.

The right ways of smoking are predetermined and sanctioned by the group. For but one example, cigarettes are not to be inserted in a nostril and the smoke inhaled by that route. To do so would simply be wrong.

If there weren't an inherent centrifugal movement of consciousness, there would be no need to limit it, no need to incite a centripetal countermovement. The enlarging movement is an inheritance from animal consciousness: something catches a creature's eye and it looks around to see what's causing it. The creature expands its zone, its context, of awareness.

What distinguishes the centrifugal capacities of human consciousness is the extraordinarily greater potential range of them. We are not only in the world as are other creatures. We can be aware that this is the case, can form ideas of the world as world. For example, we can ask how far the universe extends, what caused it, and where it will ultimately wind up.

It is just the awful potential range of the centrifugal tendencies of consciousness that prompts the centripetal. For who wants to dwell—who dares to dwell—on where the world is taking each of us: to aging, to old age if we're lucky, and to death? Or to those horrendous accidents that so far, probably, have happened only to others, but might happen to us? Or to those moments in which we have regretted our past mistakes and compounded foolishnesses, and might regret them again?

The expansive, centrifugal movement of consciousness is sensed to be dangerous. If one's child dies, say, one feels the potential for never-ceasing, ever-grinding grief, for hopeless wishing the death were not so. One is drawn down that path. Doubtless this is why saints are held up as role models. Whatever the event, they see it in perspective, in proportion; it is experienced in the largest possible context. Their example pondered may help us learn that each of us is responsible to deal only with the life that is given us and that remains to us. We are not gods.

Saints are unusual, exceedingly rare. Most people tend to live in dim awareness that if they don't distract and confine themselves by ceaseless noise, say, they will encounter pain that might be insuperable. They may encounter pain rooted at the sick heart of themselves.

Centrifugal movements of consciousness threaten to move into areas that we cannot foresee and control. As I mentioned in the introduction, there are moments in which we glance out of the corner of the eye, and sense what stands beyond, and in excess to, all that we can categorize and know. We sense a brute presence. The inference is immediate and unassailable: it must be what we don't know we don't know. No end of sights, sounds, smells can touch this quavering experience into life. A passing shadow in a forest; suddenly seeing myriads of insects hatching on a stream; a passing scent that reminds of something we cannot say; a turning in the stomach at the first sound of a name, but nothing more is revealed. At times of stress particularly, the abundance of Nature appears unboundable, as eluding our ability to forecast and control, as frightening.

So a centripetal, self-limiting movement of consciousness is triggered. I mean that on the same dim margins of consciousness in which the potential for pain or panic is encountered, there is generated a movement to limit consciousness. This limiting movement is neither completely focal and voluntary, nor is it completely automatic and involuntary. Let us call it semivoluntary.

People in the grip of this self-limiting dynamic will probably be annoyed if what they are doing is pointed out to them. Annoyed and disturbed. But not nearly as much as they would be if rudimentary and quite involuntary distortions and limitations of consciousness were to be exposed to their sight, assuming that to be possible. For if a behavior is at least semi-voluntary, one could, in a moment of relative calm at least, imagine doing something else. But if some belief or behavior is involuntary, if it is utterly taken for granted and amounts to an automatism, there is no alternative to choose. One is trapped.

One is trapped in the group reality into which each of us is born and which we must take completely for granted. Groups limit their experienced worlds in profoundly habitual and, by now, unconscious ways.

Toward exposures of the utterly taken-for-granted and involuntary I am working. I want to explain that radical convulsion of group and individual consciousness that violently extrudes from itself whatever threatens the limitations and distortions of the home group's deeply habitual ways of experiencing the world. Whatever undercuts this group's consensual reality, the automatic and arbitrary elements of its immediately lived and experienced world. That is, whatever prompts terror, whatever causes the bottom of the commonly experienced world to fall away beneath its members' feet.

Feeling terrified, the home group may counter with terrorizing. I mean the commission of genocide. I believe that no group, including our own, is immune to this possibility.[1]

*   *   *

So let us proceed to expose the strata one by one of what is progressively more taken for granted, ever more abysmally nonvoluntary. We will be exposing that which is progressively more disturbing when exposed. At bottom, the exposure is psychical earthquake for the body-bound, earthbound, enculturated creatures we are. To counteract this fear will seem to genociders the reasonable thing to do. Killing those others will appear justified in the name of self-defense.[2]

I recall a hot and very humid summer night in central New Jersey. At about 9:30 an ice cream parlor was open on a street we seldom traveled. It combined retail outlet and ice cream factory. My wife and I entered and ordered a mountain of cold sweets each. At some point I went to the men's room. As I came out a man entered the narrow hallway just before me through another door, one that must have led from the factory itself. He was roughly middle aged, and I noticed the rundown heels of his work shoes. He turned into the parlor. With a bent body and worn and weary expression he struggled to carry a huge cylinder of ice cream into the soda fountain area. Ice cream for others to eat.

At that moment I supposed that very probably the man was incapable of reflecting on his place in the universe, or of how best to live his moments in the face of the multiple alternatives open to him. His consciousness was probably limited to just getting through the day. If asked why-questions, he might have said, "I do it to put food on the table for me and my family." But in his consciousness at that moment he was probably thinking only of delivering his cylinder to the display case, getting through the rest of the day and night, and falling into bed.

What if he were confronted with the presumptive narrowness of his "God-given" consciousness? His response would be simple, founded, he believes, on self-evidence: "One has to work." Probably in finding a good reason for the limitations of his consciousness, he would control his disturbance over our intrusion.

But what if we kept at him with questions like, "Why can't we make this a just world in which wealth is redistributed, where a few don't eat sweets on the backs of the many who groan and sweat under their loads?" He would probably feel that he, really, had no alternative. He would feel helpless, probably desperate and perhaps terrified. He might have a strong itch to kill us.

*   *   *

Now let us get to levels of constriction or distortion of consciousness so completely habitual and involuntary that one could not imagine even for an instant that there are alternatives to such awareness. Exposure of constriction at this level results in violent, panic-stricken response. The panic may be limited to an individual, or—in the cases in which I am most interested—may balloon into a whole group's panicked response.

The first of such limiting and constricting features of consciousness is so fundamental and so utterly taken for granted that noticing it is agonizingly difficult (agonizing literally, as we will see). Abysmal mechanisms of defense and denial operate on this level. Only very dimly do we sense that something fearful or disgusting is there to be recognized—something on the margins of awareness—but that we don't dare to recognize it focally. It is recognized only to the extent of "not to be recognized further."

In general, constriction of consciousness is maddeningly difficult to notice, just because it's constriction of *consciousness*. What's left over in consciousness to notice the constriction of itself? The possibility of a larger consciousness is obscured, is concealed, and the concealment itself is concealed. There is abysmal ignorance: ignorance of ignorance. Life on automatic.

But I'll be more specific. For on the lived specifics pivots our ability to thoroughly describe and explain genocide (I am interested in the most arresting cases of genocide, those which generate world-historical consequences). Genocide, I have maintained, is a visceral reaction within bodily organisms to the immanent undermining of our experienced world by a foreign group's way of experiencing things. Without comprehension of our many-sided, concrete particularity and vulnerability both as individuals and groups we float off in abstractions.

But that itself is too abstract. We can no longer afford the luxuries of airy abstractions. Let us try to center down into ourselves, into our heart of hearts. Don't we tend to gloss over the possibility of endemic illusion on both the group and the individual level because we live in secret terror of what we would see if we penetrated illusion? I propose to refocus and intensify my analysis of the dynamics of illusion that precipitate genocide. This may drive home to us what is going on as we gloss over things and slide through life. We all so easily do this, individually and in groups.

*   *   *

First we should try—you as readers and I as writer—to interrupt what is probably in process: the insensible slide into naive realism, the entranced slide into the trance, the illusion, that our group's experienced world just is the world. The meaning it has is not our "construction." Oh no! That possibility is not even imagined.

Or it may be that we slide insensibly into theorizing, into the comfort of statospheric flights that take leave of our bodies—apparently. One or the other, I will try to interrupt the slide.

Recall our key insight that movement experienced to be happening in the world isn't just happening "out there," but is also happening in our own experiencing bodies. Movement experienced by us and by our culture to be inappropriate or unnatural is not merely a fact noted, but is a wrenching of ourselves that can be sickening.

Space, time, movement are not merely "ideas or images in our minds." They are habitual, cemented ways in which the enculturated and mimetically engulfed human body forms the space we directly experience, and the movements of things within it, that we directly experience. A jolt is needed to break these ways open, to expose them. Imagine again Americans being suddenly dropped into a country in which driving is done on the left side of the road. Seldom is mere reasoning with oneself, or talking to oneself, sufficient to dislodge within our bodies the deep conviction that driving on the left is wrong. Seldom do these mentalisms suffice to relieve us of a deep, visceral disturbance, something bordering on nausea for many.

Notice my experiencing of driving—rather, being driven—in Australia. It was a rare opportunity to have one's own generation of space-experienced finally become noticeable. We were in a rented car in the interior of Australia. Traffic goes on the left side of the road in Australia—a relic of the English conquerors of the continent. My wife was driving, for I feared my attention might wander, and if startled by something, I might swerve into oncoming cars and trucks.

Between stretches of monotony were times of intense concentration, coherence, and fascination. Even details on the horizon were etched for me with uncanny clarity. In touching the horizon moment by moment with my eyes, I was touching something ancient and intimate in myself. Space and time were prefiguring themselves through me. Space and time experienced were forming themselves in me. In fact, they were the encompassing ground and ever-regenerating root of myself as body and as self. What made the experience of all particular things in the world possible was itself an experience.

That is, what I always already was as the world's and the culture's creature arose alive and quivering in consciousness, seeming both inevitable and spontaneous. I felt on the verge of art. The best I could do was to hum, then whistle. I broke into laughter. My wife's quizzical look encouraged me to think that I could, with effort, explain what I was laughing about, but I was too happy to try. I again began humming and whistling.

John Dewey's words came back, but now with new life. "Form, as it is present in the fine arts, is the art of making clear what is involved in the organization of space and time prefigured in every course of a developing life-experience" (*Art as Experience*, Sources, p. 24).

I hypothesize that if group members' generation in and through their bodies of their spatiotemporal world-experienced is sufficiently disrupted, the very identity and reality of the things they experience begins to dissolve. The experienced world gives way and turns infectious. One's own experienced bodily self gives way and turns infectious. We can call this ontological hysteria. It is the fertile breeding ground of genocide.

* * *

Our super-objective: We must try to grasp in the most concrete and intensified way what happens when a home group's cemented ways of constituting a world-experienced are threatened by another group's ways. If the home group's continued existence is threatened, if the illusion of group immortality is threatened, then the very solidity of the ongoing experienced world gives way. There is terror: Get 'em all, Kill 'em!

As earlier noted, an ineliminable feature of what we call our experiencing or our mental life—our thinking, perceiving, emoting life—is that each instance of our experiencing can be picked out and described only by picking out and describing what it is of or about. A particular act of thinking must be described as a thinking of or about something particular. Even if one is thinking of nothing, it is a thinking absorbed in nothingness. If one is feeling the emotion of love, it must be love of something. To feel hate, there must be an object hated.

Though moods, to be sure, have no particular, determinate objects, they reveal how we are lodged or attuned within the Whole, within a conceptually unboundable excess. We are lost in the Whole—perhaps revealingly, if questioned pointedly about it, perhaps not. And certain sorts of emotions like love or anger shade off into moods. In moments of calm, love can shade off into love of something diffuse, all-encompassing, engulfing, effulgent, such as the whole residual universe. Hate and anger can do so as well.

Let us further develop the central point for our study: the thing or object or Whole that is experienced dominates our awareness of our own experiencing of it, even to the point of eclipsing our experiencing. Ironical. So if we are thinking of things that we deeply believe will endure—stars, boulders, our own cultural group—we tend to conclude insensibly that our experiencing endures, and that we experiencers or minders endure too.

This is profoundly fallacious. It is mind's natural constriction and distortion of itself—minding or consciousness that is at best only dimly marginal. It often takes a shock to reveal the truth: our minding or experiencing of the minded or the experienced is ephemeral. It is fleeting, it can be extinguished in an instant, as can we. And who wants to acknowledge that? We are working high up in one of the World Trade Center towers, say, and the next moment we glance around and see an impossibly huge airplane coming levelly right at us and roaring. We dash away, but in an instant are incinerated. Who wants to acknowledge that possibility?

Repeat: the dominance of the minded or experienced thing is so fundamental and automatic that we forget the ineluctable fact that there must be particular vulnerable persons' minding or experiencing of it. That fact tends to be occluded, eclipsed.

Of course, in times permitting reflection, in philosophical moments, say, we can and must make this distinction between the minding and the minded, between the experiencing and the experienced. Even within one's own mental life, within the streaming of one's own consciousness, if we think of the same thing twice (the diameter of the earth, say), it's a new thinking of that same fact thought about. These distinctions are easy for me to make now as I write and as you read this book.

But in most of our moments we are caught up prereflectively in what we are thinking and feeling about. We are engulfed in it. "One's own mental life"—the phrase I just used—is a sclerotic, distracting, stupefying abstraction. It is a concocted fictional unit, an illusion that each of us is an independent existence. It is an illusion of ordinary language and everyday consciousness. The reality is that we enculturated bodily beings are caught up moment by moment in what happens to occupy us, the object of our thinking or experiencing, not the thinking or experiencing itself. And essential elements of the meanings of these objects are predetermined by our cultures.

We are caught up in the object of our experiencing, just as it appears to us, not the experiencing itself that quickly passes away. So, again, if I am thinking of something like a Sequoia that we all agree endures—thinking of it as enduring—my own passing thought of an enduring Sequoia tends automatically to be eclipsed.

The obscuring of my own thinking or experiencing in my moment-to-moment life goes very, very deep. The thing as it is thought about deeply eclipses my passing thinking, because I have early learned from my group that the thing is to be thought about in a limited number of definite ways. If my ways of experiencing deviate from the group's norm, I myself may refuse to acknowledge them. We are caught up in what's thought about in ways profoundly influenced and structured by the way our ongoing group has conditioned us to think and feel about it from the very beginning of our lives; and it continues to condition us to think and feel this way.

The thought-about stays the way the enduring group thinks and perceives it, and will continue to think and perceive it. We must think and perceive so, because even for me to think of myself as an individual requires me to think of myself as an individual member of this culture and of its world-experienced. The World Trade Center towers can't just vanish. A survivor of September 11 who was told that they had vanished could not believe it. It was impossible and unthinkable.

Again, my own passing thinking and perceiving of anything is thrown into deepest shadow. This is everyday automatism, the everyday illusion of personal immortality. The disturbance of this is profoundly disturbing to me and to anybody who endures it.

But I am working my way to the ultimate disturbance that opens the way to an understanding of genocide: the moment in which the illusion of the group's immortality threatens to burst. This is what the survivor just mentioned finds it impossible to immediately believe, for the twin towers were almost definitive of our culture. Our ongoing world, what we have "constructed" in experience, and in this case also literally constructed with steel and cement, can't just vanish!

*   *   *

Let us dwell on the pervasive reality of our group in normal, everyday life. It permeates every level of our experience. For example, to keep some of my thoughts private, I keep them shielded from others, from the group. The group is present in the background of my experiencing. When the pervasive reality of the group shakes beneath us, we experience ontological hysteria.

Say I am thinking again about the death of my child. "Child" has the meaning it has within a culture that has bred us. The culture preceded us and very probably will endure—we automatically assume—beyond the deaths of individual members. Embedded in the meaning of "my child" as I think it is the enduring and nearly static cultural component of the thought-about—call it the meaning meant. I cannot think of my particular child without implicitly thinking of "child" in general, any child. Again, this contributes its share to distracting me from the reality: namely, that my thinking of her death may cease at any instant, as I may also.

Beyond this, I am distracted from the possibility that the culture itself may vanish. For since I have been taught to think in terms coined and defined by the culture, how can I think that it may cease to be? In most of our moments, this is quite literally unthinkable.

So there is the general fact that the object of thinking and emoting shoulders aside the particular acts of thinking and emoting in which it is entertained. And there is the general fact that the object must have communally constituted, set features, that we automatically assume will endure beyond the lifetime of any particular person. Both these facts conspire to obscure the vulnerable reality of my own particular experiencing and thinking life through time. And also, of course, conspire to obscure the vulnerable reality of our whole culture itself and all its members.

In sum, since I must describe my own thinking in terms of what we take the object to be—the thing meant insofar as much of the meaning related to it endures through time—since this is so, the passing, utterly unique and vulnerable reality of my own experiencing moment by moment tends to be eclipsed. This is true for at least most of our moments. And it is true, I believe, even in the supremely limiting and challenging case of the death of one's child.

It must be conceded, however, that that death gives one a terrible jolt. Perhaps one's life is never quite the same, even though the culture moves to pull one back into the normalcy of illusional life. Perhaps one is not as apt to slip so frequently and easily into the everyday illusion of immortality. Even the illusion of the group's immortality may tremble, and do so to the point that one can acknowledge it. For one has supped full of horrors, one has tasted and swallowed annihilation, nothingness.

*   *   *

We move ever closer to the prize. It will be our ability to grasp viscerally what happens when our whole cultural group is threatened, and can no longer constitute for us its members a reliable, stable, solid world-experienced. I will proceed toward this prize deliberately, step by step.

It is only when some delay or glitch develops in the automatisms of our everyday life together that the passing actuality of my own individual experiencing life is thrown into relief. Finally acknowledged is its piercing actuality. Strange, very strange, but true. The greatly familiar and constant becomes greatly invisible.

Let us focus first on the interaction of just two members of a cultural group. Climbing in the mountains together, my companion says, "Look, there it is, the peak we want to climb." I look in the direction in which he seems to be looking and see nothing. But then we both notice that from where I happen to be standing and looking I cannot see through the gaps in the trees through which he is looking. I walk a few steps and do see.

But of course. And we tend to let the matter drop. The contingency and evanescence of my own particular existence—so subject to accident—gets numbed and concealed. My own vulnerability and limitations get concealed. My taking this group of two for granted gets concealed—lost to acknowledgement.

Let us now take an example that is more than a glitch in the automatisms of our everyday life together. Alone in the mountains, I am stepping from stone to stone across a river. I get to a place which seems as though it might be too far for me to step. I have been told that the stones are slippery, and I have direct perceptual evidence of this. But for some reason, the impulse to get across to that stone is stronger than I resist at that moment, and I lunge toward the stone.

I reach the stone with the tip of my boot but crash down on the rock and into the water. A gong rings out within me, closer than ever before a gong could have been imagined to sound. The visual field shrinks instantaneously to a point, then springs open again. I feel the shocking cold water.

Chastened and stunned, embarrassed (for others just might be looking), I try to rise and stand in the river, knowing that I—nobody but I—made that step, and if all by myself in the mountains, I might have drowned. Nobody but I struck the point of his chin on the stone upon which I had meant to alight. Nobody's blood but mine trickles down the front of my neck and off my hand as I grope to locate the exact source of the flow. My consciousness and nobody else's was nearly extinguished. For these moments at least, in shock, my vulnerability and finitude as an individual member of the group is patent, inescapable.

Let us ratchet up the degree of disturbance in everydayness and its illusions: the degree to which the habitual constrictedness of consciousness is exposed. A vast field of my quavering, threatened, twilight reality suddenly billows out, and panic or strange near panic and nausea results. The basic illusion of personal immortality has been broken through. In these moments I believe that the group that constitutes the meaning of "child" and "stone" and so on will endure even if I should cease to do so. And the stone that I was seeing and then violently feeling, that very one, will endure when I, this seeing and feeling being, cease to do so.

In these greatly shocking moments in which my illusion of personal immortality explodes, it is practically impossible to imagine that the culture itself may explode. For again, when I come home to myself in these moments—"This is I-myself, this human being!"—when I grasp for my meaning and reality in true desperation, I cannot simultaneously entertain the possibility that the cultural ground of this very meaning attained might itself vanish.

Now consider this: the urologist informs me he's detected an irregular nodule on my prostate gland. He orders a biopsy and schedules it for a week hence. I do not just fear that this body—this body that is always with me—may terminate in death. I feel the piercing actuality that I—I myself—may die. So turbid, quavering, and panicky is the reality immediately experienced, that the line that might be drawn by the reflective intellect to divide potentiality from actuality smudges and blurs. I am already in the grip of death—a grip that breaks only when I later learn that the results of the biopsy are negative.

The doctor of medicine, the authoritative member of the home group with respect to such matters, assures me of my continuing existence. Do you think that at this moment I would be able to imagine that all authorities in the culture, and the culture itself, might vanish? That way beckons neurosis, or worse.

A younger colleague is not so fortunate. A biopsy of a tumor in his colon is ordered and the results are positive. Nearly blocking the colon is a cancerous mass the size of a softball. The surgeon obligingly shows him an X-ray picture. It looks to my colleague like a gigantic yellow and black tic embedded in his bowels. No longer is elimination automatic for my friend, the warm effluvia passing easily into the water-cleansed receptacle.

His very life falls into the grip of death. He struggles to release himself, struggles with the insurance company, struggles to get the best cancer surgeon, struggles to have the date of the operation set as soon as possible. He struggles to have his life continue. That concern must, it must, dominate his attention. He cannot also think that the culture itself may not continue.

The everyday illusion of immortality: The world as experienced by me has always had me in it, hasn't it? How can this world, experienced by us all as enduring, possibly go on without me! But in these experiences in which my individual reality is suddenly highlighted, we see with ghastly clarity that the world experienced by others may go on, but I will die.

Gripped in the ultimate hysteria, we see that the culture itself may not go on.

*   *   *

I have taken steps to expose what is ordinarily hidden, the contingency and vulnerability of each of our one and only particular lives. Also the terror that occurs when the illusion of personal immortality explodes for any of us.

But I haven't yet secured the final crucial step, although we are certainly moving toward that point. It will be the explanation of the desperate and vicious response to fear of annihilation that is the group's terror. This it is that often triggers genocidal action against an alien group. Exposing this is the reason I am writing this book. True, I have suggested something about the fundamental reality of the group in its establishment of the meaning of things for its members. But now this must be revealed in its fullest intensity. If it proves to be blinding, we must be prepared for that, prepared not to become numbed in hopelessness, prepared not to turn away (recall the observation from Melville that closed chapter 1). I am trying to make the word flesh.

Why should every member of an alien group be exterminated, man, woman, child—and every possibility of such an alien, and every memory of one, if possible? The fact is, as I have suggested several times previously, but must drive home now, we humans can double dip here; we can suffer a double dose of terror. It is not just that at some shocking moments we individuals become aware of our own particularity and mortality. But at some very special moments we can also become aware, terrifyingly and unspeakably, of our group's particularity, vulnerability, mortality.

This can be unspeakable panic terror because our group doesn't establish merely the meaning of "stone" or "child," as if this were only the meaning of words. It contributes essentially to establishing the very reality of child and stone and everything else as that can be thought and experienced by us its members. When this gives way, there is psychical earthquake. Literally or figuratively, we begin to vomit out our guts. We feel utterly helpless, as if we were infants dropped and abandoned.

Why? Because we enculturated beings cannot imagine a world other than the one we have learned to live in and have become a part of. With the possible exception of saints or hermit philosophers, we cannot expect, and we cannot imagine, any other world. This one and only experienced world trembles under our feet. Everybody in our group is lost. Nobody can motion me up the trail to see the peak we intend to climb. Nobody, no looming surgeon, can bend over me and delicately, like an angel, sew up the bleeding gash under my chin. Nobody can inform me that the nodule on my prostate gland is benign.

If an alien group impinges on our own, or breaks out uncomfortably within our own, its establishment of experienced reality may so cut across and disturb our group's that our communally experienced world starts to collapse. All get caught in the grip of nonbeing, erasure, death. Everybody is threatened with panic.

For after all, given our roots as bodily beings in a material world, it is only reality as we have established or "constructed" it in unspeakably close proximity with other experiencers through the years that continues on indefinitely— or so we have come instinctively to believe. In times of psychical earthquake, however, our members cannot lose themselves in what had been the comfortable and stable life of the group and the group's world. For the everyday illusion of immortality is closed to us all. Everyday belief and everyday experienced reality is finished.

*　　*　　*

Another group's experienced world, then, can be *infinitely* distressing. Because all we can imagine is the world as we have learned to experience it. And surely there can be only one world! Surely also, we can exist only in this world! When another group's experienced reality is felt immediately to be incompatible with our own, we are faced with the possibility of nonbeing, obliteration.

This is infinitely distressing, because from being to nonbeing there is no logical bridge. There are no steps our minds can follow to get from being to nonbeing. Annihilation literally boggles the mind. For how could thinking or minding imagine itself not thinking or minding? Thought baffles and stymies itself. We are absolutely lost, terrified, sickened.

When another group's experiencing and their experienced world threatens our own shaky group's, each of us can find nothing comprehensible. Our situation cannot be comprehended, for the very meaning of comprehension and of reason is in terms of the world that we, through our group, have learned to understand as reality. The very experienced-world itself shakes. Again, the only response is absolute or infinite terror.

Terror has been potentiated to the ultimate degree and the experienced world that had at first only trembled now drops away from under our feet. We swirl in the abyss. Only a Dürer print of damned souls fluttering down into Hell can begin to suggest this. A sickening fog and quaking uncertainty besets us. We thrash and flail trying to survive.

*   *   *

The irony of our self-limiting consciousness keeps pursuing us. As I said, constrictions and distortions of consciousness tend to be missed by consciousness just because they are constrictions and distortions of consciousness. In a constricted consciousness, what's left over to be aware of the constrictions and distortions? This seems to be the ultimate constriction and distortion: "The world just is as our group constitutes it in our experience, and of course this experienced world will continue. It will continue to be experienceable by us."

Engulfed in genocidal frenzy we are not reasoning this out. Given what we automatically and prereflectively assume reality is, we cannot even imagine what it would be to be different. The uncanny explosion of the communal illusion of a stable, normal, and enduring world is incredibly stressful—incredible literally.

Understandably, we may conclude that "the unthinkable" is just that, unthinkable. Genocide is unthinkable because it happens outside the world, the only world, in which we have learned to think. It happens outside our world-experienced, that which we must believe is the world, the world in itself, the only world there could be. Since the meaning and reality of thinking that comprehends is established in the more or less normal world known and experienced, how can we who were formed there grasp the abyss of nonbeing, the abyss of Hell?

Of course, for the genociding group, it's all perfectly understandable. That alien group, those others—we ourselves, say—we evildoers must die.

* * *

But let us not conclude precipitously that despair is the only conclusion for thinking. A corollary of the limitations of consciousness is that there may be resources for thought that are easily hidden from consciousness during a particular stretch of history. Let us try to probe the limits of what constitutes mind or comprehension itself. And let us learn more about communal or corporate reality. The possibility of discovering hitherto unimagined resources for thought depends upon pushing our thinking beyond what we usually take to be the limits of thinking. Let's keep pushing.

As we have seen, in the everyday world we tend to take calm, safe, reflective moments as normative and normal, and while engrossed in them tend to forget stressful and uncanny moments. So in a period of calm we might see cultural differences as being merely charming oddities. Thus one summer day years ago in the Sierras of California, my son and I sat at the summit of a 14,000-foot peak that we had climbed. Flushed with the victory and ecstasy of intact bodies, we lay at our ease. Idly I turned the screwed cap of the metal cylinder which contained notes left by previous climbers. Sifting through the scraps, I noticed a short passage attributed to the Qur'an:

> You lookest at the mountain and deemest it affixed.
> In truth it is as fleeting as the clouds.

Charming, rendered as it was in delightfully inappropriate King James Christian-biblical English. Charmed, I philosophized on its truth. Yes, these mountains, and all else we consider to be enduring, are really as fleeting as the clouds.

But what if we were to be thrown together with Islamic people who really lived the verse's truth? Who really lived—we would probably say fanatically lived—the whole ritualized context in which the verse was embedded and that structured their world and their lives? Let's say it's Islamic terrorists who set their lives as on a pin's fee—and one's own as well. Suppose that our group is already threatened and shaky, for whatever reasons. Imagine the terror at their alien world-experienced, their alien world-construction, cutting across ours. We must live as long as possible, and we can live only in the world. These people pollute and infect our corporate body and our world-experienced. To be rid of them!

But let's further specify and point this example so that it is exactly relevant to our situation of dire peril today. Imagine that I am a fairly young man who, like so many in North Atlantic culture, knows practically nothing about Islam. Imagine I am up on the mountaintop with my young son. Imagine as well that the person who left the quotation from the Qur'an in the cylinder is returning back over the ridge of peaks after climbing still another mountain. Along with his companion he approaches us.

We conquerors of the mountains sit down and talk. At first things go well. But gradually it becomes clear that we are climbing the mountains for very different reasons. He and his companion climb within the Qur'anic attitude toward the mountains: seeing them giving way over many thousands of years, seeing them be "as fleeting as the clouds." Seeing them wilt and wither against the background of the Eternal, God, Allah. In contrast, my son and I exult in the relative changelessness and apparent eternality of the mountains, which is evident also, we think, in the stars blanketing the night sky. For us, the mountains and the stars are stand-ins for the eternal: they are mythed and framed that way in our perceivings and feelings.

But seen against the background of the truly Eternal, Allah, a mountain will crumble away before the Muslim's contemplative gaze. Time means very little. It is fairly easy for him or her to be patient, to bide their time.[3]

I see a strange expression on the first Muslim's face. His eyes seem more inscrutable than blank. But I think I begin to detect a subtle contempt in his eyes. He discourses on other verses in the Qur'an, and on passages in the Hadith, the account of Muhammad's uniquely exemplary life. I have never heard of these things. He seems to look at me as if I were stupid—even evil.

An uneasiness crawls over me. The utterly taken-for-granted context of my experiencing, my son's and my habitual way of being in the world, feels as if it's being encircled by another context, subsumed within this other, unknown context. It's very much as if the rocky ridge of ground on which I stand starts to give way beneath me. My internal bodily sensations and commotions cannot distinguish a movement in the mountain from a movement in my body. My identity, my reality, trembles and quavers in incipient nausea.

I look to my son for help. He likewise is nonplussed, but trying to smile. I feel fear all over and through me that I try to suppress and deny. I see the Muslims as enemies. I believe they may attack us here and now. We bid them goodbye as cheerily as possible, and we two start down the mountain.

What if we think of the ultimate human group, the rest of the human race, and not just 1.2 billion Muslims? And what if in our thinking of it we were not to feel confirmed by it? The very profoundest anxiety would ensue. Unless, that is, we held the rest of the world in such contempt that we were to regard them as subhuman.

But in very truth we belong in, are gripped in, the corporate body of humanity. We are not the essential consciousness. How they see us is part and parcel of our situation, our reality. We may be able to push our thinking beyond the facile conclusion that genocide is "unthinkable." We may be able to push our thinking so that it falls in step with genociders' experiencing. If we could, if we could bridge the gap, we might find some now unimaginable palliative to their mania—and perhaps some now unimaginable palliative to our terror.

*   *   *

As a warrant of our being we have learned in a visceral way that we must defer to the judgment of our home group. But situations occur in which we no longer implicitly trust the consensus of our home group to put us in touch with reality. For an alien group cross-cuts our habitual way of constructing or constituting the world-experienced. To be forewarned about this terrible danger and about our terrible probable response—is this to be forearmed? Maybe.

Now, for us, it is Islamic terrorists. Our continued existence is threatened. Perhaps a weird clarion call sounds in our ears and heads: "Terrorize and incapacitate them before they terrorize and incapacitate us." Both groups aim at genocidal decimation of the other.

We are not used to understanding ourselves in any depth. Swept along in the tide of our culture, we tend habitually to be naive realists: we know what things are because we open our eyes and see them, and what we take them to be is usually good enough to lead us around in our world and to get us where we want to go. We conclude precipitously: "So what we take these things to be must be what they really are." We have no understanding of the limits of our understanding. Particularly, I think, when the understanding of moral qualities of whole human groups is what must be grasped.

So, let us continue to approach our situation methodically. Let us use the most concrete examples of how we need the confirmation of our home group to act sanely; and what happens if we cannot get this confirmation, because our home group is encircled and discomfited by an alien one, or because it cracks internally. I will soon give an example in which the home group cracks, and there are no other human beings to orient and guide us.

In normal, everyday times, the confirmation from others usually happens. If I hear something, but suspect that "I just may be hearing things,"

I ask others, "Did you hear that?" If they listen and say they do not, I may listen all the harder. If I still hear it, I ask again more urgently, "Did you hear that?" cocking my head in the direction from which the sound seems to come. They still say they don't. If I believe they are answering sincerely, and are in a position and condition to hear real sounds, I will be disturbed. For "real sounds" within the human range of hearing, mean those that are hearable by all normal listeners.

Virginia Woolf, for example, heard voices, but she very soon discovered that nobody else could hear them. She quickly inferred that she was going mad and killed herself.

A corollary of our protracted human infancy and dependency is our fear of abandonment. Psychologists report the unsurprising fact that children who do not get the responses from elders or peers needed to confirm or disconfirm their experiencing, become disturbed, and stay disturbed as adults. Not to be able to test reality is to be helpless. One can either curl up and die, or desperately seek explanations—scapegoats. *They* disturb us, they are out of touch with reality. In effect, a home group says, "We are terrified—let's terrorize them."

Imagine this example: A subset of our home group is lost in winter above the Arctic Circle. The situation is desperate: we have only partial shelter and limited fuel and food. One of our members says, "Hear that?" Nobody else hears anything out of the ordinary. We ask, "What are you hearing?" He replies, "That minute, dry, pecking sound? Like tiny grains of sand falling out of the sky?" We listen and don't hear it. We say, "If you're not just hearing things, what does that sound mean? If it's a real sound, what does it mean for what we should do?" He says, "I've heard that the Yupik Eskimos know that that kind of small, granular snow predicts a very cold and heavy storm building up. So we'd better leave and look for better accommodations." The rest of us fear that if we leave the little we have, our straits may become much worse.

In such a situation we are lost not only in space at this time. But lost perceptually and conceptually, all yardsticks of meaning gone. We are totally lost, abandoned. We are in a mental and psychical whiteout. We don't know how to make sense of things. Does our friend really know? Do the Yupik Eskimos really know? And is our friend just hearing things now? Quarrels break out. Our community is riven in indecision and begins to disintegrate. We can't assess our options, because we don't know what our options entail, what they mean, what they are. We panic: we begin to go out of our minds.

As if this were not bad enough. But it can get worse, and perhaps it already has. For in this last example we are confronted with the dangerous power and violence of Nature. If we're not completely paranoid we don't attribute any intent to the power of the terrible storm. We are simply overwhelmed.

But in the case of the Islamic terrorists earlier mentioned, we tend to be numbed and bewildered on another level of our being. For these are fellow human beings, and they intend to destroy us. Why? We can't fully understand why. And we can't understand how our understanding could be so limited, or even that it is limited. We stumble around in the dark. We're on the verge of panic, and perhaps we can think of only one thing: Strike at them, get 'em all, kill 'em.

How do we learn to center ourselves, and to think and perceive in new ways, ones more in touch with the actual, vast, various, excess world? We may be given time in which to try to learn.

* * *

Our funded experiencing of a world experienced by us is all we have really lived and counted on. We believe our experience to be paradigmatically human experience. The world is—we assume—how we find it.

I have asked us to consider that our whole culture—not just our group in the Arctic—has been confronted with a deeply antagonistic alien group. We are in extreme distress, perhaps on the verge of disintegration. Consensual agreement is coming unstuck. What is for us the objective world is falling apart. If we can blame it on the destructive work that another group's *wrong* consensual agreement is wreaking, then it is tempting to exterminate that group. In self-defense and in good conscience.

To be sure, we have to try to get through the day, to survive, to incapacitate as many Islamic terrorist groups as soon as we can. But if we do survive day by day, how do we make the best use of our time in the long run? We have the ability to project a future. Must we human beings always remain so limited, arrogant, open to befuddlement? Must we always rush around in our SUVs, Humvees, Abrams tanks?

For the past several years we see all around us American flags. We are pulling ourselves together in a nearly forgotten sort of vital unity in the corporate body. We see spray-painted grafitti on some speeding cars: Nuke 'Em!—with American flags whipping in the wind, which is completely understandable. Many probably have to do these things to compose themselves. But is it wise for all of us to continue to do and to think such things?

I seem to hear a voice saying, "OK, but let the flag wavers do their thing undampened. What other recourse do most ordinary people have? How else can they compose themselves? We are not saints, nor are we hermit philosophers—remember? The larger stabilizing context of interpretation cultivated by saints and some philosophers is not open to us." OK, but some of us—and I trust some of us are in positions of political power—must look for other alternatives down the road, if we survive.

*   *   *

Now, some will be tempted to think that genociders are simply psychopaths or sociopaths. That is, that they are people without a conscience, without the ability to ever feel guilt or remorse. Yes, genocides may certainly catch such people up in the torrent and use them. But many more people are involved in genocides than there are psychopaths and sociopaths available. There aren't enough of these pathological individuals. The fact is, many otherwise quite ordinary people get caught up in genocidal bloodbaths (See Sources, Browning and Goldhagen on Nazis). At least some of these persons seem capable of remorse after the hysterical conditions of the genocide itself have passed. During the genocide they seem to have gone out of their minds.

But foreign as it may seem, and probably hard for genociders to remember, that earlier eruptive time is not enveloped in total amnesia: it does not simply drop out of existence for all of them. Nor does it for us, looking on, who are trying to think what some call the unthinkable. We have pressed mind—or comprehension—to its apparent limits. We have pressed it to the abyss of Hell, to some understanding of hysteria and group frenzy.

But mind or comprehension doesn't have limits in the way a tract of land has. We do not go out of our minds or leave comprehension the way we leave a tract of land. The limit of comprehension is a limit, limin, a horizon that points beyond itself in our experience. At least it does so if we can achieve a few fleeting reflective moments.

The absence of rationality and morality and normality in the genocidal abyss is what we call irrationality and immorality and abnormality. Ironically, and maybe hopefully, these negations are tied, however tenuously, to what they negate: to rationality and morality and normality. Granted, to try to comprehend or reason out and grasp the irrational is a path marked by monstrous difficulties. But mind—that is, our minding—is not simply boggled, stopped in its tracks, as it is when it tries to think simple nonbeing or nonexistence.

*   *   *

We can cultivate the hope that concrete descriptions of what people feel and do during genocidal rampages might give us some reliable feeling or idea of what is going on. Then we might hope that we can do something to stop it in the future. The next chapters will offer these examples and descriptions.

Conceptualization and concrete description must intimately intertwine and interfuse. I have produced a partial sketch of the conceptual map that I will follow in this investigation. Some more conceptual digging and filling out must be done—on the matter of undeliberate imitation of each other by members of a group, for instance. I call this mimetic engulfment. We must investigate just how a group forms a corporate individual, with castes and roles for individuals associated with the different parts, functions, organs, levels that they occupy in that gross corporate individual—head, arms, hands, eliminative and sexual organs, feet. I will take this metaphor seriously. I believe that we must press beyond concepts into evocative metaphors if we would hope to achieve what William James called knowledge by acquaintance.

I will press the question: What happens when two incompatible corporate individuals encounter each other? Does one wilt in the face of the other? Does it begin to sink in value, to descend toward the lower regions of body? To be eliminated in waste, to become waste, to slide into annihilation, nonbeing (terrifying, no matter that we can't grasp nothingness conceptually and exactly)? Does it desperately try to regain its standing by initiating a genocidal attack on the other group?

It is essential to have produced even a partial sketch of the conceptual map in advance. Without this we risk getting lost in grotesque details and horrifying incidents of genocidal rampages. We risk getting lost and numbed in our own horror. We must try to avoid this illusion: that since we are suffering somewhat in hearing about genocide, we must be understanding it. This does not follow.

We probably will persist in asking incredulously, "How could people do this to fellow humans?" But in fact they have done, are doing, and probably will do it again. Our greatly difficult job is to discover how it's possible. We must try to discover for ourselves as thinking bodies a zone of quietness and suppleness within the horror. We must try to think "the unthinkable."

I'm taking steps to explain genocide by uncovering its reasons and causes. I am assuming that this is possible. I am assuming that there is a modicum of reason open to the human race. Perhaps the events of September 11, 2001 will bring home to us that we must understand genocidal acts. If for no reason other than they happened to us. Motivated by the hair-raising urge to survive, we may begin to really think. That is, we may break our dependency on jingoism, on childish rhetoric, on journalistic glosses on the world—the world from which we cannot escape, except in death.

NOTES

1. As noted in the introduction, for most members of a culture their group's consensual reality, their culture's world-experienced, is synonymous with the world itself. This is utterly arbitrary and automatic; so, typically, only a shock can make the unreasoned equivalence or synonymity acknowledgeable, thematic. For me, one such shock was spending a month mainly in remote areas of Peru. Only looking back at our culture could I begin to tell just how enclosing and limiting, parochial, it had always been for me. Though maybe I could have imagined such an experience in theory, it was only after actually having the experience that it was completely real for me, only then did I achieve what William James calls knowledge by acquaintance. Perhaps the American administration's failure in 2003 to grasp predictable consequences of invading Iraq, which was a failure to grasp the most elemental features of the Islamic world-experienced (or worlds-experienced), will supply a shock sufficient to thematize our parochialism for a sizeable number of citizens. Juan Cole writes (Sources, 25),

> In removing the Baath regime and eliminating constraints on Iraqi Islamism, the United States has unleashed a new political force in the Gulf: not the upsurge of civic organization and democratic sentiment fantasized by American neo-conservatives, but the aspirations of Iraqi Shiites to build an Islamic republic. The result was an entirely predictable consequence of the past 30 years of political conflict between Shiites and the Baathist regime, and American policy analysts have expected a different result only by ignoring that history.

2. Brain science makes rapid strides. For example, fear reactions may occur without the person being conscious of this at all (for one study see Joseph LeDoux, *The Synaptic Self*, Sources, 2002). The brain's amygdala picks up raw data from the environment in just a few thousandths of a second and prompts fear. This may never get to consciousness; it may never be processed through the hundreds of thousandths of a second needed to register in consciousness. How culture turns on or turns off some of the genes responsible for the amygdala's responses is not, I believe, known. Suffice to say that much of life is on automatic. It does not follow from this that consciousness is irrelevant. It is through focused and disciplined consciousness that we must learn of the limitations of consciousness. Not the least of the benefits is that we will look for fear reactions that we might not have expected without the aid of brain science. To be forewarned is, perhaps, to be forearmed: to be able to catch fear reactions of genocidal potentialities before they are acted out.

3. Whoever deposited the citation from the Qur'an, using whatever translation, does cite an actual verse—sura (or chapter) 27, verse 88. Other verses bolster its sense. For example, 73:14: "On the day when the earth and the mountains quake and the mountains become (as) heaps of sand let loose" (See Sources, *The Holy Qur'an*). In 78:20 we read that—relative to the Eternal, Allah—mountains are a mere "semblance." The Hebrew-Christian Bible asserts, "A day with the Lord is as

a thousand years, and a thousand years as one day "(2 Peter, 3:8). In 70:4, the Qur'on outdoes this: "To Him ascend the angels and the Spirit in a day the measure of which is fifty thousand years." Consonant with this teaching, Muslims are enjoined to endure: "O ye who believe! Endure! Outdo all others in endurance!" (3:200). It is hard to imagine a stronger declaration of Allah's eternality, singularity, omnipotence, and omniscience than this (3:255):

> Allah—there is no god but He, the Ever-living, the Self-subsisting by Whom all subsist. Slumber overtakes Him not, nor sleep. To Him belongs whatever is in the heavens and whatever is in the earth. Who is he that can intercede with Him but by His permission? He knows what is before them and what is behind them. And they encompass nothing of His knowledge except what He pleases. His knowledge extends over the heavens and the earth, and the preservation of them both tires Him not. And He is the Most High, the Great.

In chapter 6 I stress that Islamic theology feels no incompatibility in asserting God's singularity and transcendence, on the one hand, and His sustaining immanence in the Nature, on the other. Unlike the Christian view, Nature has not simply been corrupted, and it is not simply to be controlled. God's presence can be seen, for example, in the behavior of animals. Alluding to the writing of al Buladhuri (Sources), Will Durant writes,

> As Mohammed rode into [Medina] one group after another called to him, "Alight here, O Prophet! . . .Abide with us!"—and with Arab persistence some caught the halter of his camel to detain him. His answer was perfect diplomacy: "The choice lies with the camel; let him advance freely"; the advice quieted jealousy, and hallowed his new residence as chosen by God. Where his camel stopped, Mohammed built a mosque and two adjoining homes . . . (*The Age of Faith*, New York: Simon and Schuster, 1950)

4

FURTHER CASES OF GENOCIDE: BOSNIA, CAMBODIA, RWANDA

We're here for a few moments and then we're gone. Death is intolerable: Susanne Langer puts it well. At least this is true for the ever-growing secular populations of the contemporary world. It could be argued that traditional religious systems of belief in immortality arise precisely because humans have always found death to be intolerable. But, in fact, so many traditional peoples are so intensely animated by their religious beliefs in immortality that they positively welcome death.

Whereas for contemporary secular persons, bereft of any explicit belief in immortality, the bite of death is particularly sharp. So intolerable it is for many that a strong tendency exists to stay engulfed in the enduring secular group, and to generate unwittingly the illusion of immortality. The moments in which secular people become shockingly aware of their individual reality and mortality usually lapse back into the illusion of immortality fairly soon. Of course, these are not usual times: perhaps we will not lapse back so easily now?

What if the very endurance of the group is threatened by an alien group's differing establishment or construction of experienced reality? Secularism provides no protection whatsoever against this threat, for secular people depend at least as much on the stability of their ongoing group as do religious persons (but more unacknowledgeably than do they). The incursion of an alien group threatens to deprive secular people of the haven of everyday illusion.

It is certainly terrifying when the illusion of one's own personal immortality is shattered. But when the immortality of the group is threatened? As we saw, the disruption and terror accelerate to an ultimate pitch, as if the flywheel of a motor that contains us all were to accelerate so furiously that the mechanism tears itself to pieces. When our group's construction of perceived reality flies to pieces, members' sanity and reality fly to pieces. Most are like young children lost and abandoned. They await a savior.

Ratcheted to a sufficiently high pitch through the disruption of communal or corporate reality, most individuals' experienced reality gives way. A disgusting and panic-stricken diarrhea of everything overtakes us. A flood of detritus overcomes us. Everything is infected and sloughs into the flood. The only solution that may appear in those moments may be to purge every member of the infecting group, every single "germ" that infects the Volkskörper, our corporate body, the group.

Now, for a group to launch into genocidal rampage, I believe it must already labor under considerable stress. When it is not so laboring, then, as noted, those "others" may seem to be no more than charming oddities, though possibly annoying ones. Or they may be ridiculed or caricatured virtuosically. Or, if they cannot be pigeonholed in these ways, they may be enslaved, in either de facto or de jure ways. But if our group is already shaky for whatever reasons, and they threaten to break through our partitioning or quarantining of them, great fear is excited. Members of the home corporate body may feel justified in annihilating them. Perhaps it's only a militant genocidal minority—typically with a leader—that feels this, but its hysteria is contagious. The rest of the corporate body may be drawn over the edge.

*   *   *

Let's look at other cases of genocide in the twentieth century. We have on our hands an embarrassment of riches. The overabounding fecundity and variety of Nature is intolerable to the constricting genocidal mind. It would squeeze out, extrude, excess and otherness. But at least we in this book can revel in a variety of genocides.

For convenience we could begin around 1915: The Turkish-Islamic persecution of Armenians—Christians. Men, women, children, hordes, were forced to march into deserts where they died miserably. This occurred in the last days of the doddering Ottoman-Muslim empire. The government and dominant group was also stressed because allied with an overextended Germany in World War I. Though these persecutions occurred mainly in old Turkey, before Kemal Atatürk's new regime, the Turkish government to this day denies the genocidal features of the persecution. It speaks of a civil war involving intransigent Armenian nationalists, guerrillas, and assorted troublemakers.

Though genocidal features of the persecutions have been documented by unimpeachable witnesses and incontrovertible evidence (see Sources, for example, Morganthau), the Turkish government continually denies that its country perpetrated a genocide. That is, it was not a killing of Armenians—men, women, children, the unborn—just because they were Armenians. It was a war: Turkish authorities were simply trying to kill some of the leaders and followers of a civil insurrection. This suggests the shameful nature of genocide: something that people in calm and reflective moments at least—who are not psychopaths or sociopaths—want to deny.

When Atatürk came to power, the persecution of the Armenian people did not cease. Those in the west of the country were prevented from joining their brethren in the east. As I said, following the UN's "Convention on the Prevention and Punishment of the Crime of Genocide," (Sources), I use the term genocide to mean the attempt to harm a whole people just because they are that people. Using this suitably broad definition I conclude that the persecution of the Armenians by the Turks qualifies as genocide.

However, evaluating the case carefully calls for expert knowledge (with some data yet to be made public), which I cannot pretend to have. Not only that, but some reasonable persons could argue that we have here a borderline case, hideous as the activities were. Hence I will not use the Turkish-Islamic nightmare as one of my major examples of genocide.

But needed is a word about borderline cases. Even if one concludes that the Armenian case is one of these, I want to forestall inferences that might be drawn. It might be thought that since one opts to take the Turkish case as borderline, it needn't be examined closely, not by anybody anytime. Or that it is too inherently confused to benefit from careful analysis. Or that it only seems borderline to us now. In time all may be cleared up, and then "the facts of the case" will have answered our questions definitively.

But that borderline cases do turn up should strengthen our resolve to attend closely to them—at least in a context permitting close and prolonged analysis. It's a sign that we are encountering messy, overflowing reality itself. It's a sign that we aren't merely playing with words and concepts, locking them neatly together in a kind of game. Why should we think that reality corresponds point by point with our concepts and our arrays of them? As if these concepts were tiles that could be laid down neatly next to next, so that every case and issue that could come up is covered by them? In fact

some situations are—as far as we can see, and what else can concern us?—
some situations *are* borderline. Things ooze into what intellectualistic logics rule that they are not. This reminds us of the excess that hovers about
everything we say, think, or do.

Now for another case with which, sorry to say, I don't feel competent to
deal: Maoist China. Not only is there the historical importance of China up
to our own day, and not only its sheer size, but also the genocidal features
that the Maoist revolution does present are vivid and salient. For instance,
as head of the corporate body, Mao exhibits the power of such heads vividly.
It is reported that feats of mythic proportions are attributed to him, for instance, swimming for many miles in great rivers. Also his sexual appetite is
supposed to be prodigious, something on the order of Zeus's (and all this in
a supposedly atheistic and scientific culture). He is a stealthy stand-in for
the powers of Nature itself.

It is reported that some of the women who coupled with Mao flaunt as
badges of honor the venereal diseases apparently contracted from him. As
if the power of the head of the corporate body flowed down into all its
members, but particularly powerfully into those engorging his generative
organs. In gonorrheal or syphilitic sores, do we see a rough parallel to the
stigmata exhibited by saints who identify particularly intimately with the
crucified Savior? Bloody shows and apparent pierce marks on the hands
and feet?

We easily gain a general sense of the accumulated disturbance in this vast
continental power that prepared the way for Mao's revolution. For centuries
an ancient and proud people had been plundered by colonizing European
powers. Add to this the invasion of China by the Japanese in World War II
and the atrocities committed by them. Witness the appalling destruction of
Nanking, what is called the rape of that city—in every sense. (And what cannot go unmentioned: the invasion of Korea by the Japanese and their defilement, rape, and torture-murder of their head, their queen. Even today the
Japanese nation will not squarely face the atrocities perpetrated by it. So
deeply runs the illusion of the group's immortality and grandeur.)

It might also be argued that the Mao example is a borderline case. This
will seem implausible to many. After all, a man who exceeded Hitler by a
factor of ten in the destruction of his enemies—sixty million estimated—
must be a genocider! I am strongly attracted to this conclusion. Sadly, I lack
sufficient command of the facts to use the China case as one of my major
examples of genocide. I am convinced that it could be used.

In thorough review and analysis, a certain complication would have to be
faced. It might be argued that not everything in any way touched and

tainted by the hated Chinese landowners, small and large capitalists, and "deracinated, egoistic, degenerate intellectuals" was marked for destruction or radical displacement by Mao. That is, opprobrium did not spread completely indiscriminately across all those regarded as inassimilable by the emergent communist corporate body. It might be argued that it is only approximately true that the new corporate body simply convulsed in a vast paroxysm of extrusion.

For example, certain gifted children of exterminated landowners were regarded as salvageable by the new regime. Salvageable if they denounced their parents, participated in "encounter groups" in which they ritualistically confessed their shortcomings or sins and, in general, were what has been aptly called "brainwashed." Suggested is that an infection or pollution has been cleansed. These children could be redeemed, admitted as members in good standing in swarming legions of Red Guards, their family pasts forgotten. Particularly if they were remarkably focused in their hunting down of counterrevolutionaries. This fact would have to be faced by any thorough analysis of Mao's communist genocide.

We cannot pass by without comment the case of the Soviet Union. Joseph Stalin is credited with over twenty million deaths. In one year he is reported to have killed seven million, mainly by starvation. I will not take Stalin's purges to be one of my major cases, however, because to achieve any order in my analysis of genocide, I limit it to dreadful relations between groups. Stalin's case is so much a matter of his individual pathologies—particularly paranoia—that I prefer not to use it as a paradigm case of genocide.

I would like to find a new word for what he did. He killed anybody whom he thought might conceivably threaten his individual position on top of the hierarchy. The millions he killed were mainly his own people. So mad was he that he had dozens of his chief generals killed, even as Hitler's armies beleaguered Russia's major cities. In his inner hell of delirium he suspected that some might not owe their ultimate loyalty to him.

But this case of terror and horror must be mentioned. If for no other reason than it presses into our faces the staggering central question of how shaky groups, full therefore of disturbed members, *will* have a head for their corporate body, no matter how insane he may be. Relative to this huge, grotesque reality, it matters not a bit that Russia has been home to some of the greatest scientists, artists, writers, and humanitarians of the past two hundred years.

Our identity as individual humans requires we belong to a corporate body, and—at least in patriarchally organized societies—it must have a head. The fact that the head in this case was so obviously sick, should impel our efforts to get to the bottom of the abysmal swamp of human identity and reality, of primal experiencing, and to take seriously the metaphor of the corporate body.[1]

* * *

So what are my paradigm cases? I will deal with Bosnia, Cambodia, Rwanda, in addition to what has already been covered: Nazi Germany and the genocide of indigenous peoples of California in the nineteenth century.

In each case the salient features of genocide emerge: (1) a corporate body is disturbed for any number of reasons; (2) the body recoils from an alien group that it believes or vividly imagines is infecting and polluting it; (3) the home group tries to stop its own disintegration by annihilating the other group's cross-cutting ways of experiencing the world; (4) convulsively it expels or exterminates the alien mass, while typically led by a charismatic corporate head; (5) since all members of the alien group are carriers, actual or potential, of the diseased experiencing of a world-experienced, all are targeted just because they are members. This is genocide.

Indeed, these five salient features constitute the nature of genocide, I believe (though in chapter 6 I further discuss the difficulties in pinning down the essence, the essential features, of genocide: the concept bustles and has a floating sphere of application). To be able to spot key features of genocide emerging, and on this basis to predict a particular genocide, would be explanation of the phenomenon in perhaps the fullest sense. We might at least try to predict probabilities of genocide.

* * *

Descriptions of the five paradigmatic cases of genocide must necessarily be brief and pointed. I am after truly salient points and features, and major concepts. It is easy to miss the forest for the trees.

Now that we are, for every reason, preoccupied with the genocidal aspirations of a network of terrorist Islamic groups, it is especially appropriate that we include the Serbian genocide in Bosnia. It was aimed chiefly at Muslims. Ordering our materials this way, we better see the universality of genocide. It can happen any place, any time, given the appropriate circumstances. Any group the home group considers to be alien, other, uncontrollable, infecting, can be the target of a genocide.

Which is not to say that genocide is equally likely when nonwarlike groups are involved as when warlike ones are. It is hard to overlook the role of war in Islam. Significantly, Muhammad, unlike Jesus, was a general.

The most holy book of Islam is the Qur'an. It is held by over a billion people worldwide to be the authoritative account of the Supreme Being or Allah. As I have stressed, most people in the so-called West, even those accounted educated, are ignorant of its teachings. True, the Qur'an presents interpretational problems galore, as is the case with the Christian Bible. Islamic scholars assure us that jihad, for example—roughly "holy war"—is primarily a matter of reform within Islam itself, or a matter of defensive action against opponents of Islam.[2]

But it is naive to expect to locate the essence of Islam in its remarkable Qur'an. That no more follows than it would follow that since the Christian Bible does not prescribe celibacy for priests, say, therefore celibacy is not really Christian. A religion cannot be isolated from its history and the traditions that evolve. Many millions of persons spread over the globe for nearly 1500 years, living in times, cultures, and political systems very different from one another, must produce divergent interpretations of the one holy book.

The motives of Islamic terrorists (particularly Wahhabist puritans centered in Saudi Arabia) are many, various, and tangled. Moreover, a very few terrorists armed with marvelous technological instruments can create vast devastation. In brief, their motives include: fear and hatred of Western secularism and bias; envy of Western opulence and brawny power; retribution for personal and group suffering inflicted upon them for which they blame the United States; and perhaps the projecting and acting out of strictly personal neuroses or fixations (not in every case a necessary condition for genocide). To this brew must be added their interpretation of jihad, holy war.

A recipe requires all the ingredients it specifies. The poisonous brew of global terrorism is concocted when all the necessary ingredients or conditions are present. Without the terrorists' interpretation of jihad, the brew would probably not occur. Regardless of whether the interpretation can be sanctioned by scholars, or by a sizable majority of Muslims, it is there in the book to be appropriated and misinterpreted. If indeed it is misinterpreted. Likely it is that terrorists believe that they are acting only defensively, defending themselves against American de facto aggression and terror.

More generally, strife is a remarkable feature of Islamic history (though also of Christian and Jewish). Muhammad's immediate successors embroiled themselves in fratricidal battles. From this issued the two major sects of Islam: the Sunnis and the Shiites. The fairly recent war between Iran and Iraq stems from this ancient enmity. Iranian boys were thrown into battle with the salvific words of holy war inscribed on their headbands: martyrdom means immediate entry into Paradise.

Likewise traditional Islamic criminal law is remarkably abrupt and harsh, judged from the modern North Atlantic point of view. Islam inherited the ancient Hebrew practice of an eye for an eye, a tooth for a tooth. Since a thief steals with his hand, then, once he is convicted of theft by cleric-judges ("strict constructionists") he too is to lose something: his hand is cut off. This practice was reinstated by the hyperfundamentalist Taliban government of Afghanistan.

Notice also what is euphemistically called female circumcision. It is practiced in certain Islamic societies, notably African. Unlike male circumcision, which does not injure outright the male generative organ, female circumcision involves the extirpation of the clitoris. Some have plausibly explained this as an extreme instance of a patriarchal culture's need to control all that lies beneath the top of the hierarchy. Particularly in need of control is female sexuality. When tumescent, the "little penis" impudently rivals the male's generative organ.

What we find in a number of Islamic societies, and the traditions that they actually live by day after day, is remarkably abrupt, harsh, rigid, totalizing, and extreme. No reading of the Qur'an can obviate the historical fact that not a few Islamic societies and governments have been highly aggressive and warlike.[3] Some construe the sensational early successes of Islam as engendering the belief that success is a sacrament. Reversals, then, must be interpreted as desecration caused by something alien within or without Islam—desecration, pollution, humiliation.

Ideas and beliefs have consequences, as Emerson and our American pragmatists tried to teach us. The brew of ideas and beliefs in certain sectors of Islam is as potent and dangerous, I believe, as any to be found on the planet, at least in large bodies of believers.

Along with the concept of holy war we must mention the belief in a chosen people. Jews, Christians, and Muslims all claim Abraham to be their direct ancient ancestor. For Jews and Christians, the line continues down through Abraham's son, Isaac, the progeny of Sarah. But for Muslims, the line continues down through Abraham's eldest son Ishmael, the progeny of Abraham's supposed concubine, Hagar. The divine blessing follows through the line. Hence appear radically conflicting ideas of just who the chosen people are. These ideas animate and inflame three very different histories, three very different root-paths.

Embedded in the core of each corporate body's identity—Jews, Christians, and Muslims—are radically conflicting beliefs and behaviors. This is a recipe for feverish intolerance, ontological anxiety, and genocide; and when these conflicting ideas about cultural identity are combined with jihad or holy war, we have a greatly disturbing brew. In an era of weapons of mass destruction, and their ever-broadening availability, what could be more dangerous than a few true believers who are convinced that they are enjoined by Allah to kill all infidels (those without the faith).

Especially dangerous are Islamic extremists who feel humiliated for reasons known and unknown. Known are these (let us further explore motives): that since the decline of Islam in the eighteenth and subsequent centuries, they feel overmatched by modern Western faiths, secular and religious, equipped as these are with the latest technologies, which include, of course, weapons capable of mass destruction. Finally, and in general, Islamic extremists are enraged that Western secularism imposes its will, directly and indirectly, on Islam, and, as I said, erodes the religious foundations of her states. So that little children, emerging from hovels or refugee camps, are reduced to throwing stones at well-armed Israeli soldiers, for example. So that others hijack gleaming Western airliners and slam them into our shining towers of might, turning them into furnaces that melt down into mountainous tombs on the streets of New York City.

And the Israelis? How do they exist, or try to, today? Their remnant emerges shaken and determined from a recent genocide in Europe—what they aptly term the Holocaust. Many bring with them an essentially European or North Atlantic way of thinking and being, and implant it in the bowels of the surrounding Near Eastern Muslim states. They also bring with them an internal group that considers itself to be the true remnant, the famous saving remnant of Judaism, the Jews' own fundamentalists. These simply believe that God promised this land, Zion, to them only. They conveniently forget that God made his promise to all of Abraham's descendants. The Palestinians are lucky to be there at all.

Who will save us from the true believers, the fundamentalists of all stripes?

* * *

Violated and vulnerable as we in the United States are today, we may be in a better position to see the Serbian genocide of Muslims in Bosnia and Kosovo from the Serb point of view (repeat: to get any idea of what's actually happening we need all the points of view we can get). For the Balkan area was ruled by Islamic sultans for hundreds of years—centuries of not infrequent terror. There are well-confirmed reports of Serbian skulls piled in conical mounds at very visible points on the land.

Ivo Andric monumentalized Serbian suffering in *The Bridge on the Drina* (Nobel Prize, 1961, Sources). If possible, its account became more real for Serbs than the historical facts themselves. The everyday punishment for Serb rebels was beheading. A means favored by Pashas and Sultans for special occasions was impalement. Andric describes one such execution. Michael Sells writes in *The Bridge Betrayed: Religion and Genocide in Bosnia*:

> One American reader told this author that by the time she had finished the impalement scene of *The Bridge on the Drina* she shook all over; the horror of the scene never left her. (Sources, 178n28)

I forgo the opportunity to quote Andric's account.

We may now better see the Bosnian genocide in perspective. The old ways of thinking in terms of "good guys and bad guys" and "axes of evil"— recently revived by George W. Bush—needs urgent overhaul.

*   *   *

The genocide of non-Serbs, particularly Muslims, in Bosnia occurred subsequently to the breakup of the confederation called Yugoslavia. It had been held together by the World War II hero, General Tito, until his death. That all members of the confederation existed in various states of stress for decades and even centuries prior is axiomatic, legendary. Meanings of "Balkans" spewed out from that term attest to this: "balkanize" and "balkanization" are synonymous with disintegration, tension, fratricidal strife, strife of all kinds.

An added historical word is essential. The area called Bosnia lies along the fault line dividing the Western from the Eastern Christian churches. The Westerners in what is now marked off as Croatia often referred to the Eastern Slavs—the Serbs—as Orientals, with all that connotes for the man in the street as well as for theologians. For example, the Eastern doctrine of the Trinity reflects the "despotism" of the East. It is considered to be in error: instead of the Holy Spirit "proceeding" from the Father and the Son, the Holy Spirit proceeds from the Father alone. Though no one is quite sure what proceeding means.[4]

Laid athwart this intra-Christian divide is the later occupation of the whole area by Muslim empires, hence a ferociously contested divide between Muslim and Christian. Centuries of strife between occupiers and occupied prepared for the recent genocidal events in Bosnia. Centuries of oppression by Muslim Sultans was keenly felt by all Christian Southern Slavs (the literal meaning of Yugoslavia).

Serbs (Eastern Southern Slavs) have experienced corporate identity crisis for centuries. In their highly emotional national myth, origin myth, their greatest forebear is Prince Lazar. He is depicted as a Christ figure murdered by the infidel Muslims in the famous battle of Kosovo in the thirteenth century. Their pure hero is killed by unregenerate, unwashed, unbelievers.

Hence Serb fighters killing Muslims needed not to ask for absolution before receiving the sacraments from their Christian priests. For after all, killing a cruel and tainted unbeliever is not a sin. Indeed, Muslim blood on one's hands is a kind of baptism in itself—a baptism in blood that cleanses sin (See Sells again).

Serbia's prolonged identity crisis and experience of pollution and violation is clearly etched. Thus it is not surprising that in the 1980s and 1990s attempts were made to sharply define, draw together, enclose and seal shut the borders of the corporate body, Greater Serbia. Bosnia for a long time had served as a kind of model—flawed though it be—of coexistence of ethnic and religious groups. These included Muslims, Jews, Serbs, Gypsies, Western Southern Slavs or the Croats, etc. It served as a standing reproach to the Serbian contention that ethnic and religious purity is essential for a cohesive and enduring group.

Hence Serbia under its determined head, Slobodan Milosevic, launched a brutal campaign to purge the Bosnian parts of Greater Serbia of all polluting others, all unregenerates, all non-Serbs. He had right hands in Bosnian Serbs, the fanatical nationalist psychiatrist Radovan Karadzic, and Ratko Mladic, the well-equipped, ruthless, and relentless general. There is something unforgettably, grotesquely cruel in picturing Serbian artillery safely ensconced in the mountains surrounding Sarajevo pouring shells into that nearly defenseless city. This was the very place that had entertained just a few years before that model of Western civilization, the Greek-rooted Olympic Games. Dr. Karadzic, interviewed against the backdrop of Serbian artillery in the mountains, terminated an interview with television and press in these words: "The Muslims will vanish." All of them. Thus epitomized is the genocidal vision.[5]

Let us expand this picture, and fill it in with details, so that it will in fact not be forgotten. Serbian shells tore into the Sarajevo hospital, some exploding in maternity wards. Here is a key point. As I've said, genocidal rage and fury is not content with singling out and destroying an enemy's army, and guaranteeing its own security. It must wipe out or radically displace all members of that group, the one that, it is believed, threatens to infect with their seed the functioning and experiencing of the home group.

Facts, in the usual sense of empirically, consensually confirmable states of affairs, mean very little. At work are immediately felt ecstatic transports, eruptive elations, aversive recoilings of disgust felt in the pit of the stomach. Or, if one is male, cringings in the genitals. Or, again, various omens and talismans of good or bad fortune, joyous camaraderie with kin, retching encounters with alien masses, etc.

Wild, terrified feelings and visions of what is felt govern behavior. Semblances of thinking are happening. A pregnant woman or a newly born infant is a threat because its mere presence is registered by the genocidal group. And registration of that presence is sickening; it may disturb the experiencers' precariously balanced identities. I have called it ontological insecurity. That is, the terrified insecurity of persons whose world-experienced —including their own experienced bodies of course—is disintegrating in mass hysteria. As the corporate body trembles and sinks into its lower, excretory functions, the experienced world is turning to a kind of diarrhea. The "clear" cause of this, the enemy, the polluting and infecting other, must be swept from sight or obliterated. "The Muslims will vanish."

Not only the potentiality of another Muslim must be eradicated, but the memory of past Muslims must be also. No matter that some Muslims led exemplary humane lives. A memory is also a presence within the precariously balanced remembering organism. It is too much. Thus as Nazis razed and ploughed over Jewish cemeteries—killing Jews already dead, so to speak—so Serbs tried to destroy all reminders of Muslim lives.

Look again at this picture of Serbian artillery pouring shells into Sarajevo. Let's try to imagine it as if we were painters. Imagine recording details ourselves with daubs of pigment. Can we really register, really allow within our bodies, what happened? The artillerymen turned their guns not only on the hospital, but also on the great libraries, the National and the Oriental Institute. Here reposed voluminous accounts of some strife between groups, yes, but also of cooperation and shared accomplishment through the centuries. As the ashes of books and paintings floated into the sky, the Serbs must have believed that their mission of cleansing was winning out.

Not only death camps were set up by the Serbs, but also rape camps for holding non-Serbian women, mainly Muslim (often women only nominally Muslim, modern, secularized women drawn brutally into mythlike but grimly factual reality). "Show 'em our seed" was often heard cried by Serb soldiers. For one way to defile, pollute, or perhaps neutralize alien germ plasm, eggs, and identity is to mix that identity with what doesn't belong in it, the seed of the genociders. There is another motive here, to be sure— lust.[6] (In addition to this, see the end of endnote 5, and the endnote of chapter 5 that deals with philosophy of science and the pertinence, yet insufficiency, of quantitative empirical studies.)

But the whole situation is complex and somewhat obscure. Why didn't the raping Serb soldiers feel polluted by intercourse with Muslim women? I hypothesize that after ejaculating into the bodies of the raped women, they pulled out and escaped psychically unscathed. It was the women who were left—pardon the language—holding the bag, the mixed, polluted bag. No exclusively physiological studies can adequately grasp the role of body-as-self.

*　*　*

Let us turn now to Cambodia. I am after salient features, concepts, metaphors. I try not to lose the forest in seeing the trees. It is a sickly enchanted forest that we all too eagerly, I think, want not to see, want to forget.

Cambodia. The name is tied in our minds to the Vietnam War and to the United States' terrified preoccupation with the threat of international communism. It is tied as well to the immense tonnage of bombs dropped into the land bordering Vietnam, Cambodia. As the ground shook for many miles beyond their impact, the news of this was kept from the American public. The point was to finally decimate and demoralize Vietcong guerrilla soldiers hiding out in the jungles of that land.

But unsuspected by most of us Americans, the very meaning of war had oozed and shifted in the short period following the Korean War of the 1950s. By 2004, guerrilla warfare is in full bloom, a version of it in our own land. The Korean War was a fairly conventional conflict. Two uniformed armies confronted each other across a clearly drawn geographical line. They made air and artillery incursions into the enemy's fairly obvious positions, redoubts, stockpiles, trenches, ports. (In a real sense, the Korean War has not ended; but for our purposes, I use the "bookend" dates by which we identify and delimit it conventionally.)

In Vietnam, however, the communist guerrillas melted into the civilian population and into areas of the jungle shown clearly on no "serious" map. There were no concentrations of materials visible by radar through the forest canopy. As paleolithic people used caves in which to store their few things, so did "the Cong" (sometimes also referred to by U.S. forces as slopes—sloping foreheads, mental defectives—or perhaps snakes, gooks, charlies.)

Produced in the conventional American military machine was a frustration that exploded in carpet bombing and massive efforts to defoliate thousands of square miles of jungle canopy. Hurried steps taken to seek and destroy the enemy resulted in further softening and melting of the distinction between war and genocide. Obviously, there was no way to discriminate between Vietcong soldiers and men, women, and children civilians. And, of course, countless animals and birds and plants intimately associated with Vietnamese culture went over the edge in the process. It was war waged against the fecundity and variety of Nature herself.

To get an inkling of the true proportions of the destabilization of Cambodia, we must sketch what else beside the Vietnam conflict lay behind Pol Pot's genocide there. The French had colonized the general area for a century and a half. It was called French Indochina. When the French pulled out, old tensions between native ethnic groups reasserted themselves. The Cambodian region was populated by an indigenous people called the Khmer. Traditional animosities were exercised against the Vietnamese, for example. But the Khmer peoples are believed to have had a long history of enslavement of certain populations within their own ill-defined borders (See Staub, *The Roots of Evil*, Sources, 196). The vast Buddhist community that celebrated itself at Angkor Wat is said to have been supported by slaves.

So what we see in Cambodia is a corporate body (assuming the singular can be used) in abrupt transition, fractured and disturbed for decades and centuries in every conceivable way. Prince Norodom Sihanouk, who took over as reigning monarch after the French left, was like an acrobat trying to mediate between factions in his balkanized country. More than that, he tried to mediate between a mythic past, in which kings and queens were treated as divinities, and a rude, secularized present in which surrounding warring, imperialistic nations moved to place little Cambodia within their orbits. His efforts at staying unaligned produced an amazing performance.

Pol Pot was the leader (or Brother Number One) of one of the many dissident groups hiding out in vast forests and jungles outside the capital of Cambodia. They were, in one way or another, inspired by Mao's so-called grassroots revolution. The idea was to get back to nature and some sort of agricultural or horticultural life after the long incursion of decadent Western urban ways embodied by the French, and continued by this "slippery performer," Sihanouk.

By available accounts—none of them unimpeachable—Pol Pot was a prudent, cautious, and modest man. At least he must have seemed that way to some people. While other Khmer guerrilla groups moved into eastern Cambodia to stave off their traditional enemies, the Vietnamese guerrillas who had moved in to hide, Pol Pot pulled back and bided his time. For in our own efforts to obliterate the Cong, America unleashed a bombing of eastern

Cambodia that in a few months equaled the tonnage dropped in World War II (or so it is estimated). The reign of terror, the rain of hell from the sky, not only killed some Vietnamese, but many members of imprudent Cambodian guerrilla groups who had ventured too close to their traditional enemies.

This appears to have left a power vacuum in the outlying regions, and provided an opening for Pol Pot to unleash a whirlwind genocidal scourge. In numbers killed per day or per month—mainly by hand—it rivals the Rwandan Hutus in more recent days: in numbers killed per unit of time probably both genocides outdid even Hitler's best efforts, though that agent of hell employed technological resources unavailable to them.

Pol Pot's scourge was aimed at the "decadent intellectuals, capitalist running dogs, venal shop keepers, bureaucrats, all the mean spirited," of the capitol, Phnom Penh (the rhetoric is very like Mao's). In an astonishingly short time, his forces—which had swollen around this rising new head—emptied out the capital. They either tortured and killed their others outright, or they marched whole families and larger groups into the outlying rural areas. Though ill equipped in every way for success in farming, and without experience in living off the land, the city-folk were expected to regenerate themselves in Nature, expected to scratch out a living somehow. Those who failed either starved to death, succumbed to beasts and poisonous snakes, or were killed for their failure—usually by being clubbed to death, for ammunition was in short supply.

It is estimated—only estimates are possible in that explosive diarrhea of terror and desolation—that a million and a half "degenerates" were killed in this smug puritanical genocide. Members infecting the corporate body were to be purged, expelled, the corporate body purified. Obsessive anality is patent.

To the end of his days—and sorry days they finally became—Brother Number One maintained that everything he had done was "for his country." That is, for the corporate body of "pure Khmer" he at one time headed. This idealized country he and his followers equated with the traditional integrity of Khmer people.

In her epic drama on Cambodia, Hélène Cixous offers this characterization of Pol Pot. Shown in a tirade aimed at "the effeminate" Sihanouk, Pol Pot erupts in monologue:

> I hate them all, those who haven't the noble courage to hate,
> And those who are mere dilettantes in hatred, paying it lip-service on tiptoe.
> O hatred, I shall do you justice.
> Hatred, you claim you are power, you are intelligence.

And I dare proclaim you
The true Sun of my destiny.
In return, help me tear this country from the shameful
spells of this junk Buddha.
Indecent monarchy, I hate your effeminate countenance,
Your foolish moods, your whorish profusion.
I shall tear off your silken gowns
And I shall unveil to the stunned world
Our next Cambodia, virgin, virile, incorruptible.
One fine day, beginning tomorrow,
At History's turning point,
Our insolent neighbors, those land-guzzlers,
And this horrendous plunderer, this blind ogre, this America,
Will see looming before them—
Invincible Cambodia descending from the mountains
To hound them all beyond our borders
In a magnificent slaughter.

(Sources, 15–16. Compare Richard's venomous self-introduction in *Henry VI*. Cixous wants "to follow in Shakespeare's path." David Chandler agrees with her depiction of Pol Pot's love of hatred and terror, and of his drive to defile his enemies.[7])

After Pol Pot unleashes his genocide, imprisoning Sihanouk for three years, Cixous shows Brother Number One again. Cambodia decimated, the world finally appalled, Pol Pot leaves a power vacuum of his own making in the country. The North Vietnamese invade. Pol Pot orders Sihanouk to tour the world, under subtle high-level guard, to put a good face on things. The Vietnamese approach close to the capital, but Pol Pot assures the captive Prince:

> I am letting the horde enter very deeply into the country. They advance. I fall back, I retreat, I retreat. And suddenly, I bear down upon them from all sides . . . Clack! We close our jaws upon them. And then, there, I grind them up, you see, I'll cut them to pieces; minced, crushed, crumbled, and finally, pulverized. (Cixous, 217)

As we will better see in chapter 5, Pol Pot here exhibits—with Cixous underlining it—the classic polarities of anality: power-hungry retention, then expulsion. All in the service of shoring himself up and purifying himself and his group. He retreats, controls himself, lures the enemies into a false sense of security, then drops noxious destruction upon them. That at least is his plan. Equally revealing for the hypothesis I develop: attempting to ward off the disintegration of his own world-experienced, he plots the disintegration of his enemy's. The Vietnamese will be "cut to pieces, minced, crushed, crumbled, and finally, pulverized." In other words, diarrhea of identity, personal and corporate.

* * *

Even a cursory look at the Rwanda massacres shows all the paradigmatic features of genocide: the convulsive, terrified, humiliated corporate body; the attempted extermination of all elements felt to be inassimilable and infecting; the hysterical will to survive as that corporate body in its world-experienced. Above all, terror as the parent and right arm of genocide: the terror and hatred that possessed the genociders, and the terror and despair that possessed the genocided.

As the Cambodian affair must be understood as erupting in the aftermath of colonialism, so must the Rwandan. Roughly the area now called Rwanda in central Africa was originally colonized by Germans. As a penalty imposed upon Germany at Versailles after World War I, the territory was ceded to Belgium, a country that already controlled the vast region called the Belgian Congo (I remember these names from my youth).

If possible, the Belgians were even more Eurocentric and racist than the German administrators had been. Living in the Rwanda area, comprising about 15% of the indigenous population, were the Tutsis. This people were taller and more angular than the majority, the rounder, more "African" majority, the Hutus. In other words, the colonizers had considered the Tutsis to be more European than were the Hutus, therefore more civilized and more human. Therefore, too, more to be favored and elevated to positions of authority and power in the colonial regime (though there is evidence that Tutsis were the traditional royalty in that area). Built up in the Hutu majority was dammed-up hate, resentment, humiliation (See Mamdani, Sources).

One of the great values of regarding the Rwanda genocide as paradigmatic is that it throws light on the uncanny parallel between the corporate or group body and that of the individual member of that body. As we will see more clearly in the next chapter, the hierarchy of the particular body mirrors the hierarchy of the whole group. As each individual is a body with members that descend in value and power from head to feet, so also is the whole group as it is perceived by its members. Because individual members are perceiving the group in hierarchical terms, it becomes, almost literally, a huge corporate body with "head," "arms," and "generative," "excretory," and "pedal" functions. The functions mark different castes in the social hierarchy.

In this intuitive schemata—which I argue exhibits human behavior revealingly—the more "African" Hutus were less civilized and human than were the more "European" Tutsis. Hutus, then, were tantamount to the pedal, procreative, and eliminative functions of bodies. In other words, the Hutu as "drawer of water and hewer of wood," forever menial and lowly (Note again the story of Noah's son, Ham, whom Western tradition believes angered his father—Ham who supposedly became the progenitor of Africans. Genesis 9:22–27.) And/or, the Hutu as rectum, the Hutu as shit.

If indeed it is true that in genocidal hysteria the overstressed experienced world disintegrates, it turns into a tide of diarrhea. For the infection is most naturally attributed to the eliminative organs, in this case Hutus. But now a revolution was occurring, and it was the Tutsis' turn to move into the lowly position, to bear the brunt of the destabilized majority's projected anxieties and humiliations.

There is evidence that the oppression of Hutus historically by Tutsis, and later by European colonizers, is driven by this habitual relegation of them to the level of offal. But now, when the ruling Belgian forces pulled out following World War II, this gave Hutus the chance to act on long-held grievances. Indeed, to turn the tables, or to invert the pyramid of value and power: to place themselves in the position of head and the Tutsi minority into that of rectum and waste.

When the metastable situation, fanned constantly by radio-broadcasted propaganda for Hutu Power, exploded in genocidal violence, it was the Tutsis who were immediately felt to be the infectious flux of the disintegrating world-experienced. It was they who must be discharged, annihilated. They must be annihilated if the Hutu corporate body—the great majority after all—was to regain its health. In just a few months hundreds of thousands of Tutsis were slaughtered in a whirlwind of incredible brutality.

We owe to Philip Gourevitch graphic and voluminous accounts of life in Rwanda. He arrived there just after the main explosion of genocide, but while sporadic attacks on Tutsis were still going on. The mass of Hutu genociders was still operating, but beyond the borders of Rwanda in Zaire (protected by United Nations humanitarian efforts [!], after the outside world had finally grown alarmed by what was happening in "darkest Africa"). An invading army from neighboring Uganda, led mainly by ethnic Tutsis, had driven out most of the Hutu Power forces.

Still, discomfiting and dangerous confusion and terror held sway in Rwanda, nightmarish chaos. Probably Gourevitch risked his life to probe into places he went, gathering data. We owe him a lot; his book is a journalistic and reporting feat (*We Wish to Inform You that Tomorrow We Will be Killed Along with our Families*). It is a considerable achievement for a young man. (Could an older person have withstood the sustained stress?) His detailed and unflinching account of what he directly experienced, the fresh evidence left by the genocide, is a necessary condition for beginning to understand what went on there. Which was: the killing, mainly by hand, using stones, machetes, and clubs, of approximately a million Tutsis in a few months.

It is necessary to read accounts like Gourevitch's to begin to grasp genocide's hell. We need to know just what it sounded like to walk through unburied Tutsi bodies, now partially covered by weeds, and left as a "living memorial" to their slaughter in a churchyard. Just what does it sound like to hear and to feel the crunch of children's skulls under one's feet?

And yet, for all his book's value, it is not sufficient to understand what went on. Probably it must inevitably glance off the actual moment of hysterical, wildly emotional slaughter: the destruction of what was already shit to its equivalent mess before one's eyes, which feeds one's hungry and beleaguered heart. Gourevitch's attempt is gallant, but remarks he makes indicate its shortcomings. For example, he asks, without answering, Why didn't the Hutus who were slaughtering by hand grow exhausted before they did?

The question shows a telltale conceptual inadequacy. His careful observation, diligent search, and honest reporting do not penetrate to the experiential level of what was actually happening in the roiling and reddened streams of genociders' and genocideds' immediate awareness. That is, experiencings of a disintegrating world-experienced—on the spot, at the time. What was going on was in fact a virulent form of insanity, a form of demonic possession. (On possession, see my *Wild Hunger*, chapter 7.) As some schizophrenics work nonstop for forty or fifty hours before collapsing, so the genociders were so insanely adrenalin pumped that they did not feel the exhausting effects of tremendous exertion the way normal people in normal times do. There was nothing normal about it.

This is very hard to get used to and to concede. Most of us are sustained day by day by our more or less normal worlds-experienced. Why try to break out from the limits of our world-experienced, when these very limits mark the structure that orients and sustains us daily? How can we, even if prompted, imagine what lies beyond the limits of everyday, normal anticipating and imagining, the normal world-experienced? How can we imagine "the unimaginable"? Or how can we think "the unthinkable"? Why try?

Because without a concerted attempt we have no hope of understanding our subject, terrorism and genocide, not in the slightest. I think that a certain distance of more or less calm detachment, coupled with firsthand accounts of genocides, may give us some understanding of the "unthinkable." The word may become flesh, at least to the extent of creating a knowledge-by-acquaintance sufficient to change behavior.

Besides, if we were to claim to know that genocide is literally unthinkable or unknowable, that would be dogmatism cleverly disguised. As Charles Peirce said, it would be to block the road of inquiry. The gravest intellectual sin would be committed, one with the gravest consequences for our survival.

Perhaps for now, we should just keep certain scenes in mind. Hutus seemed to be engaged in a kind of magical as well as violent undoing of the Tutsi epoch. These tall, lean-faced folks were thought to be foreigners, those who had come some time ago from a region up north. They were to be sent back where they came from.

There is a large river flowing out of Rwanda to the north. Thousands of Tutsi bodies were thrown into large lakes, but also into this river. Washed up on one of its banks was this sight: A mature Tutsi woman was found drowned, along with four infants and young children, perhaps her own progeny. These latter, also drowned, were found tied, each to one of her four limbs. No other marks of violence were found on her body or on the infants' bodies.

Now, what hypothesis might begin to explain such a thing? We can try at least to extend our conceptualization beyond the everyday normal world into the actual but "unimaginable." As we noted, it might be said that genocide does not happen in the world, but outside it. Which means that genocide assuredly happens, but outside our normally structured world-experienced with its standards for thinking, feeling, and knowing. (See Todes, *The Body as the Material Subject of the World*, Sources). It happens in the vacuum left by the collapse of the normal world, in an experienced world so habitually warped in fear and disgust that certain types or castes of humans appear to be subhuman, or appear to be waste.

To say genocide is unimaginable means we can't imagine it happening in a normal world-experienced. "Unimaginable" connotes "not normally imaginable," which implies "not imaginable in a normal world-experienced." Yet it happens!

But while reflecting and writing about this are we not necessarily in our normal world-experienced? How can we know the eruptive abnormal world? This is a good question. Still, we are not helpless in answering. There are at least a few accounts by genociders of their own experiencing while caught up in the contagion (see, again, Gourevitch). In addition, we too have had moments of shock, great disgust, panicked helplessness, and perhaps murderous impulses. These experiences can be appropriated and extrapolated to what we take to be the limit to generate some feel and idea of genocidal madness. (With regard to shocking impulses and shocking results, recall my overstepping myself in crossing that river.)

*   *   *

As was often the case in the nineteenth and twentieth centuries, it was not scientific historians or planners stuffed with facts and theories who best foretold events—or analyzed and accounted for past ones. It was artists, poets, novelists: those in command of mythic tropes and metaphors, those who kept their probing sensibilities on the actual pulse of humans caught up body and soul—as we might say—in a turbid, roiling, mythic torrent. This is an abysmal level of reality, a rushing underground river roaring in the darkness, untouched and unimagined by modern science and Enlightenment.

Thus Tolstoy in *War and Peace* gives us a great account of the later age of Napoleon. For he sees it against the ever-present but easily ignored backdrop of abiding Nature, the vast sky and the clouds moving imperturbably across it, wounded soldiers looking up into it. Or the vast snows that entrap the military genius, Napoleon. Thus Joseph Conrad in *The Heart of Darkness*, written in the early years of the twentieth century, best foretells the fortunes of the century—one we can call uncanny. He foretells it in a simple image that opens his book. A gunboat from an unidentified country pours its cannon fire into the jungles of Africa. The message is clear: undirected fire, uncanny breakdown of the experienced world in terror and frustration, voiding of intelligent thinking. I early cited Melville's account of the numbing effects of misery on witnesses who feel helpless to change things.

*   *   *

In the five cases of genocide I have focused, shared attributes of genocide emerge. Sameness appears vividly through the many instances that differ in other respects (recall the shared features listed above).

We are ready now for an all-embracing theory of genocide that more deeply unpacks the interfusing identities of individual and group. There are no easy answers here. Individuals are not mere chips from a block, the group (though this appears at certain times to be the case), nor are groups determined by simply adding up the individuals that compose them. We are essentially individual and essentially communal. We live the paradox. Each member pours into the whole from its unique position or point of view, and the whole pours back into each of its members as only it can there and then. Though the everyday illusion of group solidarity and immortality is terribly strong, it is not impossible for some members to acknowledge that their home group is limited, and that we either find humanity as a whole the fittest object of our ultimate loyalties, or risk the genocide of the human race by the human race.

NOTES

1. When the intolerability of death is linked with the reality of the self's bodily being and its primal experiencing, otherwise fantastical happenings become believable. Thus Stalin's idea that Lenin's body be embalmed initiated a whole embalming industry, replete with science, technology, and public relations. For, as the dictator intuited, on the primal level of experiencing, no clear distinctions are made between body and self, and between sleep and death. Thus Lenin's immaculately embalmed body in its marvelous sarcophagus and mausoleum tends to appear as if the man were merely sleeping ("I'm standing beside Lenin," said the American scientist Fertridge . . . "I really feel I'm looking at the man sleeping. You find yourself walking on tiptoe so as not to wake him," see Zbarsky, Sources, 91). Later the U.S.S.R. made gifts to other communist governments by embalming their dead leaders. For example, while American bombs fell heavily on North Vietnam, the Hanoi government, in cooperation with a large contingent of Soviet embalmers, took elaborate measures in the jungle to protect the body of Ho Chi Minh. "Ho's body was regarded as sacred, and they knew that its capture or destruction would deal a fatal blow to the morale of their troops. . . . Meanwhile in Hanoi work had been going on in secret that would soon result in the largest mausoleum in the world. It was a kind of gigantic Roman temple . . . designed to be visible from the country miles around" (184–86). In touch with the reality of primal experiencing, we are ready to take seriously other events equally fantastical. Thus in 897, Pope Stephen VI had the corpse of Pope Formosus dug up, dressed it in robes, and tried before a council; the corpse was condemned, mutilated, and thrown into the Tiber (*Cambridge Medieval History*, III, 67). Sadly, this is not completely unbelievable. So much the self belongs to the body that even the dead body holds tightly the aura of that self. (I owe these references to Frederick Kayser.)

2. See Sources, Fazlur Rahman. Also Martin Marty and Scott Appleby (Sources, 846) who define jihad thusly: "Struggle, usually an internal process against bad habits or irreligious behavior. The term also denotes war as in the service of religion, although the circumstances justifying such a struggle are the subject of considerable debate."

3. Many Western readers construe the rapid expansion of Islam from the seventh century on as simply bloody and greedy conquest. This is dangerous over-

simplification that doesn't discern a central motive force of Islam: an ethical-religious ideal. The Islamic scholar and believer, Fazlur Rahman, helps us grasp this. Muhammad and his followers believed they had received from God a moral vision of a new social order of justice and egalitarianism for the earth:

> Whereas the Muslims did not spread their faith through the sword, it is, nevertheless, true that Islam insisted on the assumption of political power since it regarded itself as the repository of the Will of God which had to be worked on earth through a political order. . . . To deny this fact would be both to violate history and to deny justice to Islam itself. To us there is little doubt that this fact, coupled with the inherent Islamic features of egalitarianism and broad humanitarianism, hastened the process of Islamization among the conquered peoples. (*Islam*, Sources, p. 2)

4. The fault-line separating Westerners from Easterners, Occidentals from Orientals, does not merely divide Croats and Serbs. Nothing better exemplifies the blurring of fact and fiction, of fact and fantasy, in human affairs. The fault-line coincides very roughly with the respective spheres of the Western and the Eastern Christian churches. Some, of course, will think of these as themselves fantasy systems. But even if we assume this, we dangerously oversimplify. For fantasies are lived by real humans in real situations: fantasies have behavioral consequences that form traditions for living that build up over generations. For hundreds of years, ways of responding to Muslims as "Orientals" and "exotics" inclined Westerners to ignorance of Islam that is life-threatening for us all. (As I write, Franklin Graham, Billy's son and heir, who believes that Islam is an "evil" religion, preaches in Iraq. General William Boykin, attached to the intelligence division of the Pentagon, thinks that our advantage in this death struggle with Islam-militant is that our God is the true one, theirs is false. This self-serving myopia would be tolerable if only these Christians' lives were at stake, and not also mine, and the rest of humanity's.)

Many Christians' crushing ignorance of, and animosity toward, Islam did not end with the lugubrious demise of the Christian crusades in roughly the twelfth century, but continues to this day. Nor is the animosity against Islam limited to the charge that it corrupts Christianity and occupies its sacred places. Some Christians also charge Islam with fouling the source of Western philosophy and science, Athens. The fact is, Islamic scholars, thinkers, scientists and mathematicians built on Greek accomplishments, and without Arabic numerals, and Arabic mathematics generally, there could have been no scientific and technological awakening in "the West" in the sixteenth century to the present.

The fact/fiction of West against East reached one of its tragifarcical climaxes in the early years of the nineteenth century. Contemporaneously with Lord Byron's expedition to free Greece from Islamic-Ottoman rule, Beethoven wrote music for a production of *The Ruins of Athens*. This cantata-play features the wise Minerva, unchained after centuries of captivity under the Turks, who reviles the "barbarous" Muslims for their ignorance of Greece. She hears two of them discussing the use to be put of a sarcophagus taken from the Parthenon: they suggest a trough for their

Pasha's horse. The reduction of Islam to a caricature comes through also in the "exotic" Turkish Style cropping up by demand in some of the music of Mozart and Beethoven, and continuing at least as late as Saint-Saens. When I was a child, one form of boyish ridicule was to drop to our knees, bend forward until heads touched the ground, and repeat "Allah, Allah" at those whose presumed dominance we derided. A stunning example of the weird irrelevance of Islam crops up in William James' influential article of 1897, "The Will to Believe." Here he argues that freedom emerges when we face genuine options, one feature of which is that the alternatives must be "live," the choice must make some difference to us emotionally and existentially. Whether or not to believe in the Mahdi—the last leader of the faithful who has yet to appear according to some groups of Muslims—exemplifies a dead option for us. That this ignorance has only recently begun to crack in some quarters evidences a crucial failure of North Atlantic educational institutions.

The vast majority of U.S.-sent troops to Vietnam, and more recently to Iraq, were ignorant of those cultures. This ignorance befuddles and frightens, and is exacerbated by features of guerilla warfare: populations with no uniforms or insignia. The overlap with genocide is considerable: soldiers with little idea of who they are fighting or why, aside from the primitive perception that they are *other* and so must be *wrong*. In the last weeks of 2003, reports of a U.S. "Tiger Force" in Vietnam began to leak out. The My Lai masacre was no isolated incident, apparently. A U.S. sergeant, now near old age, interviewed by ABC evening news (11-12-03), spoke to this effect: "I *knew* who they were. I could smell them. The hair stood up on the back of my neck. I would shoot them in the back." When the interviewer asked him if he had been temporarily insane, he replied, "Anybody in that situation would be temporarily insane."

Decades ago, John Dewey saw what our hyperspecializing culture, obsessed with short-range interests, was heading toward: "The world seems to be mad in preoccupation with what is specific, particular, disconnected" (Sources, *Experience and Nature,* 295). Representing The Heritage Foundation, Steve Forbes in a public letter (11-03) bewails that a percentage of our young people don't think that our values are superior to other cultures'. The problem goes deeper than that. I suspect that many young people hardly know what a culture is. When with young people, I get the impression that most of them believe that what's around them there and then is just the way things have always been everywhere. Evident is an individualism or atomism that pulverizes any sense of developmental continuity in definite situations (and of course any sense of what Black Elk called the mystery of growth). Most of the young have little or no idea that groups are corporate individuals that became what they are by developing in time, often painfully, through certain circumstances. No idea, for instance, that there have not always been many women in classrooms. No idea that this is a change that resulted from a culture's wrenchings and convulsions over centuries. No idea that here there has been a shift to registers of reality hitherto unsuspected; that events are unimaginably overdetermined; that much of history happens behind our backs; that there is an unboundable excess always at work. [Probably only the greatest art articulates this sliding into hitherto unsuspected registers, this work of the excess and of spontaneity. I am thinking now of the slow movement of Beethoven's 29th piano sonata—particularly in Gould's performance, and of the same movement of his 32nd and last sonata—particularly in Schnabel and Ugorski's performances.] On orientalism, see Edward Said, Sources.

5. Did the Bosnian Serb leader, Dr. Karadzic, mean by "The Muslims will vanish" that they would be so terrified that they would vanish from Bosnian territory (as well as some being killed)? Or, did he mean vanish from the face of the earth? Perhaps, caught up in the frenzy, he himself didn't know? The question of intent is significant in defining genocide. As mentioned, I agree with the framers of the UN's "Convention on the Prevention and Punishment of the Crime of Genocide," that terms, including "intent," should be used and defined fairly broadly. Thus article II: "genocide means any of the following acts committed with intent to destroy, in whole or in part, a national, ethnical, racial, or religious group, as such . . . " For example: "Causing serious bodily or mental harm to members of the group," or "Deliberately inflicting on the group conditions of life calculated to bring about its physical destruction in whole or in part." So it is immaterial exactly what Karadzic meant by "vanish," for if the residue of the Muslim population were to vanish from their Bosnian home territory, because of their terror, this was calculated to bring about "serious bodily or mental harm." The term "genocide" can be usefully used in this fairly broad sense, for it suggests a key feature of genocidal fear and aggression: that the disturbing or "polluting" targeted group be removed from the daily and direct experiencing of the genociding group. For some home groups that experience other groups as polluting, it is enough that the others get out of the home group's sight, and/or off their land. On the other hand, the Nazis—and I believe the Hutus—insisted on simply exterminating their others. But I don't take the intent to exterminate to be a necessary condition for applying the concept of genocide. Being a stickler for using terms only in the narrowest and most precise senses may obscure fundamental and generic, but foggy, aspects of acts and events—particularly the phenomenon of pollution (I am indebted to acute conversations with Dr. Cedric Tarr).

6. As noted in the introduction, many factors produce genocide, for it shares certain features with conventional warfare. To the extent that it does, conventional empirical studies of warfare—e.g., economic, sociological, psychological, demographic—apply to the explanation of genocide also. Thus Stanley Milgram's experimental studies of the power of authority to sway people to do what they believe is wrong are relevant to explaining genocide (see Sources). Likewise classic studies of group panic can contribute also (see Sources: Bartholomew, Amin, Small, McFarland, Connor, Ulman). But to get anything like an adequate account of genocide, all these factors involved in conventional studies must be caught up in the larger context that includes the X factor—the dread of group pollution and disintegration of consensual reality that plays the central role in my hypothesis. How, for example, is the experimentalist to factor out measurable features that would distinguish group rape in a genociding situation from group rape in some other situation?

Could reliable data from contrasting situations be gathered? If it could, and if we found that some men are significantly more inclined to rape in genociding situations (which I think is likely), we would still have to explain why. I believe we would have to adduce the X factor.

Socioeconomic inequities, for example, can fan the flames of ethnic hatreds (see Amy Chua, Sources). But why are the flames fanned so high, so rapidly, so insanely? What but the X factor and ontological insecurity can begin to explain the off-the-charts mania of Serbian genociders, for just one instance? Chua summarizes reports:

> In the Serbian concentration camps of the early 1990s, the women prisoners were raped over and over, many times a day, often with broken bottles, often together with their daughters. The men if they were lucky, were beaten to death as their Serbian guards sang national anthems; if they were not so fortunate, they were castrated or, at gunpoint, forced to castrate their fellow prisoners, sometimes with their own teeth. In all thousands were tortured and executed.

(Her sources: Roy Gutman, "Death Camp Horrors," *Newsday*, Oct. 18, 1992, p. 3; and Laura Pitter, "Beaten and scarred for life in Serbian 'rape camps,'" *South China Morning Post*, Dec. 27, 1992, p. 8.)

The smallest member of the camelidae family in South America is the vicuña. These animals group together in family-like bands headed by an alpha male. When a contest occurs for this position, combatants will try to bite and injure the rival's genitals. This suggests that in genocidal rampages regression to trans-species forms of aggression and domination occur.

7. Pol Pot's love of hatred is also noted by David Chandler in *Brother Number One* (Sources, 103). After capturing Phnom Penh, Pol Pot introduced a reign of terror: "The Red Khmer held that . . . those who had not taken part in [the victory] were enemies. With victory, there was to be no consensus or healing. . . . To those who had welcomed the Communists' victory this policy of hatred was bewildering. Most of the people in Phnom Penh were poverty-stricken refugees . . . they were ready to help the Red Khmer. Now that the war was over, everyone longed for guidance and support. But as Pol Pot declared in 1977, 'class and national hatred' rather than the prospect of building a just and happy country had produced the victory. To follow through, hatred had to be maintained; enemies had to be treated as they deserved to be. Overnight they became 'new people,' or 'April 17 people'—[purged], less than human, without privileges or rights."

A THEORY OF GENOCIDE AND TERRORISM

And Jesus . . . saw much people, and was moved to compassion toward them, for they were as sheep not having a shepherd . . . he beheld the city, and wept over it.

—Mark 6:34, Luke 19:41

History is a nightmare from which I am trying to awaken.

—James Joyce

Aristotle believed that the common run of persons live like cattle. I think Jesus was closer to the truth: they live like sheep. That is, they flock together like sheep, whereas cattle—though they too are herding animals—tend to move out some on their own. Individual cows show a degree of individuality, at least in good weather. Of course, grazing sheep will wander off in any direction. But at the slightest sign of danger they bundle together in tight flocks: the group appears to be a corporate individual with a life of its own. But it looks wayward and helpless. The flock bobbles and trembles, proceeds tentatively here, tentatively there. It longs for a leader of some sort to guide it. The sight prompts Jesus to weep, as it might conceivably prompt us to do also.

Of course, we could maintain that it is not politically correct to mention such things, not in a democracy, and then we might quickly pass on to some other topic. But we would be neglecting to study an urgently important question about ourselves. Why must we flock together so tightly, excluding thereby the richness and variety that others could bring us?

*   *   *

We face a paradox: we are essentially individual and private, but also essentially communal and public. The paradox is subtle: it is not like simply asserting that squares are round. The public and private are aspects of one changeable, complex, often troubled creature. Coordinating the aspects is greatly difficult; it is not easy for us humans to live in fulfilling ways. Do we so fear ostracism and abandonment, so fear being too different even from members of our home group, that we go along with others to the detriment of our individuality? And if the home group itself is threatened do we bond ever more tightly still?

The erosion of ritual life in the West exacerbates the perennial problem of coordinating our public and private aspects and learning how to live. For in traditional societies, each person must face *individually* the rigors of being initiated into the elders' *group*. Now, for many, we have children trying to initiate children . . . into what? Only people already matured have any behaviorally effective knowledge of adulthood. Only when initiates believe that they have been accepted by true adults is their initiation viable. More and more in a society obsessed with consuming, the young and the old are divided, and this happens because of the different ways in which the groups are targeted by marketers. They are separated, divided into target-objects, not integrated in a developmental continuum that includes all body-selves, body-subjects, in the most intimate and crucial cooperative task.

Western philosophical and scientific thinking has dazzlingly illuminated our individuality (at least certain aspects of it). And also, it must be acknowledged gratefully, cast some light on features of our communal being—particularly on our rights as individual members of larger political bodies. When the ledger is toted up, however, emphasis has fallen eccentrically on our individuality.

And indeed, on our individuality distortedly understood. For this has been construed simplistically, as polarized against our communal feature. And the communal has been misunderstood as well, just because of the polarization. In fact, our individuality and communality are intricately and integrally intertwined, in a way that is most difficult to step off from and to see, track, understand. This is why genocide, among other pivotal phenomena, has proved such a vexing matter to grasp.

We cannot be described simply as individual selves or souls ensconced in public bodies. I believe we persons are bodies that have a claim to our own space: especially that space right around and near each of us, and, with peculiarly acute emphasis, that space within each's envelope of skin. Any uninvited entry into any of the orifices of the body is a violation not only of the body but of the self. Our primal claim to space must be unpacked and exhibited.

I argue that the group is a corporate body, and that any uninvited entry into this larger body is a violation of all the members of this body. When the complex and precariously balanced interchange between individuality and community, between privacy and publicity, and then between home group and other group threatens to break down completely, genocide can follow. We are easily violated, easily terrorized at every level and moment of our being. As I will argue more fully later, human identity involves an identity problem. We humans are peculiarly caught up in excess, in overabounding life itself. We are animals caught both in our animality and in our talking, writing, symbolizing. We are the animal that endemically dreams, both sleeping and waking. (I am indebted to Kierkegaard on this point, as on many others.)

Roughly, as we have begun to see, genocide follows this way: we become developed humans because of our undeliberate imitation of others in our surround who are already more or less maturely human. A contagion of mimetic engulfment occurs in infancy. Maturity begins to be gained when individual body-selves form a modicum of self-responsibility and initiative, or autonomy. We go along with the group when there is no reason not to. But if there is a reason not to, we begin to act on our own.

We are individuals-in-community, and each cultural community generates its own world-experienced. Each culture belongs in its world-experienced, belongs in its own cosmology—better, belongs to it, is led around by its fundamental meanings, beliefs, assumptions about the world.[1] The primal, "default or ground zero" position of the corporate body and its commonly shared and fused experienced world can be threatened, particularly by incursions from an alien group with its own distinctive experienced world. Then there can occur supercontagion, a regressive movement in which the home corporate body works and sweats desperately to reconstitute or re-glue itself by exterminating or expelling alien elements. "We are the fundamentally human society, the universal consciousness!" Genocide.

*   *   *

We are individuals, yet we are bonded into groups. And our groups themselves are individuals, but of a different order. Moreover, both individuals and groups are immensely vulnerable, easily violated. Not easy to think through! We need an explicit and thoroughly developed theory of genocide. Our immediate problem with Islamic extremists will not be soluble without a solution of the background difficulties. Sadly, our "best" educational institutions ill prepare for this work.

The West gained its initial stunning purchase on the physical world through analysis and objectification. Our science, technology, military might, and commerce are now changing the globe, and of course ourselves, with eruptive and stunning rapidity. The pre-Socratic Greeks, for example, factored out of the flux of events what they considered to be the enduring elements: for instance, water in its various states—solid, liquid, gas—was thought to be the root cause of all events and of all things.

The rise of modern science in the West in the seventeenth century also owed much to analysis and objectification. Isaac Newton, for example, made the great progress he did by building up wholes conceptually and experimentally through "the simples," the "unsplittables" or atoms, that composed them. Even twentieth-century physics focused profitably for a while on subatomic "particles" (but superstring theory's construal of forces as harmonic interrelationships or interfusings of incredibly short "strings" may have ended the profitability of this atomism).

But analysis and objectification, ever spreading over the globe through ever-expanding North Atlantic commercial and military culture, fancies itself to be the only respectable way of knowing and being. This utterly imperialistic attitude presumes to say what the sanely and scientifically experienced and experienceable world is. That is, it presumes to say what the world is.

The great price paid for this triumph is greatly hidden. Automatic analysis and detachment takes a detached and analytic attitude toward everything, including of course ourselves and our ever-ramifying subjective and intersubjective experiencing. We are not just objects! But living within the scientific Western worldview we picture ourselves as particular objects to be scrutinized and pinned down *in the world*. This means that the living of our everyday lives gets pinched and occluded: our immediate experiential involvements in surrounds and in unwitting exclusions; our involvements in other experiencing subjects, in wholes, and in the *Whole felt as Whole*. But thereby a factor hugely constitutive of us is overlooked. I mean the mythic and primal residues in our experiencing, the ways we live the background World inherited from our deep past.

As noted, and I'm noting it yet again, despite areas of consummate precision and sophistication, scientific research is typically naively realist in its general approach. No clear distinction is made between objects in the world experienced detachedly as "out there in the great container of space ready to be measured," on the one hand. And on the other, the world itself as we are caught up in it immediately in our subjective and intersubjective experiencing: that primal, moody, mythic engulfment and involvement that creates the basic erotic level of world-experienced, world-meant, world clutched and hoarded as ours. The world can be regarded as a collection of measurable objects only after our primal involvements and selections in the World as a whole have been secured. Since this has a mythic dimension, let us capitalize it, as I have done, call it World or the Whole.

When this primal level of experiencing and world-experienced is over-looked—all hyperstates of immediate selection and involvement—the ec-static transports and destructive smearings of genocide, say, must be over-looked as well—or simply not understood. "Why, our world-experienced is just the way the world is! We are righteous, they are evil."

A hyperstate such as genocide is overlooked, or misunderstood, at least when we try to think about or theorize about it, when we try to describe the experiential aspects of the phenomenon, the full *what* of it, and to locate its causes and conditions as best we can. The sheer avalanche of genocidal fury and shock, the *that* of it, so to speak, has at least been reported sufficiently. In fact, to grow weary of hearing about it is a danger. Perhaps a prurient fas-cination with genocide replaces hard thought about it. But more likely, we just look away and grow numb, as Melville discerned.

To grasp our flowing, elusive, compelling, exclusivistic experiencing of the primal World-experienced is greatly difficult. To reflect upon it in typi-cal scientific ways tends to freeze it; as reflected, it is objectified; we lose the awareness of the ongoing and "constructing" subjectivity that we indi-vidually and corporately are. This always remains at the heart of ourselves incompletely knowable, essentially elusive. Something pulsing, alive, spon-taneous and naturally buoying (to whatever effect) always flows at the heart of us in the shadows (even to commit suicide we must be minimally buoyed to do it). To try to turn around quickly enough to grasp it, as William James puts it, is to miss it. For to be reflected in an instant's reflecting leaves that reflecting itself unreflected, and so on in every succeeding instant. Nietz-sche makes the same point: the acrobat cannot jump over his own shadow, cannot detach himself from it—the shadow sticks to him. Carl Jung also agrees.

But, obviously, we must make some headway here if we would grasp those tortured periods of experiencing that we call genociding. Concepts are good for only so much. They must be supplemented by metaphors. Why? Because concepts are applied primarily to objects only, and, more precisely, to those which possess the necessary and sufficient conditions for applying the concepts.

Only metaphors evoked by artists, shamans, priests, priestesses, poets can evoke and vividly reveal our ever-ongoing immediate experiencing of the world-experienced. For a famous example, James spoke of the streaming of our experiencing. "Streaming" suggests not only the flowing of it, but glimmering reflections thrown off the stream's surface. These reflections are often fantastical, for evoked are mythic associations from primal sources of humankind within our lineage: reveries and daydreams of dominance and submission, say, or radiant, fleeting images of incredible power and potency (recall communist Chinese depictions of Mao, for instance: degenerate myth). As Dostoevsky put it, "Nothing is more fantastic than reality itself"—particularly the reality of our own immediately experiencing selves lodged in our immediately experienced World. Science with its finely diced-up objects and its calculations is marvelous, but it is not adequate to grasp ourselves and our immediate, profoundly parochial experiencing of our World-experienced.

*　*　*

Some nineteenth- and twentieth-century thinkers have tried to completely rethink the interfusing and interfused natures of individuality and community, of experiencing and experienced, and of past and present. They attempt to short-circuit or abort the now automatic movement of detachment and analysis into atomlike parts or objects. They try through various methods to engage us in our immediacy, to describe to some degree the experienced world as we get caught up in it spontaneously (see Ramsland, *Engaging the Immediate*, Sources). This can be described as uncanny or magical: weird fusions, confusions, ecstatic transports, immediate discharges of fear and fury, strange feelings of relief, etc. As I've said, we should speak of genocides as ontological hysteria. These thinkers—myself among them—try to lay out in sketch a playing field for a theory of genocide that doesn't prejudice us to favor scientific objectivity exclusively: a prejudice that detaches us and limits in advance what can be discovered about the gruesome phenomenon.

I remember being a young boy observing turkeys in pens in the desert of California. When one or two turkeys would begin to gobble, the gobbling would often spread through the whole group in a wave. The gobbling of the first had ceased when the last birds at the end of the wave began their grating, rumbling chant. I can still hear in memory that wave. I knew it was an important event, and somehow gave important meaning to other similar events, but I couldn't have explained why. I had yet to encounter the distinction James made between knowledge by description and, on the other hand, direct, involved, heated (or chilling) knowledge by acquaintance.[2]

Our immediate sensuous and emotional involvements in the world around us provide fundamental meaning—personal meaning that spreads itself in what we later learn to call symbols. Something greatly important to us in an experience spreads in a symbol that concentrates and epitomizes the importance. This symbol-tripped spreading supplies continuity, energy, momentum, connectedness, orientation in our lives. Think of the power of the cross, or of the Islamic crescent.

It is primarily artists of some sort who form symbols, images in matter, metaphors that epitomize, intensify, and clarify our immediate sensuous experiencings of the World-experienced. Music, of course, leaps to mind. We can easily understand how ancient sages (and our own Thoreau) could speak of the sound of a stream as the sound of praying. It is Nature supporting and buoying us in a way, and at a level, that eludes our conceptual and our conventional scientific grasp.

So it is not surprising that it is artists who best communicate our immediate involvements with things, with animals, birds, persons, mountains, lawns, lights and shadows, claps of thunder, deaths. And it is they who best resuscitate and communicate the ancient mythic residuum still active in us. Sometimes artistic disclosures throw us back on our own experiencing as ours, ours! Throw us back on all the often uncanny involvements that make us what and who we are.

And so it is not surprising when the artist-writer Elias Canetti grasps for us in sensuous symbols and metaphors the immediate reality of mimetic engulfment in groups: the engulfing power of groups epitomized in images of rivers or the sea, images that capture the density, growth, and infinite openness of being carried along in crowds, large or small:

> The sea is multiple, it moves, and it is dense and cohesive. Its multiplicity lies in its waves; they constitute it. They are innumerable; the sea-farer is completely surrounded by them. . . . The dense coherence of the waves is something which men in a crowd know well. It entails a yielding to others as though they were oneself, as though there were no strict division between oneself and them. There is no escape from this compliance and thus the consequent impetus and feeling of strength is something engendered by all the units together. The specific nature of the coherence among men is unknown. The sea, while not explaining it, expresses it. . . . Waves are not the only multiple element in the sea. There are also the individual drops of water. It is true that

they only become drops in isolation, when they are separated from each other. Their smallness and singleness then makes them seem powerless; they are almost nothing and arouse a feeling of pity in the spectator. Put your hand into water, lift it out and watch the drops slipping singly and impotently down it. The pity you feel for them is as though they were human beings, hopelessly separated. They only begin to count again when they can no longer be counted, when they have again become part of a whole. (*Crowds and Power*, Sources, 80)

Part of the skill of the twentieth-century psychologist, Jean Piaget, was his patience in describing exactly what he observed in children. Before he tried to explain their behavior he tried to describe what was going on immediately, what was being expressed momentarily by them as whole bodies, whether they could say this or not. Thus he could capture the reality of mimetic contagion within groups, not so unlike contagion between turkeys:

The child often imitates without being aware of it, merely through confusion of his activity or his point of view with those of others. The child's egocentrism is essentially a phenomenon of indifferentiation, i.e., confusion of his own point of view and that of others or of activity of things and persons with his own activity. . . . [I]t is both suggestibility and unconscious projection of the ego into the group, and lack of awareness of the point of view of others and unconscious absorption of the group into the ego. In both cases it is essentially unconscious. (*Play, Dreams, and Imitation in Childhood*, Sources, 73–74)

But is "the ego" an observable reality? Isn't Piaget at this point giving us atomism and reified abstraction, the sort of thing we expect from the West? Yet aside from Piaget's apparent inconsistency, he is giving us important insight into mimetic engulfment in the corporate body.

Note also the similar virtue of the psychologist-philosopher Maurice Merleau-Ponty: he also describes what's being immediately experienced and expressed before he tries to explain it. Thus in his own studies of children, he notes mimetic contagion between them. One instance reveals everything: A teacher slaps the hand of one of the children, who begins to cry. The other children begin to cry. One of them, not the one whose hand was slapped, cries out, "The teacher hit the hand." The hand. That is, the child has not perceived the individual hand of that other child as that other child's hand. As actually experienced in the actual experiencing of the child who made the statement, the teacher has hit any hand in the group, or, hit the corporate individual's hand. It is this, once observed and described, that must be explained, and it is not easy.

To complete this initial survey of mimetic contagion, note what some psychologists have recently concluded about infants just ten days old picking up facial expressions from their parents. A few decades ago it was received wisdom that infants only appeared to be smiling, but that this appearance was not a manifestation of friendly feeling, but was caused by stomach gas contorting the face into a semblance of a smile. But careful observation and experimentation ruled out the gas account. The conclusion to be drawn was that a parent's smile directly irradiated the infant's body and face, and reproduced itself, in some straightforward way, in the child's good feeling and in his or her rudimentary but real smile. In other words, the corporate body feels good, and individual members all participate in this good feeling.

What spreads contagiously most easily and momentously? Terror. The genociders and the genocided catch each others' terror. It is a self-potentiating circuit—a fascinated frenzy that feeds on itself.

*   *   *

It would be nice to say that the thinkers just cited typify the Western or European-rooted intellectual stance. They do not (although there is a long tradition in the West of artists and mystics who grasp reality as immediacy and engulfment). There is a deep countertradition among intellectuals that seems devoted to systematically covering over immediacy, suppressing it. This is found mainly in the detaching and analyzing habits of most scientists, but also in many Anglo-American analytic philosophers today. This stance colors and slants most of the Western world, particularly as Muslims experience us. Muslim militants typically perceive us as being remarkably fragmented and shallow, as being fixated in a narrow range of attention, and as lacking deep belief and conviction—lacking belief sufficiently deep to die for.

Automatic detachment and analysis became habitual with René Descartes, and with the British Empiricist philosophers and psychologists who followed in his wake. The Renaissance European man, Descartes, was brilliant in many ways, but as a thinker about the human condition he was greatly misled, and he is greatly misleading. He attempts to explain "the mind" before describing accurately what is to be explained. Following the general natural-scientific bent of his time, and some of science earlier, he endeavors to explain things by first breaking them down into their simplest components. So he assumes that there are "simples" out of which mental phenomena such as thinking, desiring, and feeling are built: simples such as sensations, images, or atomlike ideas. When these occur "in the mind," and they correspond to things "outside the mind," we have knowledge, and only then.

But these "simples" are not what is really encountered immediately as the human organism and the rest of the world interact and interfuse moment by moment. They are the wizened fruit of a premature causal-explanatory analysis that has occurred automatically, and that has forgotten itself—an intrusive reflection that distorts and conceals what is prereflectively given. If we describe the world as actually experienced in our actual, immediate experiencing, we find an interconnected and interfusing planar or fieldlike reality—however rudimentary, vague, shifting, and smeared most of it may be at any moment. Gestalt psychologists and phenomenological philosophers have tried to describe this.

We get from Descartes and his many followers a vivid picture in which there is an individual mind or consciousness inside an individual skull, the mind full of supposed atomlike mental entities. We are pictured encapsulated, walled off from the rest of the world, with only natural science and elaborate argumentation left to reassure us that there is a world out there at all. This picture of human mind is disastrous for grasping mimetic contagion: how we are immediately caught up in the world around us. It is disastrous for grasping that supercontagion, genocide.

Descartes' picture is insidiously misleading. For it contains a particle of truth: namely that there is an individual and private aspect of our experiencing or minding. Recall my earlier account of falling on a stone in a river, striking it with the point of my chin, my field of consciousness nearly vanishing, shrinking to a point before re-expanding. There's an element of personal privacy here; nobody else was experiencing this at that moment exactly the way I was.

But the personal privacy is only an aspect of a whole processual system of experiencing in which a whole human body is engaging immediately in the whole environment. The event of deciding to step and then falling bears the unmistakable message of my particular, contingent, and particularly impulsive and vulnerable physical-psychical being.

The well-functioning brain is a necessary condition for normal consciousness. But it is only a necessary condition, however fundamental, not a sufficient one. It is only an aspect of the whole flowing contextual and cycling reality in which my organism and the rest of the environment are interflowing and interfusing instant by instant.

Descartes' picture conceals the fact that the brain is only a fluctuating aspect of the whole. The brain must be functioning within a body that is functioning in an environment, which includes of course the culture and its experienced world. Only after realizing this can we reliably investigate what many call the psychological level of this single, complex being. The true picture must include the patent fact that we don't immediately experience mental "simples," which are then built into wholes, but rather a field in its throbbing, flowing, fluctuating wholeness. This generates the intoxicating trance: this world-experienced is the world, is identical with it.

The true picture will leave room for physics, physiology, and brain science, but they will not enter prematurely. Their analysis into simples (if that is what they are doing) will not atomize and falsify the description of our immediate experiencing of ourselves caught up as only we can be in the surrounding and sustaining world. The hard sciences will be available to assist in explaining how we are radically porous, open, limited, vulnerable to the contagious influences of the world around us.

There is an element of particularity and privacy in our lives all right. But it must be understood in bodily terms: as we aware body-selves who have an abiding claim in our culture to our own space, both within our body's surface, and close to these surfaces outside them.

All this is essential to making sense of ourselves-in-the-world, better, to making sense of our worldly-aware and unwittingly selective body-selves. Our privacy, understood as we immediately experience our bodily selves, can be so violated, and our sense of ourselves and the rest of the world experienced so imperiled, that we lash out to destroy the alien beings who violate us, lash out to try to subdue and to quiet psychical-physical earthquake. When this happens, we bond furiously and incandescently with others of our group in genocidal rampage. Because each of our vulnerable bodily selves is threatened simultaneously.

We are speaking of privacy and inwardness, the particularity of the individual body-self living into its possibilities in the world, and enduring the world's jolts on the way. This must be understood in a context of conceptualization—and ultimately metaphorization—utterly different from Descartes'. Needed is the context of world-experienced understood this way: as a vast circulating Whole of energies pouring through nodes within itself, which include our own enculturated organisms. Everything is open to, and is flowing into, everything else, in one way or another, to one extent or other. Our integrity and sanity are in need of constant support and protection. As the contemporary physicist John Wheeler put it once, There is no *out there* out there! (Tor Norretranders, *The User Illusion*, Sources, 201)

I will say more about why things are sometimes experienced as alien and disturbing: alien and disturbing because polluting. As we have seen, things perceived to live and move inappropriately, unfittingly, in space and time, are experienced as disruptive and poisonous to the point of threatening our continued ability to live.

There is no need to try heroically to jump from sensuous experiencing to theorizing about ourselves. Sensuous experiencing, directly described, and properly rendered and epitomized in art and in symbols and metaphors, is the best beginning for grasping our actual lives as body-selves.

*   *   *

As I earlier sketched, there are thinkers who resolutely oppose the whole scientistic, prematurely objectifying, analytical, and naively realistic drift of so much Western thought. This drift trends toward shipwreck, even as we live and breathe today. How long can humankind hold off our probable self-destruction?

Some of the most important of these now unfashionable thinkers are North Atlantic philosophers themselves who appear at the turn of the nineteenth century into the twentieth, and through the twentieth (though typically peripheralized by academic-analytic philosophers.) They are, however, moving clearly toward intersection with indigenous and "backward" modes of thought. Indeed, toward intersection with what we can discern of paleolithic modes of being and thought. (See my *The Primal Roots of American Philosophy: Pragmatism, Phenomenology, Native American Thought*, 2000 Sources.)

I have been particularly influenced by the later explorations of William James, and also by how these were continued by Alfred North Whitehead. I will only occasionally cite these thinkers, however, preferring to create a new organic unity of thought, if at all possible. Furthermore, they did not, as far as I know, say anything explicitly about genocide and terror.

I agree with James that if we succeed in describing the experienced world just as it appears in our experiencing immediately, we encounter a reality anterior to, and more fundamental than, the distinction we draw between subject and object. We are porous, open, participatory beings. The coldness or sharpness or solidity of things is not just "out there" as properties of such objects. Such properties or characteristics infiltrate, flood, permeate, or contort our very being as perceivers, rememberers, forecasters.

In fact, James asserts, the very same—numerically identical—hardness, say, that figures in making up or constituting a stone wall's reality through time, figures in constituting ours when we are perceiving the wall (particularly if we bump against it or trail our fingers across its surface). That hardness, that very same, that one hardness. Or, that very same, that one warmth of another person's body that figures in constituting that person's reality through time also figures in constituting our being through time when we embrace that person.

It's simply not the case that there are feelings, or images, or ideas "in our minds" that do or do not correspond to something "out there." That's Descartes' dualistic psychophysical picturing of us, as if we were detached and encapsulated minds or selves. What could be more alienating? No wonder that indigenous people find so many of us modern Westerners to be rootless, superficial, weird, driven, and dangerous.

Of course, there is some distinction to be drawn between knowing and the known. In the career of the stone wall, say, through time, its characteristics or properties such as hardness are locked into its other properties such as height, thickness, position on the earth—as long as the wall stands at all. But in our careers as knowers and experiencers of the wall, they need not be locked together. I may be remembering the hardness of the wall dissociated from its other properties. Or I may be fantasizing about its hardness without specifying that it's the hardness of the wall. Immediately experienced by me, hardness may fuse with any number of things, or with the World-experienced as a whole. I may habitually experience the Whole world as hard, obdurate, impenetrable, intransigent, as may my home group also. If this were to be so, a depth psychologist (or a mythologist) might become greatly interested.

So, no matter how strange in various ways all humans might be as organisms, we are members of the physical world, and appallingly open to chance, to violation. Or to being exhilaratingly caught up in some group or other that has formed or is forming in the world. Or to being caught up in a fanatical group's frenzy. We are not hermetically sealed subjects, nor are we objects neatly set off from objects around us. How is the world experienced in our primal, fluxing, disintegrating, regenerating, degenerating, interfusing experiencing of it? In the world as actually experienced, nothing is as neatly enclosed and separated as our European intellectualistic logics assume that it is. Vicious intellectualism is the view that characteristics not explicitly included in the definition of something are excluded. Actually, things overlap with, or ooze into, other things—to various degrees—in the messy, actual World as it is immediately experienced. With sundry consequences, things merge in various ways with what intellectualistic logic says they are not.

We are disclosing the basis of our undeliberate imitation of others, mimetic engulfment, and also the extremer forms of this, contagion. To various degrees things irradiate each other and absorb or repel each other. The parent's smiling face and attentive body pour a distinctive configuration of photons and pheromones and heat waves into the infant's body: it is possessed to some degree by the parent's body. But this is just one of a countless number of examples that could be given. There are no "minds" sealed off in their mental "contents" from other minds. Those are reified abstractions, not realities: philosophers' fictions. They are remnants of atomistic, dualistic, and mentalistic thinking, and they generate endless distractions, estrangements, and befuddlements.

* * *

We are disclosing the basis for the experiencing of disruption of identity, also of pollution. Our smoothly functioning, experiencing organisms, caught up mimetically in our group, generate a world-experienced; and as long as things go well, the generating is mostly automatic. If the experiencing is both smooth and creative, it's a humming of the organism drawn into its future. It's a humming and honeying sense of one's own being and well-being and one's possibilities, which is simultaneously a celebrating of oneself and the world in which one lives.

But we are essentially limited, open, vulnerable. Hence, as I have already sketched, and particularly if we feel shaky and down, some other human group's mode of being and experiencing the world may loom menacingly before us. Our immediate reaction will tend to be fear or terror. We fear that we cannot assimilate the foreign group's mode of experiencing. We fear that our experienced world cannot accommodate the others' experienced world looming before us and threatening incursion. The other group intrudes into our space as we immediately constitute or construct it as ours. Violated, our experienced world threatens to fall apart. Moreover, entranced, we do not distinguish our experienced world from the world itself, the only one there is. So the world threatens to fall apart.

The honeying experiencing of smoothly constituting an experienced world for ourselves threatens to dissolve into a stinking tide of refuse. We dread to fall into the lower, eliminative functions of body, personal and corporate. What is the answer? To turn all those others into waste first: they are excess, to be left out, to be wasted. We want to find them a bloody mess of flesh and bones already moldering there at our feet.

* * *

To develop these points I appropriate features from what Whitehead calls his cosmology. The universe is an evolving organismic whole: as I said, one

sea of energy pours through each node of itself—however, whatever, wher-
ever that node may be. What we call things in the broad sense (for example,
persons) are evolving assemblages of actual occasions. Actual occasions occur because they pick up, sweep up, take in from the world around them in
the manner and point of view peculiar to them—at least as long as they are
sustained in existence. This "prehension" is undeliberate: given the universe
pouring through itself, and pulling itself within itself, things fall into place
through a generic aesthetic fittingness. The universe grows at each moment
by budding out of the preceding moment. As the evolving whole surrounds,
pervades, and sustains us, we are formed and fashioned. We are ever-
emerging creatures, largely unconscious, mimetic, tremulous, vulnerable.

If we dilate our awareness, and at the same time keenly observe, we detect some of this formation of self as it is happening. Detectable is a shadowy and slippery mimetic interchange between this body and other elements in the surround. (It is my own body, but it is not objectified: in this
stretch of experiencing I am not thinking explicitly and clearly that it is individual at all.) The experienced world tends to take on the features of the
organism experiencing it. But it's not a one-way street. The experiencing organism tends to take on the features of the things experienced.

To articulate this more exactly, as the body is irradiated by the surrounding world, the world-experienced is invested automatically with the quality
of the body that is experiencing it. Hence, one's body-as-experienced (one's
"body-image") is not confined within the surfaces of one's individual organism, but floats and blurs with the surround-experienced. It blurs ecstatically
with the surround and with one's group. When that group is menaced by another group, members must also be menaced in dread and disgust.[3]

Note Alexander Pope's couplet concerning experiencing—negative in
this instance:

> All is evil that the evil spy,
> As all is yellow to the jaundiced eye.

* * *

I ratchet up the intensity of the points just made to unlock the conundrum
of genocide. Why do people do it, why aren't they content with destroying
the other group's armed forces, or just kidnapping and incarcerating their
leaders? Then the other group would be putty in their hands—so one might
think. But one would have to touch them!

Whitehead says the whole universe pours into and through each node of
itself, so we prehend or take in the whole universe (though doubtless the

closer parts more intensely than the farther). In any case, we prehend a vast whole of the surrounding world. This pours into our nervous systems from every side. As I've earlier noted, on the level of what we sense immediately (I won't say perceive), it is electrochemical events in our brains. The course of experienced events—events as experienced—turns on electrochemical events in the brains of individual human organisms. But—and this is an utterly crucial point—these organisms are mimetically engulfed tremulously in fellow members of the home group.

Here is the keystone in the arch of my hypothesis concerning genocide: The brain is not a sealed atomlike thing. It functions as a stage in surging brain-body-environment loops of energy exchanges. The brain functions in human bodies caught up in frequent mimetic contagion.

We shouldn't forget, moreover, that basic neural pathways were laid down in primal mimetic contagion and fusion with others in infancy. Much of this primal mimetic residuum remains throughout adult life.

On this utterly prereflective and primal level, we don't make the distinctions that we take to be clear and fundamental when we are somewhat detached and able to reflect, nor when we are stanced and set to expand our store of knowledge by description. We don't calmly and neatly say, "This is our group, that's the other group. We can keep to our path, they can keep to theirs."

Particularly if our group is already disintegrating, particularly vulnerable, we are in danger of picking up mimetically on the other group's way of experiencing the world. This does not jibe with our deeply trusted, habitually experienced world. This is the ugly, stomach-turning dissonance which we experience immediately as, "Their way of being is inassimilable—they infect us."

In the grip of panic, we are unable to make the distinctions that in normal circumstances—at home in our group—we make tolerably well. At least when there is a clear need to distinguish between the head of my own body and the head of the home group's, I can do this well enough to survive in my group. Or, when there's a need to distinguish the head of our group from the supreme head of the universe, God, I do this tolerably well in normal times. That is, I do not prostrate myself before the king (or president?) with quite the same absoluteness and avidity with which I prostrate myself before God during a religious ceremony. Moreover, in more or less normal times we all can distinguish between any other group's head and way of experiencing the experienced world and our own head and way of experiencing.

But in the grip of panic fear that the other group's way of being in and experiencing the world may mimetically engulf us in it—what happens then? Lines of demarcation and identity blur and smear. Most excruciatingly, their corporate head threatens to engulf ours, and with this we are disoriented radically and begin to go to pieces. The inclination to fuse ourselves back together through exterminating the other group may be actualized suddenly.

A king rules, it was believed, by the grace of God. A Pope is God's vice-regent on earth. German soldiers marched into battle in the First World War with belt buckles inscribed, *Gott mit uns*, God with us. Islamic terrorists believe that it is their God-given duty to destroy us. If fundamental distinctions could be made clear, we might see, for example, that their God and ours must really be one and the same. But prevailing is only a vast, vague, sickening sense that they are not us; that they have developed through history in a fundamentally foreign way. Before we disintegrate and turn into garbage or filth, we turn them into this. We are the master race, they are filth.

This kind of smearing on the primal and prereflective level of experiencing still prevails for us body-selves today. For as bodies in groups we have not changed all that much. The fact that some corporate bodies are democracies that, during normal times, allow many different perspectives and arguments to be aired, provides no guarantee that conditions will not suddenly be dire. Even the troubled democratic whole may fuse together behind some genocidal leader.

On the immediate, heated level of experiencing that I am trying to disclose, members are caught up in corporate bodies. And corporate bodies may threaten to smear into other, incompatible ones. Nobody is thinking, in any of the usual, honorific senses of that term. Two corporate bodies may not "smell right" to each other. This may be due to a divergence of behavior on a level that the reflective intellect—if it were operating—would regard as insignificant. Some difference in hygienic matters, or culinary ones, or in social relations—as in what counts as acceptable physical distance in social interaction, etc. But immediately, as the corporate bodies threaten to rub up against each other, the difference radiates in a nauseating panic throughout the corporate bodies and their members.

* * *

Matters come to a head. Let us concentrate on particularly provocative differences between corporate bodies: on matters of hygiene. Hitler inflamed his followers by blaming Jewish bankers for exacerbating the economic woes of Germany after the First World War. He blamed their love of "filthy lucre." It may be no coincidence that just before this time Sigmund Freud and Karl Abraham were formulating ideas that equated money and feces on the subconscious level of minding. Briefly put, the infant in toilet training exchanges his bowel movements for praise from his caregivers. Or again, he may refuse to move his bowels because holding out for a larger reward; he "hoards his treasure," etc. Moreover, infancy is not simply outgrown, not simply detached and left behind.

Now notice how these ideas fit in with those pertaining to individual and corporate bodies, and the different levels of value, from the top down. Hitler said such things as, "The filthy Jews' money-grubbing hands are taking the food out of our mouths." He was not saying that they were merely depriving good Germans of food! That doesn't begin to communicate the offensiveness and violation he was attributing to Jews. He was saying that they were mixing the lower levels of body, specifically the excretory functions, with the noble mouth, face, head.

Moreover, it was their excrement. No mixing could be more polluting. He was charging Jews with an inexpressibly nauseating violation of non-Jewish Germans. This was the sort of charge that would incite many more or less ordinary Germans to genocidal mayhem, and would incite many professionals and intellectuals to systematic, cold-blooded, mass murder.

Adjustment of levels between bodies, individual and corporate, is the most important adjustment of relations between persons. Thus invalids desiring to be cured requested merely to kiss the hem of Jesus's garment, for his curative power was believed to flow down from his head and heart through his body into their suppliant mouths. Thus the Orientalized Roman Emperor, Diocletian, decked opulently and bejewelled, could be approached only by kissing the hem of his garment. Thus, as mentioned, some women who cohabited with Mao flashed as badges of honor—as stigmata perhaps—the venereal sores contracted from engorging his genitals.

Even today the obeisant Catholic will kneel and kiss the bishop's ring as an expression of obedience both to him and to the corporate body epitomized by him. Japanese bow, lowering their upper body vis-à-vis the other in a conventional sign of respect; this is a lingering shadow of primal body-mythic reality. An ultimate sign of contempt is to fell an opponent and drag his body in the dirt, as Achilles dragged the body of Hector behind the chariot, though we doubt this is the ultimate sign of contempt. For forcing someone to consume human waste must be profoundly degrading.

In times ripe for genocide, corporate bodies threaten to smear into an impossible whole, a polluting and disintegrating mixing of these bodies. In a genocide—or in very many of them—a corporate body reconstitutes or regroups itself just in time by exterminating the other group and its experienced world. "Manifestly, there cannot be another world-whole. There is only one world, and ours is it!"

* * *

We can very concisely sum up this theory of genocide. Before any things in the world can be picked out, objectified, measured for the purposes of science and technology, we bodily beings must possess a primordial, moody sense of all things involving each other. It is a visceral sense of the unimaginably vast bolus of involvements that we call the World itself. Whatever our habitual attunement within the Whole, it pervades and colors all our situations; it gives them their ambient and emotional quality and charge. It is the constant and contrastless taste of things. It may never become focal in our attention. But it is the ultimate context, the erotic and electrifying context, within which all things find their place and can begin to receive an identity in our experience.

Emphasizing subjectivity, as I am doing, does not land us in subjectivism or mindless relativism. John Dewey, for example, noted that everything picked out, every "this" in our experience, emerges at a point of stress within a whole system of meanings and interests installed in a culture. Its demarcation and individuation as a this, a referent, is our attempt to resolve the stress. Does the resolution endure through our ongoing experiencing? That is, does what we have picked out and individuated stand the test of our experience? For instance, picking out driving on the left side of the street as *the* correct way: does that work for a culture? If it does, it has been tested, and has not been found wanting.

As Dewey puts it piquantly, things or practices are human needs turned inside out. Needs being met count as tests being passed on the nature and reality of what meets them. Every effective focusing presupposes the functioning cultural matrix, the vast majority of which must be utterly taken for granted. So all creativity in a culture presupposes a vast ground that cannot all be questioned at any particular time. To be forced to question everything at once produces convulsions. (See his *Experience and Nature* and *Human Nature and Conduct*, Sources.)

Primordially, the world for us must be spatial-temporal-cultural-bodily-habitual. Space and time are generated by and for us enculturated bodies within the circumpressure of our experienced world. Space and time are anticipated in patterned ways by our aware bodies in every move we make, every attitude we take, everything we do and undergo. As I've said, following Dewey, art can bring this to the focus of awareness, can make it thematic.

The unexpected can happen at any moment. We are vulnerable bodies in space and time, and are conditioned by our cultures to act so as to protect ourselves and to find our way. When other cultures intrude upon us, when they ride roughshod over our habitual ways of constituting space, time, culture, body, ourselves, we experience this primordially as wrong, as evil. And they seem to get away with it!

Our white-hot feeling of being imperiled and violated can be so disturbing that our generation of experienced space, time, and appropriate conduct—our habitual context of interpretation—is skewed and begins to wilt. Things in the world no longer retain their identity long enough to be identified as what they are. The disintegration of the experienced world is a basal loss of integration and coherence, a loss of Worldness and selfness. It is nauseating disorientation, a kind of diarrhea—the metaphor is apt. For we are essentially enculturated bodily beings who must order the value and meaning, the very identities, of all that is experienced by us—we must order our bodies and, indeed, all matter. When this ordering and patterning is disrupted, the world-experienced collapses like a tent with its poles kicked out from it. (Our bodies are understood in some way hierarchically by all cultures. Can the hierarchical ordering in corporate bodies themselves be altered? This key question will be taken up below.)

As noted, we should speak of ontological hysteria—that which concerns our very being. We should speak with Macbeth of weird beings who infect the air through which they move. Yet again we see that this opens the door to genocidal attempts to incapacitate the alien modes of experiencing and being that violate, infect, collapse us.

*   *   *

My assumptions are radically anti-Cartesian. I do not believe that mind and body are different substances, in any sense of substance, but rather are two different aspects of one reality: human organisms caught up in their environments through energy exchanges. As Dewey put it, the actual referent and unit to be dealt with is ourselves, each of us a brain-in-body-in-environment—with environment obviously including the cultural surround within which we are squeezed into shape—more or less. Understandably, then, I welcome new discoveries in brain science that keep pouring in through the literature (for example, Joseph E. LeDoux, *Synaptic Self*, Sources). They connect us to lizard and rat.

Studies of incredibly rapid fear reactions in the brain's amygdala are especially significant. Many of these reactions never reach full consciousness, that is, the focus of consciousness where they can be acknolwedged as what they are. Or they do not reach consciousness at all. This discovery increases our ability to grasp automatisms of a group's panic reactions, the corporate individual following its leader as nearly as inevitably as a lizard's body follows its head.

There is a hidden danger, however, in these valuable brain studies. The danger is inherent in the whole bias of Western science and philosophy in favor of the particular and individual at the expense of the corporate and communal. The inevitable corollary is to favor "bottom-up" over "top-down" explanations (recall Newton's and Descartes' attempts to break down Nature into "simples," and to use them to build up wholes conceptually). The scientific ideal is to hold various measurable "simples" (or "variables") constant and to vary others experimentally and to see what happens.

As I've mentioned, what each of us immediately senses (again I don't say perceives) are electrochemical reactions in each of our brains and skulls. This is true, but for that very reason can be insidiously misleading. Because that truth feeds into the bias that favors the individual, particular, and easily measurable over the messy and the communal. Concomitantly, it feeds the natural-scientific bias for controlling certain variables and varying others. For it is simply a fact that human corporate responses are more difficult to control and study scientifically than are brains studied in relative isolation of the environment.

I don't believe that this is an insurmountable difficulty, but it is one. When LeDoux, for instance, distinguishes between short loops and long loops of synaptic connections in the brain, he is leaving conceptual room for discovering neural correlates of various corporate responses in experienced situations. I wonder if scientists will find neural circuits in the brains of fearful genociders that can be distinguished neurogenerically from the fear experienced by the genocided. They should try to find such.

LeDoux's idea of long loops also opens an area for better understanding the powers and limits of individuals' reflection—their powers of taking thought—to counter genocidal reactions in the group. For, again, he opens an area of correlation between neural-empirical inquiries and conceptual-phenomenological ones. I can only suggest this: that some of the loops will be longer than many empirical scientists will expect. For the structure of reflection as actually picked out in our experience—to be discovered only phenomenologically—tends to be more complex and strange than most empiricists want to grasp (compare, say, Kant and his idea of the spontaneity of the will when faced with the dictates of ethical reason).

People's ability to reflect during times of genocide is notoriously limited. These immediately exhibited limitations, along with the participants' constricted and frenzied worlds-experienced, must be described in their own terms, phenomenological and experiential ones. But neural correlates discovered and described in their own empirical terms—nanovolts for example— might conceivably help us expand the limits of reflection. Through properly timed and calibrated chemical and electrical interventions and learning programs?

I also suggest that a culture's erotic "construction" of a world-experienced is matched in members' brains by long synaptic loops that integrate indefinitely many shorter ones. I am looking for neural correlates of what James calls the residual or background presence of the world or World.

But the danger is to think that ever more and more empirical-scientific studies of the brain in only restricted interaction with environments will be sufficient to grasp a phenomenon such as genocide. There is no substitute for the conceptual-phenomenological distinctions and topics that I have stressed in this book (though not excluding metaphorization). For example, the elemental distinction between experiencing (or minding), on the one hand, and the experienced (the minded), on the other.

Brain studies help us understand the ineliminable element of particularity and privacy in our experiencing—the excess in which we individual experiencing bodies are caught up. Brain events in your skull must be distinguished in some primal way from those in mine. This ineliminable element of particularity and privacy helps explain how some misunderstandings arise between members of even well-functioning cultures. No two individuals will ever know *exactly* how the other is experiencing any given thing.

But we have all been mimetically conditioned to notice what the whole culture takes to be essential. That is, we agree on the gross things to be experienced, and their gross features. For example, "The sun is up"; "These edible things are in front of us, those inedible ones are to the left"; "That other thing is taboo, it pulses with power, do not touch!" etc. Even to speculate on how the other is experiencing any given thing, we must agree that it is that thing we are experiencing somewhat differently.

Moreover, within any given culture misunderstandings can often be cleared up: "Oh, now I see what you mean." "I hadn't thought of that angle on it." But misunderstandings between members of different cultures tend to be much more difficult to clear up. A member of one culture may never be able to imagine an angle on the world in which something apparently innocuous—a little worm, say, or an oddly shaped leaf—could be experienced as pulsing with evil power. In one's own experienced world, these things may not be noticed at all. Hence genocidal leaders feverishly reiterate that those to be genocided "live in a different world," or, better, a lower, quasi world. "They violate the fundamental structures and rules of the world. Get 'em all, kill 'em."

* * *

The theory that is emerging can describe, retrodict, generally account for, and possibly even predict genocides (with some degree of probability). Moreover, as any good hypothesis should, it is able to do the same for other quite different but related phenomena. For example, ritual human sacrifices to a deity can profitably be construed as a way of preserving the ultimate home group, the ultimate corporate body with its cosmic head. For instance, the Aztec practice of sacrificing human beings to feed the hunger of their sun god.

The theory also helps us grasp how wildly many people react to the head of our own nation-state. The United States is now almost completely secularized, so it would appear. It is grounded in the rational and scientific principles of the Enlightenment-influenced founding fathers (insofar as it is grounded at all). Our head, our President, is not to be distracted, not to be serviced sexually by an adventurous young woman in the precincts of the White House. As head of our corporate body, he is defaming and weakening it. I imagine that President Clinton, with his finely rationalized intellect, must have been brought up short by the explosive reactions his philanderings generated.

The theory of genocide I am developing should alert us to possible trouble spots on the globe, enable us to sketch the probabilities of genocide at a particular time and place. The theory should have some predictive power. Empirical inquirers can follow up on this down the road.

* * *

As I have maintained from the beginning, I am supposing that genocidal aggressions occur between groups. This remains a constant in my analysis. But it's as if a thundercloud would race across the sky and blacken the sun. The looming shadow of various forms of terrorism and guerrilla warfare falls over the world since the Vietnam War a few decades ago. The great threat now is no longer vast armies, but small cells of individuals, interlaced cunningly and secretively through large corporate bodies such as ours: cells that possess modern miracles of communication and assorted weapons of mass destruction.

As the line dividing civilians from military personnel dissolves, likewise does the line dividing war from genocide. But with no improvement in the situation. This development inclines the world toward genocides of monstrous dimensions. For victory cannot be gained through the decisive event of the annihilation or surrender of a whole army. The question arises imperiously: How can there be victory unless we kill or incapacitate all of them? (See this chapter's endnotes, also those in the next chapter.)

*   *   *

At this point we can hope to introduce the ideas of projection and scapegoating without oversimplifying the hypothesis concerning the causes and conditions of genocide. We need not be seduced by the atomistic connotations of the phrase "individual person"— or "individual group." By now we should grasp just how precarious, vulnerable, dissolving, at times scattered, our essentially enculturated body-selves are. Thus we should grasp fairly easily how and why projection and scapegoating happen.

It is all too easy to have our thinking co-opted by misleading visual images or metaphors before we know it. Thus in thinking of projection we tend to be seduced by the image of a self-enclosed entity such as a blockhouse used in conventional warfare. In it a slit is placed, through which a beam of blame and aggression is sent out at those encroaching others. "It is not we who are aggressive. Oh no, it is they!"

As we are immediately involved in the situation experientially, our troubled and aggressive tendencies are indistinguishable from theirs; so we escape blame, we think. Identities blur. Scapegoating: *they* take the blame for our anxiety and animus. In the case of guerrilla warfare and terrorist groups interlacing across the globe, the anxiety and dread felt by our home group feeds on itself with especial avidity, because we cannot decisively locate the enemy. The dreaded other corporate body easily takes on a spectral quality: he hovers everywhere and nowhere; he haunts the world. Home group paranoia is a distinct possibility. (Of course, demagogic or just stupid political leaders manipulate the masses by claiming to pick out and locate the corporate body; for example, "If we fight al Qaeda in Iraq we are better off than fighting them here.")

And all this occurs on a level more immediate and abysmal than the rational, deliberative intellect can imagine to fathom. The only proper words for such exchanges are magical and uncanny. With them we get to the roots of behavioral contagion. In certain hysterical and orgiastic states, like evokes like in such inscrutable ways that the distinction that can be drawn—A is like B, but A is not B— washes away completely. There is only a throbbing smear or blur. And ironically, these hysterical or orgiastic states occur most cataclysmically when we are confronted with an other group overwhelming in its otherness. One way, of course, of being overwhelming is to be multiplex and unlocatable. "They're going to kill us" mirrors and excites magically "We're going to kill them"—somehow.

Anthropologists speak of "primitive" or indigenous persons' sympathetic magic, that is, their conviction that like produces like, or that parts are interchangeable with wholes. When caught up in anthropologists' scientific stance—in their distinctions, detachment, objectifications—most of us today think that this belief in magic is ludicrous. Thus when primitives believe that to damage a hair from the head of an enemy damages that person, even if that person is unaware of the loss—for most of us in the "enlightened" West this is incredible. Or, to think that imitating the falling of rain in a rain dance prompts actual rain, that likewise seems incredible.

But it should be clear that when aware persons are interacting in anything like an emotional way, sympathetic magic of the most momentous sorts goes on anywhere anytime. What we do and think springs back upon us: what is projected onto the other springs back upon ourselves without our realizing that this happens. To feel fear tends to excite fear in what surrounds us, and this increases our fear (though the fear may be quickly overcome in aggression). To be aggressive excites aggression. One ambient and emotional quality permeates whole situations, and the various beings party to them.

Or, on a more subtle level, to think of happiness, say, as something to be conquered (as Bertrand Russell did think of it), tends to conquer our attempts to achieve it. In his last notes before his untimely death, Merleau-Ponty blurts out, "Reversibility is the absolute truth." (*The Visible and the Invisible*, Sources)

Happiness evokes happiness, fear evokes fear, aggression evokes aggression: reciprocity is immediate. This occurs on the magical level—unwittingly, prereflectively, and at its greatest, hysterically and orgiastically. Fearful, disturbed for whatever reason, the home group projects its collective fear and aggression onto the alien group or groups. "Get them before they get us, infect us—get 'em all." Scapegoating. Rational thought is corrupted before it gets started. Only rationalization remains—if any thought does at all.

That we need to understand myth and magic to get a secure purchase on human reality appalls the rational or secular intellect. And to get a secure purchase on myth and magic we need metaphor: A is B! Regardless of distinctions the rational intellect will make when and if it regains its senses: "Well now, really, A is like B in a certain respect; but A is not B." As F. M. Dostoyevsky put it—and it bears repeating—"Nothing is more fantastic than reality itself."

*　*　*

We can get only so far with philosophical-conceptual (actually phenomeno-logical-conceptual) analysis. It is necessary but not sufficient to get a handle on genocide. Abstractions and conceptions cannot fully communicate the shuddering encounter with alien group bodies in their concrete presence here and now. These are corporate bodies that are threatening to destroy the world-experienced-by-us, and of course ourselves in it. As I've shown, I trust, this may trigger that supermimetic contagion and frenzied bonding within the home group that is genocidal rage and terror. We should speak also, as does Tolstoy, of the fascination of frenzy.

Now I want to approach this whole matter more sensuously and concretely, more along the avenues of the arts. What best communicates the sensuous, the immediate, the concrete and the magical—yes, it is art and metaphor. If we were somehow to participate in an actual genocide, our mental equilibrium and judgment would probably be so upset that our ability to clearly describe what was happening would be passingly small. Many participants in actual genocides cannot remember the events clearly. They are too discontinuous with their later more or less normal life, their thinking and speaking. The context for grasping any particular event—any particular "this"—has fallen to pieces. Their genocidal acts turn to dust in their memories.

What happens when our corporate body encounters another corporate body and cannot stand up to it? This of course is a metaphor, and it will be a pivotal one in this book.

First a general note about metaphor. The Greek roots of the English word are telling. Meta-phere: to displace or transport. A meaning that is habitually and literally applied to one thing is transported to apply to something else. For example, "The road is a ribbon of moonlight." "Ribbon" refers habitually and literally to certain sorts of ribbony lengths of fragile matter that can be handled right there in front of us. Why not be content with that? Why extend or transport the word to refer metaphorically to a road's undulating moonlit surfaces?

Once the question is asked, we can begin to see the answers. Because literal and habitual meanings usually refer to things experienced as objects. But, as we have amply seen, experience that objectifies presupposes a prereflective, pre-objectifying, predetaching, primal level of intuitive meaning-making, a level of experiencing typically built upon but not acknowledged. It is this primal level of meaning that is made by human organisms in their subjectivity and intersubjectivity—in their ecstatic corporeality and intercorporeality. And made spontaneously and ecstatically as organisms engage immediately in the world-experienced—in its hot or cold, attractive or repulsive, supportive or fearful, right or wrong sectors and moments.

As I said, in an effective metaphor (meta-phere), meaning is transported and extended. The whole pre-objectifying, prereflective, and preconscious body-self expands its involvements in the world ecstatically. It cannot say straight out what it is doing. It intuits connections on the expanding margins of its awareness: new angles and perspectives on a topic are gained that could never have been deliberately projected or planned, not even imagined before. Fresh perspectives, fresh and enlarged meaning, startling new clarifications, illuminations, intensities.

In other words, it's the primal sort of meaning that we must grasp if we would hope to understand the ecstatic reality of genocide and terrorism—the most baleful forms of ecstatic transport. So our excited metaphors can hope to catch glimpses of genocide and terrorism.

Will we ever have enough metaphors? I think not—and in principle. For words, even brilliantly creative ones, give us only suggestions of the realities of experiencings. True, they can break us out from the congealed constrictions, the crusts, of literal, prosaic, objectifying speech and thought. They jolt us, and we glimpse features of reality not discoverable otherwise.

But they do not cease to be words. Moreover, they themselves tend to congeal, to become encrusted: if not freshly motivated by situations, they lose their ecstatic and explosive power to reveal (take the current overuse of "He's *cool*"). We can, for example, become fixated on, fascinated with, merely visual metaphors—for instance, "points of view," "perspectives." There is always an unboundable excess that works in and through us situated bodily beings. This must be grasped—insofar as it can be so—with the help of tactile, auditory, kinesthetic, and olfactory metaphors. As if a burrowing mole were to sniff something at a certain sector in the ground relative to its body. With respect to genocide, bodily, intuitive, preconscious and subconscious selves must be allowed—calmed, encouraged—to wrap themselves around intolerably obscene matters, as closely as they can do so.

We are bodily beings, but ones that generate thought and feeling of a variety of sorts on a variety of occasions. We have no direct awareness of our own brains, but these are necessary for our feelings and thoughts. The streaming associations, presences, patterns—forming, breaking up—of mind (better, minding) itself. Ghosts and spirits of the dead populate us, and things that are far away and inaccessible are presences that pass through us. This is the organism's total, fathomless processual life, the excess that we live and are. In a traditional Korean lyric, spirituality of mind is exemplified:

> If you die, become a flower,
> I a butterfly then would die,
> To flutter about you in springtime

We are those primates who can picture ourselves dead, and turning, say, into flowers and butterflies. Strange animals we are! So close always to oblivion, happily or unhappily; and when our world-experienced or minded is pulled out from under us by those encroaching others, we can reduce them to oblivion before they reduce us to that.

I will weave theorizing together with serious metaphorizing in a cable of alternating strands (metaphors upon metaphors). Metaphor is not a second best. Much better than do literal thought and conceptualizing about objects, perspicacious, timely metaphor can grasp near the heart of our bodily-minding selves—our complex, ecstatic, shifting and flickering worldly subjectivity and intersubjectivity: our snakelike subjectivity and intersubjectivity.

*   *   *

When we use metaphor and call the leader of a group its head, what are we led to expect, and then to find, that we wouldn't have been led to expect and to find without it? We expect that if the head is badly damaged, the rest of the corporate body will also be. Whereas if another part of a corporate body is badly damaged, say the left arm, then though the whole body will be affected, it will probably not break down. (But when Robert E. Lee lost his right arm in the Civil War, Stonewall Jackson, the whole body was seriously affected). Notoriously, when the head of a corporate body is killed or badly damaged—thrown out of action—the whole body tends to become demoralized and to crumple.

Perhaps our leaders today hope that this will happen if we can kill or capture a terrorist head, Osama bin Laden. But what if there are many heads separated greatly in space but tightly integrated through attitude, information, and belief, and through shared ends and means? What if it would be more profitable and meaningful for our experience if we picked out and individuated such a "this," an individual more broadly integrated and based, or even scattered? What if our very survival depends upon thus shifting our thinking? (In Arabic, *al Qaeda* means "the base," but, more imaginative than the West typically is, this group is not based in any particular place.) The gravest danger is that terrorists will outthink us, that they will reduce us to sitting ducks frozen in outmoded paradigms.

Now, we might have illuminated this vexing complexity without the metaphor of the head of a corporate body—and its variants—but I believe it augments our need and ability to know. For one example, the metaphor helps us to understand how bumbling, incompetent heads often stay in power so long: it's the aura of their power—residual mythical and magical power—as heads of vast corporate bodies. In addition, we are helped to understand how the United States could have been lulled into a frothy dream of security. The dream springs from our shared assumption that the head of our vast and mighty corporate body must be perceiving and acting intelligently. But what do "body" and "mighty" *mean*?

Let us press our quest to know what a corporate body is, and what happens when our corporate body encounters an alien one and cannot stand up to it. Or alien ones. As we directly take in the world in normal times—assuming we are erect, competent persons, looking out levelly at the horizon—we take in first and foremost other such competent heads balanced atop their backbones who also look out levelly at the horizon. (Canetti speaks of the moving forest as a paradigm symbol that the German army and people use for themselves. John Dewey employs the pregnant phrase, rectitude of organic action, to describe an ideal for all human beings—uprightness that is simultaneously physical and moral.)

What is submissive adopts a lowered posture and position. It is beneath the head, and suffers a grave diminution of power, status, and value. This is true within individual bodies, within corporate ones, and between corporate ones. And it is true of both human and nonhuman animals. The metaphor pays off in knowledge. We are led to expect, and then to discover, that if, for example, the feet of any body get too close to the head and mouth, there occurs the revulsion of pollution. (In *Ulysses* James Joyce depicts Molly Bloom and her husband sleeping head to feet, not head to head. This together with Molly's allusion to fellatio in her soliloquy contribute to the book's erosion of conventional social structure and taboos that literary censors rightly detected. Advertising laxatives on television at dinner time continues the erosion, I believe with momentous, probably unmappable, consequences.)

Hence, we are led to expect that in the hierarchy of value incarnated in conventional corporate bodies (one body at one place) there will be a class or caste of persons within that body that are experienced as being so low and polluting as to be untouchable. We are led to expect what we do find: that untouchables reside not only in India, but in places we would not otherwise have expected. Say in academia: in branch campuses of research universities, in community colleges, or in schools of education. The power of this stigma—bodily-mythic again—is so great that it brazenly defies rationality. A person's actual intellectual accomplishments are typically invisible.

Now we have a better idea of what happens when one's corporate organism runs up against an alien one that it cannot stand up to. One that it believes collectively—contagiously—may be superior to it. Its belief in the overwhelming validity and appropriateness of its world as it experiences and constitutes it—that grounding, stabilizing, empowering believing—begins to disintegrate. This may prompt, in enabling circumstances, a genocide of the others: the reduction of them to garbage or filth.

What if—as is the case in our dire situation—there are many heads of a corporate body? Aren't the risks of our demoralization even greater? What if we can't even imagine what would count as genociding them?[4]

* * *

In his magisterial three-volume work, *The Philosophy of Symbolic Forms*, its second volume *Mythical Thought*, Ernst Cassirer unpacks brilliantly the metaphor of the corporate body. With great discernment and sensitivity he distinguishes the levels: the head or chief setter of policy; the right arms, the executives who carry out the head's orders and plans; the trunk and support staff who support those above them; the "go-fers" (gophers) who "step and fetch it" or who function in the mail room; and finally the lowest, those who handle the filth, the eliminative functions, janitors and sewer workers, untouchables.

Cassirer's systematic work prompts another statement of my views. When a group is wobbly, and cannot stand up to another group, the preeminence of the home group, and the stability and coherence of its experienced world, begins to collapse. It falls toward the lower regions of body. Its world begins to disintegrate, as if in a tide of diarrhea. This is revealing metaphor because it suggests both the disintegration of the world-as-experienced and its subhuman, disgusting, wastelike status.

Even when we limit our thinking to the conventional corporate body located in a fairly well defined place, so pertinent is the metaphor: the thinking corporate head slumps and begins to lose its organizing and directive power. Given the parallelism between levels and valuations of the corporate body, on the one hand, and the individual body, on the other, all members slide toward waste and the subhuman.

Yet again, the subhuman, concretely and immediately understood, corresponds to the lower regions of the body—in both individual and group bodies—particularly the eliminative functions. So, if our disintegration can be laid to polluting and infectious others—subhuman, subrational, wastelike others—we can restore our integrity and control. Stop our disintegration. Exterminate them. This accounts for the peculiarly disgusted recoil-in-attack of the genocider confronted with the to-be-genocided.

Not only is Cassirer's archival, archaeological, and folkloric scholarship impeccable and replete, but he is a perceptive and empathic person. Yet, he still labors in the afterglow of the Enlightenment, the settled belief in ever-advancing science and reason, in ever-greater analysis and objectification, in ever-greater control. He still labors in the biased belief that we Westerners have advanced all along the line, and that we feel obligated to drag the rest of the world along with us. He brilliantly unrolls the tapestry of mythic consciousness and metaphor. Yet he believes that it will fall away and be left behind. He believes that mythic consciousness is quickly becoming passé generally, and in enlightened circles is already dead.

This is egregious error, as Charles Peirce put it, one that spawns countless other errors. As forming a coherent and vital framework for lives, mythic consciousness is undoubtedly giving way. Agreed. But great funds of it, knots and coils of it, still endure as correlates of our personal-communal bodily and emotional being. They lie concealed like mines, ready to explode when a careless foot steps on them. (It is reported that a professor of philosophy in a United States research university was so incensed at a colleague who aired Christian views, that he planned to sue him for championing cannibalism. That is, for adhering to the doctrine that salvation occurs through ingesting—in the symbolism and ceremony of the mass—the body and blood of the Savior. Such bumptious naivete dressed up as scientific sophistication, such literalism and adolescent rationalist ardor, boggles the mind. Confronting now the essentially mythic but very real culture, Islam-militant, as we are—such bumptious naivete is greatly dangerous.)

Fortunately there are artists and writers employing sensuous images, symbols, and metaphors who see deeper into the perennial human condition than do most professional conceptualizers and cerebrators. In fact, from Greek myth, we have available a metaphor that can, possibly, put us in touch with our present dire situation: that of the Hydra. Cut off one of its heads and two more grow in its place.

To look again at a matter mentioned above: We might think that secular persons' experience of the head of the secular state would be very different from religious persons' experience of the ultimate Head, the God of the universe. But there are reasons to deny this. Entering the Christian cathedral, believers are enclosed in a structure shaped like a giant cross, ensconced in the symbol of ultimate love and suffering: God's reclaiming of us sinful creatures through the sacrifice of His Son. Believers, properly attuned, are engulfed in the suffering and saving body of the God-man Himself. They know with certainty that Jesus Christ is head of the church.

This would seem to be poles apart from secular experience of authority, but Leo Tolstoy gives us pause. Drawing on his experience as an army officer, and employing his great powers of observation and description, he focuses attention on the ever-archaic body-self, individual and corporate. He conveys to us the experiencing of a young officer in the presence—shouldn't we say Presence?—of the Czar. No gulf separates the religious believer in the Presence of the Head of the universe from the soldier in the Presence of the head of state. Yes, this state head is still entangled somewhat in the religious consciousness of nineteenth-century Russia. Yet note how Tolstoy speaks to us even today through the character of the young officer, Count Rostov, about how the life of the whole corporate body stems from the Czar, Alexander the First, the head of this Body. The Czar is reviewing the army:

> It seemed as though not the trumpeters were playing, but as if the army itself, rejoicing at the Emperor's approach, had naturally burst into music. Amid these sounds, only the youthful kindly voice of the Emperor Alexander was clearly heard. He gave the words of greeting, and the first regiment roared "Hurrah!" so deafeningly, continuously, and joyfully that the men themselves were awed by their multitude and immensity of the power they constituted. . . . Rostov, standing in the front lines . . . experienced the same feeling as every other man in that army: a feeling of self-forgetfulness, a proud consciousness of might, and a passionate attraction to him who was the cause of this triumph. . . . Every trait and every movement of the Czar's seemed to him enchanting. . . . Stopping in front of the Pavlograds, the Tsar said something in French to the Austrian Emperor and smiled. Seeing that smile, Rostov involuntarily smiled himself and felt a still stronger flow of love for his sovereign. He longed to show that love in some way and knowing that this was impossible was ready to cry.

Later:

> And Rostov got up and wandering among the campfires, dreaming of what happiness it would be to die—not in saving the Emperor's life (he did not even

dream of that), but simply to die before his eyes. (*War and Peace*, Sources, 263-4, 275)

It makes one think of other cases of potent lodes and fragments of myth still alive in fractured secular societies today. For example, movie stars, gaseous giants created by the media. These are often very ordinary persons whose images are multiplied billions of times electronically, radiated into the atmosphere, or out of it entirely, and bounced from satellites to points all over the earth. How entrancing and rare—almost numinous, heart-thudding—actually to be in the physical presence of one of them. And one finds oneself standing there stupidly, faced with a tinny incarnation, some ludicrous epiphany, of a god or goddess. And it may dawn on one—or it may not: A fraud has been perpetrated on us, and upon the world at large.

These media giants must be careful not to overexpose themselves. For the magically magnetic aura surrounding them can vanish, leaving them naked and alone. Mimetic contagion disperses in a vanishing cloud: silence, then emptiness. Is it the emptiness of a culture hollowed out at its heart? We shall see.

North Atlantic culture is largely secularized. But most people are still mesmerized by the heads of various groups. When these collapse, we all tend to collapse. We lack self-reliance and independent judgment. We might learn something from the hunting-gathering life in which we were formed tens of thousands of years ago. From the evidence we can still glean from hunting-gathering peoples who survived into the twentieth century, there were no single chiefs. There were specific chiefs for specific tasks that pressed upon the group at the time: hunger boss (rabbit boss, say), water boss, diplomatic boss, sickness boss, etc. If we could approximate to this form of life, there would be less chance of helmeted heads of corporate bodies clashing. In other words, if we were more deeply democratic the world would be safer. Members might be less cemented in the corporate body, more tolerant of differences, less subject to compulsions and terrors. Needless to say, we would be able to think more effectively about al Qaeda.

*   *   *

In our eruptive age of electronically dispersed information, we can at least try to communicate to Muslims not yet ready for martyrdom that there is more to North Atlantic culture than consumption manias, more than capitalist exploitation of everything and everybody. This exploitation includes the pandering by the commercial media to appetites for violence and prurience worldwide. This is an abuse by parasitical members of Western societies of a singular accomplishment of their groups: that the citizenry consents to be governed, but does so only if it possesses certain rights, such as those of free speech and press. We can try to communicate that a cost of these rights is that they can be abused, and that they are being so.

As Justice Oliver Wendell Holmes put it, we do have the right to free speech, and we hold that principle dear. Nevertheless, it is not excusable to cry Fire! in a crowded theater when there is no fire. Great principles are effective only when they tie into the whole fabric of a culture's beliefs and practices. There is no substitute for awareness of present and actual situations and what they demand of common sense and concern. In neuroanatomist LeDoux's terms, the great principles correspond to certain long loops of synapses in the brain.

But to be effective in everyday, actual life, these must be connected to numerous little loops that correspond to immediate awarenesses of the present and actual situations that hold us moment by moment. Our current North Atlantic culture is so huge and so fragmented that many persons cannot or will not identify the good for themselves with the good for the whole culture.

As mentioned, the ultimate loops correspond to our residual awareness of the Whole universe—its abounding circumpressure, as James wrote. A culture's religious rites and rituals perpetually formed and re-formed its members' bodily senses of what was appropriate and what was inappropriate, right and wrong, in situations. Religious rituals don't merely connect us with what we take to be supernatural. They reground us in the natural world that, as Islamic philosophy puts it, reflects the divine through countless interweavings and facets. Religious rituals, the greatest of all loops, engage innumerable smaller ones. Ever-regenerated religious faith is an endless source of energy for engagement. I take up these matters, and also the ominous decay of constructive rituals, in what follows.

*   *   *

My theory of genocide is now completed, but only in sketch. It is too schematic to provide the guidance and motivational muscle needed to effectively face the challenge of genocide today. The conflict with Islam-militant may lead to the use of weapons of mass destruction, even to the incineration of the planet's life. Wouldn't this be genocide on a scale never previously seen or imagined?

I have described this book as a progression in intensity. What is progressively intensified is the meaning of the facts, a whole new way of thinking about them that renders "the unthinkable" thinkable, understandable, to some extent. There is meaning necessary for accurate knowledge about genocide. But there is also meaning necessary for knowledge by acquaintance with it—meaning that is planted in our whole bodily selves engaged and vibrant in the actual world around us. Progressions in intensity concern this latter meaning most centrally. There is something essentially repetitive and ritualistic about them.

We can try another angle on this, another metaphor: it is like tightening a screw. One turn, then another, and another, and maybe a final half-turn that locks the meaning in place, that entails commitment. I have already used metaphors in the present chapter. I propose to use more. Metaphors are variations on a phenomenon that approach it from this angle, then from that; that place it in this unexpected context, then in that. Startled, we may be awakened to what is actually happening around us, and to what we are doing.

I myself was startled as I rewrote the next chapter. The rewrite was a variation that allowed me to see what I hadn't seen before. That is, that a strange kind of humor may be essential for the most effective response to the possibility of the incineration of the planet, the possibility of pan-genocide. The problem with "page-turner" books is that readers tend to turn right through the excited emotions that, if they had been lived through and screwed down, might have led to committed action.

In the next chapter, the penultimate one, I will further thicken up and intensify the spectacle of genocide by assembling as many different viewpoints on it as I can imagine. The point is to bring genocide down to earth, to make it a concrete reality right here among us, to make it three-dimensional, to prevent it from being a mere abstraction, a mere accurate but dead speech. Inevitably this effort triggers the attempt to reinvigorate constructive and expansive ritual that could integrate us with what is actually happening in the world.

As primordially erotic, a culture's identity-building is only partially conscious and deliberate. It is not classroom-rational; it gains little or no attention in the clinical Western university. What throbs and attracts us as right has a mythic absoluteness and ultimateness about it. Likewise, what throbs and repels dreadfully as wrong has this absoluteness and ultimateness. Cultures that have grown up in different circumstances couple with their surrounds in ways that produce divergent hot spots and cold spots, different fervent valuations and devaluations.

In the next chapter I search for means to hold off genocide in a new vision of all humans belonging erotically in Nature. It is a vision that integrates previously separated visions: from the Qur'an and its paradisal limning of Nature; from a revived Western sense of the sanctity of individual life and its attendant rights; from biology and evolution; from artists. That is, from overabounding Nature as the matrix in which our species evolved and took shape. It is a matrix that held for 99 percent of genus Homo's existence, and which supplied the basic patterns of the great religious rites: daily, monthly, seasonal, and generational regenerative cycles. Nature with its overbrimming fullness of life, which includes of course the evolved human organism, is what all humans share.

I can hope to excite an expansion of erotic appropriation, so that all of humanity and all of Nature is believed to be, fervently felt to be, ours—but not in the sense that we own it. I can hope that we can acknowledge boundless excess, waste that is not repulsive but is attractive. We are members of the Whole in our being, so probably this expanded erotic appropriation would bring us home to ourselves. It would be the most concretely centering and energizing experiencing imaginable.

Typically we are aware of each other as aware of ourselves (though TV and moving pictures short-circuit this regenerative cyclicity, this reciprocity). The size and depth of the self is a matter of the ecstatic reach of what we can make our own. So the greatest size and depth of ourselves would be our awareness of all humankind's awareness—actual or possible—of ourselves. The being of the self is this magical reciprocity, this magical intercirculation of regenerative energies, within the corporate body of humanity. Magical, why not? It would include our awareness of the dead, their presence to us.

*   *   *

As far as I know, all settled cultures feature a pivotal rite at the close of the year in which the gathered harvests are celebrated and the revered dead are evoked. In our culture it is All Hallows' Eve—in its currently degenerated, commercialized form, Halloween. In Celtic times it was Samhain (Sow-an). Such rites of evocation and invocation reconnect us with the dead who nourish us, reconnect us with those in whom we were mimetically engulfed—plant and animal—those who authorized our being. Nature and, of course, our human ancestors built an experienced world in which we can have a place. Primal peoples believe that the dead still have their own domain somewhere in Nature. To lose them is to lose their stabilizing, empowering, numinous presence.

When these stabilized and stabilizing rites of invocation and evocation are lost, the erotic energies that build an experienced world stray—they find ephemeral outlet in rave parties and the sexual riot of daisy chains, say. Note the words of Jean Markale in *The Pagan Mysteries of Halloween*:

> Samhain feasts, which end in general drunkenness, are primarily orgies in the exact sense of the word, which is to say the "collective exaltation of energy," that potential energy that resides in every individual and sometimes needs to find expression through recourse to more or less magical rituals. There is a tendency to consider the orgy to be a manifestation of degeneration, even an aberrational slide into "the hell of vice" and total debauchery. Certainly the contemporary example of various orgies—sexual "daisy chains" and other rave parties—are rather distressing in their mediocrity and vulgarity, but they still testify to an unconscious search, by debatable means, for the higher state to which all human beings aspire. The orgy is a sacred ritual whose objective has unfortunately been forgotten: to surpass the human condition by awakening all the resources of the individual in order to reach the supernatural and the divine. (23, Sources)

I would add genocide to the list of sacred ritual orgies whose "objective has unfortunately been forgotten."

Might we find a sacred ritual of orgy-like passion focused on the preservation of life on this planet? And can we do so with the proviso that what we mean by "surpassing the human condition" is "surpassing the present human condition of dangerous xenophobia and technological trance"? Can we forget the supernatural long enough to open up and spread out the natural and re-root ourselves in it? For the human condition holds more possibilities than have yet been imagined.[5] They overflow our categories, topologies, taxonomies, classifications, conceptualizings.

* * *

I look at the people around me: changeable, vulnerable, needy creatures like myself; prey to illusions, excitements, disappointments; engulfed in groups, or greatly lonely; sometimes heroic; sometimes abashed, panicked, terrified. Incongruous, laughable, but it is a fact: the world is in these hands, ours.[6,7]

NOTES

1. I am not saying that there is no overlap between cultures' experienced worlds, that there is nothing that members of the different groups can agree about. They

can agree about a lot. For example, the rain has stopped, the dinner is served, the sun is up, that thing there is an animal, etc. But what allows referents to be jointly pointed out is only a portion of the meaning that each culture brings to bear on the referent in question. For example, an indigenous group may believe that a bear is a spirit creature with numinous powers. Whereas a secular and scientific culture sees only a species of carnivorous mammal. The total meaning in one world-experienced, and the behavior incident upon this, can be vastly different from what it is in the other. Scientific and technological cultures, obsessed with denotations and referents, tend to miss the extent of this gulf.

2. The sort of knowledge by acquaintance I stress in this book is knowledge of mimetic contagion or mimetic engulfment (my *Role Playing and Identity*, Sources). As usual, artists best grasp this, or particularly acute observers such as Aaron Burr. Note how Gore Vidal transmits one of Burr's accounts of Thomas Jefferson:

> I have not the art to give a proper rendering of his discourse, which came in floods. He seemed to think aloud and, as he did, one was obliged to think with him, in the process becoming so much a part of his mind that each time he hesitated for a phrase, one's own brain stopped all functioning and waited upon his to think for us all, to express for us all. What a devilish gift! (*Burr*, Sources, 259)

3. The manners in which individual members are caught up mimetically in the corporate body of the group can be directly detected, but the detection requires the most focused and sensitive—the most intricately oriented—phenomenology. I have spelled this out at greater length in my *Role Playing and Identity* (Sources, 21-29 [note Paul Schilder's work on body-image, how it floats, expands and contracts, transposes itself] also note pp. 92-131).

4. Pollution in the full or existential sense involves moving and connecting improperly in space: particularly mixing levels of the body, individual and corporate, that should be kept separate. Muslims are unbaptized, unwashed; city dwellers are degenerates; Tutsis are the lower and alien people who have gotten the upper hand; Jews are filthy with money; "Digger" Indians delve in the earth as if they were animals or subhumans. I believe we will see the same pattern in nearly any case we are tempted to call genocide. Take the rampage against indigenous Mayans in Guatemala, going on with greater or less intensity for decades. (See Victor Montejo, *Death of a Guatemalan Village*, Sources.) People who some claim to regard as "communist subversives" are demeaned by goons in forms of address such as "shit face"—a vivid mixing of what ought to be kept separate. Or they are tortured by being dropped into deep pools of human waste, and, as Montejo reports, some plead to be killed. (One translation of Qur'anic verses [56: 40f] renders a punishment for those in Hell: "The drink of the damned will be boiling water and filth.") Marguerite Feitlowitz (see Sources) documents similar violation and defilement of "subversives" under the military junta a few years back in Argentina. Nazis would not allow death camp victims proper facilities for hygiene, etc.

Note also CIA operations that destabilized or disintegrated "socialistically inclined governments." For example, Prince Sihanouk was undermined this way, which opened the door to Pol Pot. A similarly regarded government in Guatemala received the same treatment, which opened the door to the fascist-style, landowner, genocidally inclined regime: a government that was a reliable trading partner for our corporations. The United States shares heavy responsibility for these genocides. There was a rational component in fear of international communism, also an hysterical one. In retrospect can we sort out these components?

There has appeared (2002) an article by Tim Gulden, issued under the aegis of The Brookings Institution (see Sources), which deals with violence in Guatemala, 1977-1986. The study is valuable both for its subject matter and for its highly mathematical and empirical methodology. Gulden finds suggestive patterns in a data base unique for its fine-grained spatial, temporal, and demographic discriminations. His study agrees with my overall hypothesis that there are fundamental differences between conventional warfare and genocide. In the former, killing is done instrumentally: it is a means for achieving the incapacitation of an enemy's (say an insurgent group's) armed forces. Whereas in genocide, the killing seems to be an end in itself. For the genociders, the others are intrinsically disgusting or evil. (Of course, on my view, genociding is hyperinstrumental in the sense that it works to preserve the genociders' peace of mind, even sanity.) In a number of ways, Gulden's greatly precise discriminations are valuable, e.g., a tipping point or precipitating point for genocidal violence in Guatemala was reached in situations in which the genocided group, the indigenous population, reached about 25 percent of the local group. This suggests that a percentage much less than that was not regarded as a threat to the established group sufficient to precipitate mass killings or repressions—its genocidings. Gulden's use of the data base also suggests a significant fuzzy or grey area between conventional warfare and genocide. In the mountainous fastnesses of northwestern Guatemala, the government's killers could not easily identify whatever leaders of "the insurrection" might conceivably have been involved. So an excuse for killing indiscriminately—"Warfare!"—may have contributed to the genocidal violence against indigenous populations that occurred in the remote mountainous areas (recall parallels in the Armenian genocide treated in chapter 4). I hope that Gulden's exacting mathematical study will excite others of the sort. As I detail in the next chapter, with respect to the horrifying, complex, and dangerous phenomenon of genocide, we need all the points of view we can get to "corral" it and to begin to focus on it.

5. *Newsweek* (11-10-03) quotes Sen. Trent Lott on an alternative solution to keeping peace in Iraq: "If we have to, just the mow the whole place down, see what happens" (23). Assuming he said that, and that he intended it humorously, is this humor that aids us in our present situation? Or does it dangerously tempt us with possibilities? The ease of flippant remarks implies that we can specify what would count as "mowing them all down, seeing what happens." But can we spell this out—dare we? S. Ackerman and F. Foer (*New Republic*, 12-1 & 8-03), report that

President Bush interrupted a meeting between Condoleezza Rice and three senators to boast, 'Fuck Saddam. We're taking him out.'" (17). This eruptive bravura stance borders on humor, but is not humorous. Under great stress and/or temptation, do most people have any clear idea of what's moving and motivating them?

6. Attend carefully to Regina M. Schwartz, *The Curse of Cain: The Violent Legacy of Monotheism* (Sources). When groups form their identity around a single supreme head, around their God, they tend to brutally exclude other groups. "For there is only one world, and one Creator-head of it, and it must be as we conceive it all." Others must be wrong and subversive. The trickiness of it is well understood by Schwartz:

> This book is about violence. It locates the origins of violence in identity formation, arguing that imagining identity as an act of distinguishing and separating from others, of boundary making and line drawing, is the most frequent and fundamental act of violence we commit. . . . Violence is the very construction of the Other. This process is tricky: on the one hand, the activity of people defining themselves as a group is negative, they are by virtue of who they are not. On the other hand, those outsiders—so needed for the very self-definition of those inside the group—are also regarded as a threat to them. Ironically, the Outsider is believed to threaten the boundaries that are drawn to exclude him. (5)

Although Schwartz does not develop a pollution hypothesis in the gestalt of corporeal ways in which I do, her book should be read in its entirety. Valuable analogies are drawn between groups and the body of the land believed to be theirs. The relevance to the Palestinian-Israeli dispute is striking.

7. This chapter on theory has not been written for philosophers in the technical academic sense of "philosopher." Indeed, these persons have often impeded investigations into our primal experiencing. I do rely upon William James, John Dewey, Maurice Merleau-Ponty, Alfred North Whitehead, Susanne Langer (see Sources). Hilary Putnam should also be consulted. He holds unimpeachable analytic credentials, but is much more open to the actual scope of our experiencing—and to what is regenerative in that experiencing—than are most "analytic" philosophers. See particularly his *The Many Faces of Realism* and *Renewing Philosophy* (Sources).

6

CENTERING-DOWN INTO THE IMMEDIATE: VARIATIONS ON THE THEME OF GENOCIDE

Civilization is the thinnest crust over the deepest volcano.

—Friedrich Nietzsche

It is certain that never, before God is seen face to face, shall a man know everything with final certainty. . . . For no one is so learned in nature that he knows all . . . the nature and properties of a single fly. . . . And since, in comparison with what a man knows, those things of which he is ignorant are infinite . . . he is out of his mind who extols himself in regard to his own knowledge.

—Roger Bacon

The main reason Western rationalism has failed to explain genocide is that, enamored of universals and general theories, it has failed to come to grips with the particularities of the human condition. This body, these arms and legs, these bowels, those looming others, this moment of being cornered by them.

But there is no escaping some form of thinking, some general ideas and theories! I have chosen to think by way of writing. If the writing communicates, if it directs my and my readers' attention to the vexing phenomena of genocide and terrorism, so that we come to be more familiar with their twists, turns, and impacts, it must involve some general ideas. Not without reason have some termed these phenomena "unthinkable," for they seem to elude the reasons and ideas with which we think, and by which we make sense of the world. It's as if genocide and terrorism happen outside the world, or in a hellishly lit netherworld.

But I must assume that what I just wrote makes some kind of sense. What kind? Well, we all do have some idea of what it's like to leave the ordinary world of sense and to walk into a kind of nonsense. But, it's not the kind exemplified by, say, square circles. These we believe are impossible: we don't think they could ever be actual. But we don't doubt at all that genocide and terrorism are actual. We point out unquestionable instances of them and may feel nauseated.

So we do get *some general idea* of what they are, even when we keep calling them "unthinkable." We get some of this idea through recounting the many factual accounts of particular cases available to us. We get some idea through shared concepts. We also get some idea by discovering apt metaphors. For these don't just treat us as thinking and feeling objects getting in closer accord with other objects. Apt metaphors feast upon, unpack, and develop our actual experiencing as subjects, body-subjects: the often fantastic associations and reflections glinting off our streaming experiencing in the immediately experienced world moment by moment. To use a stock example, to say "the road is a ribbon of moonlight" jolts all of us into a fresh viewpoint, a novel angle, so that we see how roads in moonlight do actually look to us sometimes: like luminous ribbons showing us the way.

An apt metaphor (*meta-phere*) transports us so that phenomena no longer present themselves in habitual, encrusted ways, but variously. Metaphors are spontaneous variations on phenomena that build them out in previously unimagined ways, illuminating facets and sides of them never before made focal, or even suspected. We are finite beings. We may sometimes speak of "the God's eye point view," but—though this seems to make sense and is good grammar—I doubt that we get any informative idea of what is supposedly being talked about.

Isn't it true that all our knowledge is perspectival, that each of us sees only one aspect, one side, of anything at a time; and, moreover, that we can't imagine what would count as any number of us seeing all possible aspects or sides of anything? When knowledge reveals something of any actual thing, isn't it because we accept our condition as ambulatory, bipedal animals with eyes on only one side of our heads; so that, for example, we must face what we immediately see? In other words, when our knowledge reveals something of any actual thing, we must be conforming to our limits as finite beings.

In fact, isn't it essential to the very meaning of "actual thing" that it presents itself to our immediate experiencing as "never completely knowable" by anybody or by any group over any length of time? Strange, but isn't it true that the most "concrete" and "three-dimensional" account of anything depends upon our essential human finitude?

So, isn't "the unthinkable," aren't genocide and terrorism, just extreme cases of this principle? Why should we reasonably expect anything like complete knowledge of anything, least of all knowledge of these grotesque phenomena? Shouldn't we be content with distant approximations?

I propose, then, that we take as many different viewpoints as we can on these phenomena. Metaphors are spontaneous variations of viewpoints, their very unexpectedness or shockingness essential to their strength. I suggest now that we methodically and systematically vary the phenomena. Both the spontaneous mode of variation and the systematic have their own distinctive strengths, and we need all the help we can get, faced as we are with phenomena as difficult, repulsive, and elusive as are genocide and terror.

$$* \quad * \quad *$$

Needed are variations on the themes of genocide and terrorism, examples of them that reveal the torments of the flesh immediately experienced. As outlined in the introduction, this book offers a progression in intensity. More than accurate knowledge by description is required if we would know in a way and to a degree that may effectively curtail our genocidal impulses. We need knowledge by acquaintance, and we approach this best by centering down into the immediately experienced world through variations on the relevant phenomena that screw them down, so to speak, within the immediacy of our bodily selves.

Now is the time to deal with the general account of waste that I mentioned in the introduction, to particularize and concretize it. The account takes off from the dim sense of excess, of what's left over after all attempts at knowledge by description. It is the unclassified, uncategorized, unknown—waste, in other words. Under certain conditions, this easily leads to the sense of what is to be wasted—those disturbing others.

Along with Western rationalism's preoccupation with general accounts and theories goes its emphasis on the mental. And, indeed, on this construed dualistically: on the mental as over against, and superior to, the "merely physical." This dualism forfeits our ability to understand genocide, for only as bodily beings, body-selves, can we begin to understand it.

We experience waste firsthand every day in our ever-regenerating, processing bodies: in our body-selves every day. Western rationalism all too easily concludes that there is no discoverable reason for genocide, that it is literally unthinkable. But if we attend closely to our own bodies, and to corporate bodies' parallel features, we begin to grasp why we would want and need to turn those others into waste before, we believe, they turn us into that.

In philosopher Jean-Paul Sartre's trenchant novel, *Nausea*, the main character, Roquentin, declares,

> People who live in society have learned how to see themselves in mirrors as they appear to their friends. I have no friends. Is that why my flesh is so naked? You might say—yes you might say, nature without humanity.[1]

The nakedness of the flesh—that is, it cannot be grasped exhaustively in any set of our concepts. It overflows all these: it is an excess, waste. Nature without humanity. Are we approaching, at long last, our scurrying, anxious non-human kin, the lizard on the fence, the rats in the wall, as Emerson has it?

> I realized that there was no half-way house between existence and this flaunting abundance. If you existed you had to exist all the way, as far as mouldiness, bloatedness, obscenity were concerned.

Sartre does not shrink from the anal connotations of this excess, this overflowingness, this waste:

> Had I dreamed of this enormous presence? It was there, in the garden, toppled down into the trees, all soft, sticky, soiling everything, all thick, a jelly. And I was inside it. . . . I was frightened, furious. . . . I shouted "filth! what rotten filth!" and shook myself to get rid of this sticky filth, but it held fast, and there was so much, tons and tons of existence, endless: I stifled at the depths of this immense weariness.

Clearly, Sartre is pointing out not just the excess or waste, the overflowingness, of living things. As a first grip on what he is getting at, we might think of bacterial propagations, or of swarming, countless insect life, or of numberless pupas hanging in jungles, or of mammals' profusive propagating—rabbits, say. But no, Sartre is propounding a sweeping position on all things in any way experienceable, and he is suggesting that a fear of being swallowed up in waste can motivate genocides: It is *they* who are waste, offal. Get 'em all, kill 'em!

No doubt, this is powerful stuff. Nevertheless, to get from his metaphysical position—yes, we can call it that—to genocide, steps must be filled in. Why is all waste soiling filth? Why not beautiful waste? It would seem to be so if one took an elevated ecological position on the regenerativity of Nature. Birth, Death, Rebirth!—the most ancient religious attitude of humankind. Things must die and feed back into the earth if new things would live. Recycling.

But it is just this elevated, tranquil ecological point of view that Sartre's Roquentin does not take, and one must ask why. There are reasons for his attitude that are not clear. It is mainly when people are in dire peril that they project their fear of waste and disgust with it onto those others. It is when they try, crazily, to flee their own bodies, so that their bodies' vulnerable contents cannot, they hope, be smashed out of them, or be poisoned. Is Roquentin in a perpetual state of dire peril? It is not made clear.

The danger of all-sweeping philosophical positions and their attendant mentalisms is that all-decisive bodily and situational particularities will be swept under the rug. Thus I have not begun my account with any such positions, nor, as you will see, will I tie everything together in a concluding position of this sort. But we will not be left with nothing.

Not least of the particularities is the particular way a particular people has its past funded for it. (Roquentin rattles around loose, as if he derived from no tradition.) Thinking that a people who have, they believe, left their superstitious past behind them are less liable to genocidal behavior—that is probably erroneous. For to snap loose from the past is to lose touch with the vast domains of our ancestral foundations, which include, we dimly sense, what we don't know we don't know. Hence staying in touch with these foundations may render us less likely to panic when glimpsing the vast excess left over from what we know, and from what we know we don't know—the amorphous domain of what we don't know we don't know. "This enormous presence all toppled down into the trees."

So I prefer to think of Sartre's metaphysical sally as a greatly valuable variation on the theme of genocide and terror, but a variation among others. How many variations will give us a perfectly adequate account? The question assumes that there is such an account, and I am greatly suspicious of that assumption.

Trying to evade the clutches of abstractions, generalities, and mentalisms, I will now mobilize concrete examples, and make methodically as many variations on the theme of genocide and terrorism as I can imagine. Seen up close from many different sides, we can approximate to an account of what they actually are. In the end, we will see that the essence of

genocide cannot be precisely pinned down, but, again, we will not be left
with nothing.

*   *   *

How do we learn not to overreact to overwhelming variety and abundance,
to differences, in short? This is a hugely difficult question, the ultimate
question for our survival. Let's look at it first from the point of view of our
biological background.

From the start, this book has been inclusive and integrative. I have
claimed that the conventional natural and social-natural sciences can contribute to understanding genocide. These investigations assume the existence of a world of interacting objects or events that can be measured and
studied empirically. But I have also maintained that there is an X factor in
genocide that can be grasped only when we delve into how any group
comes up with any notion at all of a world. This is a prescientific matter that
all sciences must simply assume if they are to begin being scientific. Scientists must awaken from sleep, get to the laboratory, not mistake the coffee
urn for the cyclotron, etc. Different cultures' primally experienced worlds,
even when overlapping at crucial points, can be violently incompatible, poisonous of each other.

I offer here only one example of a natural science making a contribution
to grasping genocide. It is a simple example from evolutionary biology. It
presupposes sentient organisms in the world. These are not simply objects,
for they are supposed to be capable of experiencing. But the experiencing
supposed is relatively simple powers of animal perception. It is not that enculturated human experiencing that builds up the primal experienced world
that all empirical theorizing and investigation presupposes. Yet, acknowledged or not, it is presupposed by all theorizing and investigating. With this,
we will re-engage with Emerson's shocking observations about our neighboring kin: the lizard on the fence, the rats in the wall.

Deeply rooted in humans' evolutionary past is the instinct to note differences. Without automatisms of eye movement, for example, animal organisms of any sort could not survive. For we must note instantly changes in
the status quo that may portend danger and may mean our deaths. We must
exaggerate differences before settling down again into routinized life. (Recall Joseph LeDoux's work: the brain's primitive amygdala receiving practically instantaneously fear-charged data from the environment. Contemporary science complements and deepens Emerson's insights concerning
scurrying, anxious creatures, our hard-to-acknowledge kin.)

This rooted instinct to fearfully react to differences is still with us. But now it can be seen to feed into the primal ways in which human cultures form experienced worlds. It feeds into the ways cultures make their surrounds their own erotically, the way they form the basic meanings in which, and through which, their members live. The fearful instinct to note differences feeds now into ideologies, worldviews, whole modes of existence and presumed righteousness. It is here that we must pursue the X factor in genocide. For a prime example, certain segments of Islam, and dominant forces in North Atlantic culture, are now on collision course, the consequences of which may be fatal.

*   *   *

This book is mainly focused on the X factor. Before any more new variations or examples—before "performing variations" become routinized method—let's consolidate and intensify what I believe this book has achieved to this point. We have seen (1): That we are radically open, porous, participatory and vulnerable creatures who become human through mimetic engulfment in home groups. (2): That a fundamental feature of our being-in-the-world is that we live in the world as experienced and interpreted by our home group. (3): That a necessary condition for most genocides is that another group can, in certain circumstances, threaten the integrity of our world-experienced; this is countered by *Get 'Em All! Kill 'Em*. The terrors of genociders and those to be genocided feed on each other.

We have just taken a recollective point of view on my whole hypothesis concerning the X factor. I propose now to further thicken up the theory of genocide by systematically concentrating and directly comparing as many more viewpoints on genocide as I can imagine. The more aspects of the phenomenon that are revealed, the more nearly concrete and adequate will be our picture of the "unthinkable." As I said, I doubt that we can imagine, with any intellectual integrity, God's point of view, "perfect objectivity." Fundamentalists of all stripes merely spout torrid words. They have fallen into a corporate trance that they want us to join.

Let us try now to share the point of view of some genociders. As early as the introduction, I sketched what I take to be the viewpoint of Islamic terrorists. At this juncture let us try to take Nazis' point of view. These instances of their once great culture operated with what might be called Germanic precision, methodicalness, thoroughness, focused attention.

We have underlined our human tendency to overreact to differences—to introduce and to exaggerate traits that differentiate. As thinking animals, we can even slice apart our own consciousness. This is what Robert Jay Lifton calls doubling. Nazi doctor-genociders who were not outright psychopaths sealed off from the rest of their lives their murderous roles while on duty in the death camps. They could do this with a degree of success.

If Nazi doctors with a remnant of conscience could seal off their murderous roles in the camps from their everyday awareness outside the camps, they could more or less protect themselves from guilt. To disconnect from their murderous roles, they could make them nearly unrememberable, unthinkable in that basic way. They could allow their social and ideological environment of the Third Reich to erode and crumble all normal standards of judgment and evaluation, of empathy, knowledge, comportment. Their experienced world while on duty in the camps could become, in a real sense, another world, one outside the usual or normal world, at least of Nazi times.

Lifton nudges us toward the point of view of the Nazi doctors themselves. One of his unforgettable portraits is that of a Doctor B. He is unusual in that he is not just another SS officer, not just absorbed in the world of Nazi ideology. He retains some footing in the more or less normal world of pre-Nazi times. And yet, when Lifton interviews him a second time a few years after the war, he frosts over and becomes impatient with Lifton's questions. "You were not there." The clear implication: you cannot understand. Doctor B. does not even now, after the war, cleanly dissociate himself from his uniform, his flag, and his S.S. colleagues and superiors. He terminates the interview because he wants to go skiing. He is still doubling, disconnecting, protecting himself. He lives, like many do, in a self-protective trance.

*   *   *

Now let us consider some points of view on "the unthinkable" from surviving victims of the Nazis. Perhaps the most searing account (I am not trying to rank accounts along this parameter) is that by Auschwitz survivor Jean Améry. He records how unspeakable physical torture erodes body, soul, and mind—to frame our identity in a traditional tripartite way (Sources, *At the Mind's Limits*). I am not up to summarizing his report. Even to select some quotes seems presumptuous to me now.

I turn to Primo Levi's account, also of Auschwitz, in *The Drowned and The Saved*. Recounting his release:

Coming out of the darkness, one suffered because of the reacquired consciousness of having been diminished. Not by our will, cowardice, or fault, yet nevertheless we had lived for months and years at an animal level: our days had been encumbered from dawn to dusk by hunger, fatigue, cold and fear, and any space for reflection, reasoning, experiencing emotions was wiped out. We endured filth, propinquity, and destitution, suffering much less than we would have suffered from such things in normal life, because our moral yardstick had changed. (75)

We can detect some connection to the normal or thinkable world. For, as we have noted, irrationality, immorality, insanity, unthinkability are, as negations, necessarily tied in some thin sense to what is negated by them: rationality, morality, sanity, thinkability. Greatly precious in Levi's report are his words, "Any space for reflection was wiped out." That is, as bodies and as body-selves, the victims' space was violated, both the space very near them, and the space within their bodies. Not just their bodies understood biologically as organisms, as little more than objects, had been violated, but their minds and souls, their subjectivity linked in intersubjectivity, their body-selves. They could hardly think or judge at all: their moral yardstick had bent or wilted. Maybe our minding—or mind—cannot think its own complete absence. But in retrospect at least it can, with effort, think its own grave impairment.

Levi continues his account of the profound, uncanny, terrifying damaging of themselves:

[T]he just among us, neither more nor less numerous than in any other human group, felt remorse, shame, and pain for the misdeeds that others and not they had committed, and in which they felt involved, because they sensed that what had happened around them and in their presence, and in them, was irrevocable. Never again could it be cleansed; it would prove that man, the human species—we, in short—had the potential to construct an infinite enormity of pain, and that pain is the only force created from nothing, without cost and without effort. It is enough not to see, not to listen, not to act. (86)

Pain inflicted on others: the only force created from nothing—a diabolical perversion of God's alleged power to create *ex nihilo*. So fluid, oozing, engulfed, and fantastical is our reality. Aspects of reality cannot be kept neatly isolated, as our intellectualist and conceptualist logics try to keep them.

Again, Dostoevsky is right: there is nothing more fantastic than reality itself. As we are immediately caught up in the stressed world, A does not resemble B in certain respects. A *is* B. The victims cannot cleanly dissociate themselves from the victimizers. We are all engulfed in the corporate body of humanity. When that turns rotten, as it was experienced in the death camps to do, all are affected.

With particular poignancy and horror these victims' body-selves had been broken into. The genociders insinuated themselves into their victims' body-selves: this to the point that the victims could not clearly distinguish what they themselves did from the criminal acts committed on them.

When the distinction between I-myself and the other—my other—is so deeply smeared, pollution and impairment of self have reached their unspeakable nadir. Levi felt himself identified with a potential for inflicting pain that had hitherto been unimaginable and unthinkable by him. "We, in short, had the potential." His very self teeters on the brink of the unthinkable. But being an extraordinarily strong and intelligent person, he is able to think the unthinkable—to a remarkable extent.

Levi reports his experience that what had happened was unredeemable. To our list of strange relatives—rationality/irrationality, thinkable/unthinkable— we must add redeemable/unredeemable. We can barely think unredeemable. We hang on to it ever tighter when we realize that Amery certainly, and Levi probably, committed suicide. Once the torturers had violated the bodily-soulish-minding bodies of these extraordinarily strong, determined, intelligent men, the torturers were introjected. As I said, they were made a terrible part of their victims' own selves. We can barely think this. But it is not simply unthinkable.

We have been trying to feel our way into the point of view of some of the victims of genocide. We now face the most difficult category of victims: those so deadened and, in a real sense, dehumanized and unselfed by unremitting terror, deprivation, and misery that, even if they survived, they have written and spoken nothing. (In the camps they were called zombies or sometimes Mussulmen—a terrible slur on Muslims.) Who speaks for them? I don't know.

I have relied on the empathic powers, focus, and mental dexterity of artists before, and will do so again, hoping to approximate to the unthinkable. How about "The Man with the Hoe"? Poet Edwin Markham writes of a man worn down into subhuman status through pitiless poverty and toil:

> Who made him dead to rapture and despair,
> A thing that grieves not and that never hopes,
> Stolid and stunned, a brother to the ox?

. . .
Whose breath blew out the light within this brain?

Markham's poem has been classified as social protest. The pitiless exploiters of humankind—slave drivers, greed-maddened capitalists, *patrones*—appear as the answers to his questions. Worthy of contempt and condemnation they are, but the blame to be placed on those who genocide is of a different and more portentous genre, for it implicates people who are pitiless and . . . ? Levi: We—we all—have the capacity to inflict pain that we could not have imagined before. What are we to say of the human race's capacity for omni-destruction, ultimately for self-destruction, for genocide?

*   *   *

Edmund Husserl, regarded as the founder of twentieth-century phenomenology, used a method he called free variation to sort out the essential features of any thing, event, phenomenon. We take features of something and vary them in our imaginations. Those that cannot be varied without the phenomenon vanishing are essential to what the thing is. (For example, though a square can be of any size, color, texture, material, its having four equal angles and sides cannot be varied.) Husserl thought that there was a thorough set of variations, a set that established the essential features, the essence, of any phenomenon.

I have been varying points of view on genocide. I cannot hope to have fully exhibited its essence, however. I cannot hope to have revealed all that is invariable of it. So-called existential phenomenologists reject what they call the abstract, mathematical, conclusive, or definitive pretensions of Husserl's method. No refining down to pure essences can occur in the human realm. There is not only our complexity but our freedom and spontaneity—both for good and ill—and nowhere are these features more evident than in cases of genocide, and in how we might respond to them. Indeed, Husserl himself once sketched this existential position.

A square's essential features can be precisely and conclusively defined. It's what Husserl called a formal essence. But there are "material essences" (or "experimental" ones), Husserl notes, whose spheres of application are floating, those that have fuzzy boundaries of application. A simple example of this is "notch." When we vary its shape freely in the mind's eye, we cannot tell exactly when the phenomenon vanishes, cannot tell when the indentation or depression ceases to count as a notch. An indefinite number of borderline cases present themselves.

An immeasurably more complex material essence is exhibited by genocide. Much earlier we noted some borderline cases. Here we should flash another caution. We should be reluctant to state definitively what the essential features of genocide must be—that totality of conditions necessary for every application of the concept of genocide. The actual phenomenon overflows—to some conceptually ungraspable extent—our powers of conceptualization.

A moment's thought might make this obvious: Constrained by numberless factors as it doubtless is, human consciousness exhibits, nevertheless, an inherent complexity and spontaneity that, I believe, cannot in principle always be described, let alone predicted. Nor can the scope of its possible activities be, in principle, precisely demarcated. (Unlike today's computers, which function linearly, the human brain functions in parallel. The complexity is mind-boggling.) Even with respect to the weather, the level of complexity is such that, in principle, it cannot always be predicted. How much more so with human beings! Dostoyevesky in *The House of the Dead*, writing of prisoners in Siberia, gives us a taste of it:

> [T]here is no phenomenon more curious than these strange outbursts of impatience and obstinacy. Often a man will suffer in patience for several years, resign himself, endure the most savage punishments, and then suddenly erupt over some trifle, some piece of nonsense, almost over nothing at all. In one view, he may be termed insane. (35, Sources)[2]

Let us pause on this point for a moment. Socrates and Plato have been called ethical optimists, that is, they thought that if people only knew what goodness is, they would not act contrary to it. Aristotle disagreed. He thought that sometimes people act out of "sheer devilry" (what Edgar Allen Poe seems to have meant by "the imp of the perverse.")

So with respect to genocide: someone might cite cases in which a home group does not, apparently, feel insecure, nor does it dread being polluted by an alien group. Nevertheless, it kills or incapacitates all members of that group. Why? Who knows? Maybe out of sheer devilry, or the imp of the perverse, or to prove, like rabid sportsmen, that they can get 'em all.

Let us vary again the phenomenon of genocide to see the problem of trying to pin it down decisively. Imagine a situation of extreme scarcity of food.

The environment and the available technology cannot sustain the number of people who regard this area as home. Imagine also that there is a sub-group of this culture in this area that is thought by the majority to be expendable in times of great emergency. To avoid general starvation, this minority group is genocided by the majority. Whether such a thing has actually happened or not, we can imagine it.

Now, we might say that there is a formal aspect of the concept of genocide: killing, or at least driving off and incapacitating, all the members of a group just because they are members of that group. Let's say that this formal criterion has been met in this case. If so, it might be thought that a conventional study, elementary economics, can explain this case of genocide: there is no need for my elaborate phenomenology of clashing world "constructions," points of view.

But we would forget at our peril that we've been talking merely about a formal aspect of the concept of genocide. Typically this phenomenon as a whole is an instance of a material essence if there ever were one. Greatly floating spheres of application are exhibited by it—perhaps we should say turbulently floating and fluctuating spheres. So, we might think, a conventional science, economics, can explain this one case. But the danger is to infer that a congeries of conventional natural sciences and social sciences could explain all more complex cases.

The danger is to forget that there are different sorts or orders of complexity. The temptation is to do what Ptolemaic astronomers did to preserve their geocentric theory of the rotations of the heavens when faced with new observations: they kept adding epicycles to the plotted orbits of the planets. In our case, the temptation is to keep adding conventional scientific explanations. But the conceptual space easily becomes so cluttered that any need for a sweeping conceptual revision is obscured. I, of course, have supplied such a revision, and it seems to describe and to begin to explain cases of genocide that are by far the most interesting ones, and the ones that are most significant historically as well.[3]

Moreover, I am far from admitting that concepts—no matter how good—are sufficient for addressing phenomena, particularly those of human relations.

*　*　*

Significant though these conceptual and definitional difficulties are, they should not deter us from trying roughly to locate the essential features of very many cases of genocide, to rough-in the material essence of these cases.

A living residue of Husserl's method of free variation can be found, for example, in Karl Jaspers' philosophical thinking, which can be classified as existential-phenomenological. These variations help us roughly to locate the nature of very many cases of genocide. Jaspers describes "boundary situations," great decision points in a human's career, such as marriage, divorce, killing people, or one's own aging and death. We can also speak of boundary situations for a culture. How we confront and react to these awesome boundaries tells us a lot about who we are. They are revealing variations. Do we melt down, wilt, vanish, or do we find new strength beyond what the normal routine would have led us and others to expect from us?

What I am doing with the variations I am conducting is more along the lines of existential phenomenology. We are exploring "the unthinkable" in human existence. We are probing into the unknown, or at least the only partially thinkable. Among other things, we are testing metaphors, but are not claiming definitive, literal conclusions. We don't aim to talk only about objects.

After all, metaphors are sorts of variations, as we have said: they place phenomena in contexts and relations that do not literally apply to them (it is concepts that apply literally to objects—but we are not just objects). Metaphors are not second best. Recall what was argued in the last chapter: it is just metaphors that have a chance to suggest the evolving, flowing, flickering, often dreamy—or nightmarish—complexity of our subjectivity and intersubjectivity. As William James put it, metaphors pump free air, and fresh air, around things experienced in our experiencing. We can begin to turn things in our minds, unhitch ourselves from the stale, constant, contrastless "taste" of things in our experience. That is, gain release from mimetic engulfment, life on automatic, the technological trance, the life of turkeys.[4]

*   *   *

I have given special attention to Cassirer's metaphor of the corporate body, and its various levels, functions, and values. We have found that it has led us to expect, and then to find, connections, insights, and hypotheses that we wouldn't have found without the metaphor. Particularly is this the case with patriarchal societies, of the type of the three great Western religions. I want to further intensify this metaphor now.

The question has been raised several times: What happens when two corporate bodies encounter each other and one cannot stand up to the other?

What happens when the head of one sinks and the whole body fears to be ingested by, and destroyed in, the other corporate body? Particularly in the lower, eliminative regions of that corporate body. We dread becoming the worst of menials—mere waste, offal. This is all metaphor. But it is greatly helpful to thought. The radical extremes of genocide find a radical hypothesis to describe and perhaps to explain them.

What if an important aid in educating ourselves to resist the temptations of genocide is to push an imaginative variation: to try to think and experience human groups without single heads? Would members of such groups be less susceptible to genocidal urges in the face of the threatening other group (assuming a system of terrorist groups, say, can be spoken of in the singular)?

We face a decision, a boundary situation. How do we deal with our terrible vulnerability and fear as body-selves conditioned in local environments and hitherto competent, more than likely, only there? One very tempting reaction to our vulnerable condition is to ensconce ourselves ever more tightly in our patriarchal corporate body with its gleaming, helmeted head, terrifyingly armed. But corporate bodies are now on collision course and, very possibly, fatally. The most daring and creative thought and action is required.

* * *

Pursuant to making a choice at the boundary, let us look into human identity as involving an identity problem. Let us look at ourselves as organisms that can form experienced worlds, and can even come to believe that we have located our place in the cosmos. Fundamentalists of all sorts desperately need to believe that they have precisely located their place in the cosmos (there are secular fundamentalists, ones who don't believe that they are such).

Can any other species ask the questions, Who am I? Who are we? If not with language, can they think such self-interrogations? Elephants are reported to linger over the corpses of their fellows, perhaps to "fondle" some bones with their trunks. Is this fondling? Do they have some vague but real sense that these corpses are ones of their own species—do they have some general idea of this? Or do they know that this particular instance was *that* kindred individual who no longer lives? (See Bradshaw, Sources.)

I don't know. I would not be surprised if we discovered someday that some nonhuman creatures have a degree of behaviorally significant self-consciousness as individuals and as groups. Some psychologists claim that when chimps have a colored dot affixed to their foreheads, then are shown their faces in a mirror, they put their fingers to the spot. Does this suggest they have some sense that that is an image in front of them, and that it is an image of themselves—of themselves altered? Do they have some sense that that body imaged before them is theirs—a taproot of the sense of self? Might they sense, though not say, "That body there is myself. What has happened to me?"

Humans certainly do have the capacity to ask and to think, Who am I? Who are we? The capacity may be left unrealized very often indeed, and that is interesting. But it is evident that we do have it. (Socrates endangered his life teasing and taunting people to exercise the capacity.) Martin Heidegger tacitly defined us as the beings whose identity lies in the capacity to throw our identity into question. Max Scheler maintained that in no other age has human identity become so problematical. I think our identity is thrown into question repeatedly, whether we can acknowledge this or not. Fundamentalists defend themselves with ever more vehement assertions of dogma.

I believe that our identity lies partly in having a distinctive identity problem. In this key respect, the other animals may be superior to us. They do not kill in sport to become recognized as great hunters. Nor do they kill all members of a prey group just to be killing all of them. Whereas, if I am right, a decisive factor in triggering typical cases of genocide is the awful fear that our identity and existence is sorely threatened by another group's way of thinking, feeling, and interpreting the world. Hence that whole group—or that system of groups—must be exterminated or incapacitated. Get 'em all, kill 'em. To feel that one's identity is so precariously balanced that it could be upset this way, isn't that to have a terrible identity problem? Might it now prove to be fatal?

There have been many attempts to define human identity, most of them laughably inadequate. The great philosopher-logician-biologist Aristotle left us a skewed, eccentric account. He pigeon-holes us as rational animals, and exaggerates the significance of our "godlike" rationality.

This whole taxonomical point of view seemed incredibly alienated, distanced, one-sided, obsessively analytical to Christian thinkers. St. Augustine shifted attention to our immediate sense of ourselves—the point of view of personal inwardness. We not only ask, What or Who is Man (Humanity)? But also, Who am I? This is a pivotal turning, dilation, deepening of awareness. It becomes canonical and stays so for centuries in, say, the Protestant (Presbyterian) version of Christianity, the Westminster Catechism: "Man's chief end is to glorify God." In giving us our end, and making it glorification of God, something important is said about our identity as thinking, adoring, worshiping, meaning-hungry creatures.

Whole cultures can ask the identity question, first-person plural, Who are we? The answer comes in the basal store of cultural meanings, ultimate orientations and beliefs, rites and rituals. In the Islamic Hadith, or recounting of the eminently exemplary life of Muhammad, all devout Muslims are lifted to an exalted realm of individual and social responsibility. Judaism as well relates our human identity directly to the Creator. The three great Western religions underline our ecstatic hunger for meaning and purpose, a hunger I believe to be a poignant, and often in times of great stress, a desperate attempt to stabilize and ground ourselves.

But have any of these attempts to define and guide us done much to calm our identity anxieties, to assuage our terrors in the face of boundless differences, to stem the tide of genocides? This is a heavy historical question. Maybe things would have been even worse without such noteworthy attempts. However, in certain feverish states of insecurity in a corporate body, it seems plain that high Western philosophy and high religion have not only not helped, but have often been employed as rationalizations to destroy "barbarians" and "infidels"—Persians, Turks, Jews, Diggers, American capitalists, what have you. (See Regina Schwartz, Sources)

Note again the Hamitic doctrine: Noah is storied as having a son, Ham, who violated his privacy, who looked upon his father when Noah was naked and intoxicated. Ham is sentenced to be the father of "hewers of wood and drawers of water," beings low on the corporate body hierarchy. This doctrine was used by slave traders and owners to rationalize their brutal enslavement of blacks, which is one small step short of genocide in the narrowest sense, but certainly genocide in the broader United Nations sense. Christian love meant little or nothing. Though it must be said that active in the movement to emancipate slaves were certain Christians.

As always, we are trying to probe into, pry into, tease our way into that primal prereflective level of white-hot human behavior in which desperate supercontagions of human activity fuse together a genocidal group in the face of those others.

*   *   *

Human survival depends on the successful struggle for meaning on the primal level of our experiencing. However tiny and ephemeral we may know ourselves to be, we humans can yet make some vital contribution to the world—so members of vital cultures believe. Making a contribution attempts to solve our profound identity problem. Islamic terrorists believe that the global reach of U.S. commercial, military, entertainment ventures undermines the very meaning of their lives. Their contribution is to stop us.

Our challenge in North Atlantic culture is to grasp the ways that we have come to make and project meaning through the inexorable growth of our various technologies (for example, marketing commodities through electronic media). In the information revolution, this meaning almost totally eclipses on a world scale our other contributions: medical, scientific, artistic, and aspects of the political such as human rights. These contributions can be called spiritual. Let us put the mirror up to ourselves and see if we like what we see when we see what others see of us.

Both Christianity and Islam derive from Judaism, a paradigmatically patriarchal and hierarchical religion. This presents problems for those who want to live cooperatively with all living and nonliving things. For almost inevitably, a particular religionist will describe the head in terms that favor his or her home group over against all others. Later in the chapter I will treat further the problems generated by the patriarchal metaphor, the gleaming head of the corporate body.

But first I want to deal with encouraging and constructive elements in all three great Western patriarchal religions. (Might the greatest danger today be stunned, entranced demoralization and hopelessness?) All three believe that humans are made in the image of the Creator. Hence we are all creators—creators with a small "c." And indeed, all three religions have, in their various ways, been insistently creative and expansive. I think that we must call now on our shared creative gifts. We must create new ways of thinking and being. In fact, we must reason our way to new conceptions of, and metaphors for, reason itself.

Charles Peirce maintained that no reason can be given for being reasonable, for to give a reason is already to assume reasonableness itself. This is most interesting. But reason takes many forms, and indeed reason and reasoning evolve. Peirce himself was quite aware of this. He knew that the first step in philosophy is always phenomenology, always the looking around that first takes in the lay of the land, then second, that looks from this angle, then from that, then from another. Phenomenology assesses what the primary topics (or *topoi* or categories of possible things) are. And Peirce knew that this is very different from deductive reasoning: that which infers with ironbound formal necessity within certain systems of geometry, say. It also differs from modes of empirical or natural scientific inquiry. Moreover, following Emerson, he left room for affective reasoning: the heart itself is a cognitive organ, and must be protected from stunned despair.

Taking our lead from the better-known phenomenology of Husserl, we have distinguished between the search for "formal" essences and the search for "material" or "experimental" ones. In our taste of experimental-phenomenological investigation, augmented by the study of metaphor, we have seen that genocide is a material essence with a scope of application that floats considerably. Freely varied, genocide reveals horrific possibilities for human relations. We are the particular bodily beings who must make meaning all the time in the most primordial ways, and we must do so in a universe that we can never fully know or control.

Meaning-making is a constant for human beings, but all our structured worlds-experienced prove to be precarious in certain circumstances. The world can turn upon us so that we turn upon ourselves before we know it (recall Primo Levi). The distinction between self and other is not the unshakable and incorruptible matter that pure abstract reason, or formal studies, or common sense, assumes.

It has been clear from the start of this book that lying at the foundations of our lives is a primal level of reasoning that is not formalized, and that antecedes all natural scientific-technological reasoning. As noted, the latter secretly presupposes the former. The Greeks distinguished *poesis* from *techne*. Both involve making, but they are different sorts of making. Poesis makes things that are valuable in themselves. The most crucial example of all is that initial erotic involvement in which a culture makes the surround its own. Poetry and music and philosophic thought enhance that core of human life that is valuable in itself: It is the I—and we—"can do," which is manifested in reflection, appreciation, self-worth, responsibility, adoration, and celebration.

Techne, on the other hand, makes things that are useful for gaining other things, those which are useful for gaining still other things, and on and on. Techne does not create intrinsically valuable things—rather, it creates extrinsically valuable ones. Nietzsche early noted our modern slippage from our foundations of primal meaning-making—our making of intrinsically valuable things. To habitually act to gain things that are only extrinsically valuable, is to slip into the compulsion of power, for more power, for more power . . . endlessly, restlessly, ultimately destructively.

Most religious Muslims are convinced that the United States is obsessed with a very narrow notion of scientific reasoning, and with a grossly narrow notion of technological reasoning—reasoning as techne only. They believe that we are obsessed with short-term gain for ourselves of extrinsic values only, and have lost all effective conception of the ultimate intrinsic values of the sacred, the holy, the beautiful, the clarified. We are denuding, de-fruiting, despoiling the world, uglifying it, and calling it global trade, the wave of the future, progress.

Let us first see if we can exercise our most creative powers of self-interrogation, and see if religious Muslims may have a point. Then I will beg Muslims to exercise their own creativity. For we float in the same rocking boat. Our patriarchal heads (however we try to disguise ours) are on collision course. We have started down a path that will probably, I believe, lead to atomic warfare and other obscenities—a path that leads to the poisoning and the incineration of the planet.

People in North Atlantic culture like to say, let science take the lead. But as I have maintained, science—powerful as it is—is not our primordial involvement in the surround, nor does it disclose that. It is not our primordial, or erotic, mode of meaning-making. And it is on this primordial or primal level that our destiny most immediately lies. To be effective, the distanced and detached point of view of science must limit itself to what can be objectified and precisely measured. But it is just the prereflective point of view of our immediate, engaged, ecstatic involvement and first-person meaning-making that must be masked out by the scientific point of view (both singular and plural first-person meaning-making). This is where the X factor lies. With all our energy, we fly blind.

We are awash now in the latest scientific breakthroughs in genetics. Many seem to think that the same methods that led to the sensational disclosure of the so-called genetic code or genome will lead to solving the problem of human identity. They seem to think that science can satisfy our hunger for meaning and purpose. This is yet another manifestation of blind egoism and desperation, the technological trance.

For they have not thought about thinking, experiencing, and meaning-making themselves—the erotic in its deepest manifestation. The methods that led to the discovery of the gene or genes that, if defective, cause hemophilia, say, will not solve the problem that people experience as the meaninglessness of their lives. Nor will these methods cure the emotional flatness or boredom—or remove the emotional discomforts—that some give as reasons for their drug addiction. Nor will these methods grasp or cure mad corporate rushes in genocidal orgies. Nor can the methods address the grievances of vast groups of Islamic peoples, for example, who believe the United States deals unjustly and stupidly with Islam.

Take a person who does not contract the hemophilia he otherwise would have without that preventative genetic surgery of the fetus he was privileged to have received. He is still left with the question of how to make sense of his life and to achieve a sense of direction and self-worth as an individual, and as a member of a group. All the genetic discoveries in the world cannot help him. Indeed, if he had been born a hemophiliac he might have been in a better position in respect to this matter. For then he might have thought that just staying alive was accomplishment enough.

But surviving is not all that we need. We need meaningful lives lived within meaningful groups that form a meaningful, commodious, and fairly self-secure world-experienced; we need to make contributions personally and corporately. To have meaning slip through our fingers is to fall into emptiness, boredom, and restlessness. This prompts what Henry David Thoreau termed silent desperation, a kind of numbing, unspeakable terror. To feel this is often to lash out at what seems to be causing it.

Or take another case brimming with illusory potential, for it locks us into the single point of view of scientism. Very probably some people are genetically predisposed to alcoholism (an affliction that cannot happen in Islamic countries that strictly enforce the prohibition of alcohol). Assuming the genes responsible are identified, what are we to do with the knowledge? Can these genes be altered in the fetus? I don't know, but it might be worth a try.

If we could, however, we would not have cleared the path for the emerging child to live a meaningful life. We would have removed a grave danger to his life, to be sure. But the child would still be left in the situation of the person cured of hemophilia. Indeed, some alcoholics find badly needed meaning in battling their "disease," and in helping others battle theirs. A legitimate use of genetic knowledge of predisposition to alcoholism would be to educate those at risk on just how destructive drinking will be for them, how diabolically addictive alcoholism is. (See my *Wild Hunger: The Primal Roots of Modern Addiction*, Sources)

But to regard alcoholism as a disease is an oversimplification, which is typically engendered by excessive and probably frightened overreliance on medical and natural scientific expertise and data.[5] Alcoholism is not contracted as are diseases commonly and correctly so called, nor does one recover from it as do people from diseases in the ordinary sense (pneumonia or malaria, for example). It is contracted out of a need for eluding or blunting discomfort, or for suppressing one's appalling vulnerability— perhaps coupled with a genetic predisposition. Or out of a need for ecstasy to fill the emptiness of one's meaningless life, the need that was satisfied in our hunter-gatherer forebears through the skills and adventures of just staying alive. Alcoholism is a personal and also, typically, a cultural failure to root and flourish in the majestic generative and regenerative world that formed us. It is the failure of a culture to enlist its members, each in their own way, in a common cause of creativity and maintenance of intrinsic value.

*   *   *

In the beginning there is that erotic involvement in the surround in which we members of a culture make an experienced world our own. All cultures—excepting a few experimental ones in the twentieth century—have generated religions. For all people profoundly sense—if only inarticulately—that their ability to grasp reality is limited. Even today in proud North Atlantic culture we can suspect, if we think at all, that we have no idea why there is a universe rather than nothing.

We live now in a plunging, restless, technologically wired and wiring culture. For nearly anyone accounted educated to speak seriously about the holy, say, is an oddity, practically an affront. But all cultures have rooted themselves in this all-involving gut sense of the holy or the sacred. I mean, roughly, the numinous and spine-tingling sense that we are caught up in the unknown, that we are supported and nourished and righted inexplicably every instant. The basal meaning of a life is how we contribute our mite in the swirling sea of energy exchange and interdependency. The meaning of life is how, through endlessly various ways, we participate—awake—in the universe's maintenance, recreation, and celebration of itself. Talk about intrinsic values!

I think that there might be a new golden age of Islam. The first of my reasons is this: Of the three great Western religions, Islam's apologists most prize and protect the mysteriousness of the ground of all being and value. Thoughtful Islam can most resolutely oppose and debate the technological and commercial mania of North Atlantic culture that rides roughshod and deranged over the planet. It is a monomania that uproots from all traditions of meaning-making, from all forms of deeply meaningful work; that skews or destroys all settled frameworks of evaluation, all ways of distinguishing extrinsic from intrinsic values.

The greatest creativity is demanded from thinking, resolute, religious Muslims. Suddenly they find themselves at a strangely advantageous position in world history. Many have not yet been swept up in the technological and commercial mania. They retain some perspective. They might achieve a purchase on basics. Some are able to say that they can have no Western movies or TV in their houses, for example, because—and this is their reason—they must protect their families.

Thoughtful religious Muslims are placed in this unexpectedly propitious position for roughly four reasons. They possess (1) A tradition of conceiving reason to be autonomous within its domain: reason not antagonistic to faith, but not its mere tool either; thus reason as an antidote to fanaticism. (2) A deep-rooted and somewhat astonishing tradition that eschews revenge. (3) An Edenic or paradisal tradition in which Nature is experienced as sacred—a great resource in the face of current ecological disaster. (4) Finally, they possess some gift of time: they have experienced a delay in acquiring electronic technology that affords them some freshness of perspective on this technology that is no longer possible for most in North Atlantic culture. I will deal with these four factors in reverse order.

We are vulnerable, imperfect, limited, bodily creatures. Essential to our identity is an identity problem. Vital cultures supply an answer to the question, Who are we? Very often our awareness is greatly limited. Nowhere is awareness more limited than in a culture that has lost, or is fast losing, its traditional and habitual modes of creating and maintaining intrinsic value. Most in North Atlantic culture are caught up in the technological trance: absorbed in endlessly creating extrinsic values, one leading to the next, and the next and the next, in the vague and feverish hope, it must be, that enough extrinsic values will add up to intrinsic value and a meaningful life.

TV is now so ingrained and habituated as to be "normal" for us. This radical revolution in human communications and history is so completely taken for granted that the phenomenon is, for most, invisible. To allow a term from the clinical Western university, millions are conditioned from infancy to the grave to be voyeurs: to peep, to see, without being seen. By increments insidiously small and slow, we are conditioned to experience ourselves as unexperienced by others, which means, given human intersubjectivity, as not fully real. Our own agency and responsibility is masked out, self is masked out. We no longer participate fully as body-selves in the swirling sea of energy exchanges that constitutes the universe, no longer contribute our mite to it all, nor do we receive, in the flesh, others' mites.

TV technology lures one into the immediate gratifications of power over the screen. This becomes numbingly habitual. But isn't there an added hidden inducement? If one is invisible and not fully real, a kind of protection is supplied for us beings who possess a residual, though usually not readily acknowledgeable, sense of our appalling vulnerability.

More obviously, people are conditioned electronically over many months and years to believe the big lie: that meaning can be bought, that comfort and convenience and buying power are the great intrinsic values. Consumerism means getting and spending and rushing around, which means the disruption of the ritualized and disciplined life and its slow development of self and character. With the loss of rituals goes the inestimably great loss of the sustaining and stabilizing life, the propulsiveness, cohesiveness, and preciousness of life.

One need not be a Muslim to perceive these things, but it might help. Everywhere North Atlantic electronic media reach, they constrict the context in which things make sense. Who could possibly object to fast foods? But we just might discern that they disrupt the rituals of cooking and serving and partaking of food that have given some of the deepest meaning, intrinsic value, and reality to human groups from time immemorial. We do not live by bread alone, nor by hamburger meat if that is added. We are not mere engines to be stuffed with fuel. Our commercially driven technologies are destroying cultures right and left worldwide, and are undermining ourselves.

Martin Prechtel comments on the life-building role of ritually recited stories cherished by a culture: "After years of listening, a young person learns to recognize her life in stories and is guided through life by the piloting examples they contain" (Sources, 2). Prechtel taps the ancient myth, found in primal cultures, of the world tree. It is the vital fabric that holds together the heavens and the earth, the sun and the waters, in life-giving and -renewing cycles of interdependency and energy exchange. He goes on,

> The extreme and reckless pruning of this tree of life by a culture where television, advertising, media, academia and politics pander to the least common denominator; where people are not loved for their depth, but for their thinness, has left our dreams damaged. The sap of subtlety, this lifeblood of metaphor and myth is rushing spilt and trashed into a wasteland of white noise and canned laughter, with no branches to feed or flowers to force into the seeded fruit of cultural renewal. (5)

About seven million Americans use antidepressants (*Newsweek*, 7-15-02, 49). Countless millions more are addicted to this or that. In its various degrees, addiction is loss of agency, autonomy; it is impairment of self. Should we be so sure that we know what is best for the rest of the world?

*   *   *

Now the next reason for my believing that thoughtful religious Muslims are in an excellent position for lowering the chances of planetary catastrophe. It is their distinctive relationship to Nature. Recent ecological movements and eruptions in the West manifest a renewed longing among many for vi-

tal involvement in the parent of our species, Nature. Nevertheless, the main
momentum of our culture today was set in the seventeenth century by
modern Western science and technology. This carried the ideology that Nature is to be understood in mechanical and mathematical terms only.
Beauty and sacredness and the holiness of Nature are considered to be
merely our subjective opinions.

Nature, then, for us, is mainly and merely raw material to be exploited
for immediately palpable gain—a means to our own very human extrinsic
ends only. Yes, Nature is necessary for our sustenance. Sustainability
means sustaining its utility. But Nature has no intrinsic value in our experience. Notable it is that Islamic science passed through no comparable desacralization and disenchantment of Nature. The Islamic perspective on Nature can help free us from our dominant secular and utilitarian
sense of Nature, and can help supply an antidote to the spreading over
the globe of our desacralizing views and our rushing, grabbing, ravaging
practices.

The Qur'an names Adam as the first prophet, the first messenger from
God or Allah. As such, he could hardly be expected to have infected the
whole human race with his sin. Hence Islam rejects the doctrine of Original
Sin. There is an idea of a Fall, however, of a straying from God and his Paradise, otherwise why the long succession of prophets to recall us to God?

But, Muslims believe, echoes of the original Paradise sound and resound
through Nature today, if we have ears to hear them. They can be heard in the
language itself of the Qur'an, and in the liquid flowing and curling of other of
their religious-poetic writings. The Islamic mystic poet—Sufi mystic—Yunus
Emre sings,

> The Rivers all in Paradise
> Flow with the word Allah, Allah
> And ev'ry longing nightingale
> He sings and sings Allah, Allah

(Quoted in Seyyed Hossein Nasr, *Religion and the Order of Nature*,
Sources, 281.)

Nasr expands on the Sufi doctrine:

The very "stuff" of which the Universe is made is "The Breath of the Compassionate" and the existence of all things is nothing but their invocation and praise
of God. That is why the sage hears the dhiker, or the invocation of God, in the
sound of the running streams and the cry of the eagle, in the rustling of

the trees, in the wind, and the sound of the waves breaking upon the shore . . .
because Nature is not even now separated from the paradisal reality that it manifests for those who have an eye to behold the reality behind and beyond the
merely phenomenal and sensual." (291)

We must reach an understanding about the meaning of "the merely phenomenal and sensational." If we mean the attempt to build up an experienced world from bogus mental atoms (phenomenalism), then I agree that
we must get beyond this. But if we mean the attempt to describe the sensuously given surround with its horizons luring us ever deeper into the
world (phenomenology), then we should go along with this.

Once this understanding is reached, the thought I have developed in this
book feels right at home with what Nasr says. Like Islamic thought, and unlike most modern Western thought, this book's background thought never
passed through the stage in which only measured quantities constituted
knowledge, and in which Nature was divided from mind and spirit and was
desacralized.

As we have seen, William James rediscovers that we participate in the
very substance of things around us, and to think that Nature is merely ex-
ploitable stuff is to exploit and to wear out ourselves. Dewey devoted his life
to reweaving the continuity of Nature and culture. Whitehead found the divine in the essential natural patterns that prompt and lure things to resonate
and to fall together with each other beautifully.

Behind these philosophers lie Thoreau and Emerson who intuited the
malaise of modern Western persons as a kind of hyperenculturation. We no
longer feel at home in the Nature that formed us for 99 percent of genus
Homo's existence: the freely roaming ambulatory life of hunter gatherers. In
"Walking" Thoreau helps us rediscover that we walk for the sheer joy of it, the
sheer effervescence of our freedom to move as we will—and freely to be
moved as Nature would move us. (The actual roots of "wilderness": wil = will;
der = of the; ness = the place. So "wilderness" = "the will of the place" [see my
Wild Hunger, 8].) We are cultural-natural creatures: we must make the surround our own primal-erotically. But if at the same time the world doesn't
erotically make us its own—if this coeval reciprocity and inclusion are
lacking—there is vast trouble. We cut our roots, we no longer belong in what
formed us and in what must sustain us moment by moment, forget it as we
will.

Very like the Islamic-Sufi mystic who hears God in the running of the
stream, the sound of the surf, and the cry of the eagle—and very like Native Americans who speak of walking the beauty path—Thoreau experi-

ences immediately his primal resonance in Nature, his partaking in its throbbing, vibrating substances and events. Nothing divides the sounding brook and his own being: each participates in the other.

> I hear the sound of Heywood's Brook falling into Fair Haven Pond— inexpressibly refreshing to my senses—it seems to flow through my very bones—I hear it with insatiable thirst—It allays some sandy heat in me—It affects my circulations—methinks my arteries have sympathy with it. What is it I hear but the pure water falls within me in the circulation of my blood—the streams that fall into my heart? (Sources, see Cameron, her commentary on his *Journals*. The quotation is from Thoreau on pages 31–32 of *Journals* 6:562; see her note on page xi.)

The division of mind from body is some philosophers' fiction. We should speak of Earth-mind: the regenerative exchange of energies, the total adaptational harmony of each thing resonating and contributing as only it can within the Whole. There is no longer a division of mental subject from physical object, but a salvific wide-awake trance in which one thing participates vitally in another—and in countless others besides.

Emerson follows suit. He returns to the ancient mythic image of the world tree (in his case, *Yggdrazil* from Norse legend). The tree holds heaven and earth and time together in a primal humming and honeying coherence. Over 150 years ago Emerson intuited the roots of the addictions that plague so many modern "enlightened" secular humans. He writes in "Circles":

> The one thing we seek with insatiable desire is to forget ourselves, to be surprised out of our propriety . . . to do something without knowing how or why . . . Nothing great was ever achieved without enthusiasm. The way of life is wonderful, it is by abandonment. . . . Dreams and drunkenness, the use of opium and alcohol are the semblance and counterfeit of this oracular genius, and hence their dangerous attraction for men. For the like reason they ask the aid of wild passions, as in gaming and war, to ape in some manner the flames and generosities of the heart. (Sources and the main epigraph of my *Wild Hunger*; my quotation is from the last lines of "Circles.")

Addiction is counterfeit ecstasy, a galling and misleading eroticism, because we no longer trust the Nature that formed and fulfilled us to move us into right relationship, to make us its own—and to keep us its own— erotically. We think we can freely manage everything. But ingestion of substances and other actions that become addictive are counterfeits: they counterfeit freedom, ecstasy, and the regenerative cycles of Nature. They falsely promise all three.

Picking from apparently limitless resources of psychotropics, one chooses to get high after feeling low, and does feel high. But then withdrawal agonies set in, and to keep them at bay, one is compelled to take another dose of the substance or the behavior, and on and on. (Ingesting morphines, for example, switches off the brain's own naturally periodic production of morphines— uppers, endorphins—a production that does not easily recommence.) No longer matrixed in the ancient cycles of regenerative Nature in which the human body was formed, it is stressed and strained. Addictions are degenerative, obviously or subtly.

One loses the deepest eroticism and ecstasy of freedom, competence, adventure, new discoveries, one's legacy from Nature. Addiction covers the widest span: from drug and alcohol compulsions, through addictive eating disorders, to workaholism. We gain insight—most of us belatedly—into the deep Muslim aversion to alcohol: it is perceived to be an offense to the human organism and a desecration of Nature.

Jerry Gorsline and Freeman House write,

> As I walk over the hill I'm paying attention to the trees and the ground. The river comes into view and suddenly I'm stunned by the realization that I am not the same person who started the walk! I am transformed by a ceremony residing in the land itself. The place dictates the mandate for human activities there and that mandate can be perceived directly through a ceremony that lives in the woods like an almost tangible creature. (Sources)

The immediacy and simplicity of the transformative experience is dangerous in an insidious way. For how could something so simple and direct possibly be true? The taste for luxury and for comfort and convenience corrupt our bodies' perceptual-vital-spiritual life. Also corrupting is the tendency to think that we know things reliably only when we look, literally or figuratively, through some scientific instrument or other. Opponents of international capitalism are not composed only of anarchists, but also of all those deeply disturbed by North Atlantic desecration of the matrix of our being, disturbed by an anarchy deeper than merely political anarchy can imagine.

*   *   *

As I said, I believe that there is a chance that Islam can achieve a second— and even greater—golden age. World events place thoughtful Muslims in a strangely unexpected position, one that is alluring, powerful, and potentially daunting. We face now the possibility, or the probability, that technology serving fear, hate, and misunderstanding will incinerate the planet. Islam, it seems to me, is in the best position to avert this unspeakable genocide of the world's peoples.

To further explain this view, I will now interweave the third and fourth regenerative factors in the Islamic position as I understand it. That is, their tradition of overcoming motives of revenge, coupled with their view of reason as transcending merely cultural differences between thinkers.

On at least two momentous historical occasions, when victorious Islamic warriors had every apparent reason to exact revenge, they did not. They supplied deeds to back up and prove the power of their holy book's integrative and compassionate vision. Muhammad himself battled Meccan tribal warriors for three bloody years. When victorious, he did not genocide them (though he did destroy their "idols" in the Kaballa); he sued rather for reconciliation. Again, about 500 years later the warrior Saladin defeated the Christian Crusaders and regained the city of Jerusalem—the inhabitants of which the Crusaders had massacred decades earlier. And again, a suit for reconciliation. Saladin allowed Jews and Christians to leave the city or to continue there their own religious observances and ways of life.

Thoughtful Muslims can tap today the spiritual resources of these startling role models. They can look at things from the points of view of these warriors. For many Muslims today feel every motivation for revenge, and if these are acted out the incineration of the planet may follow. The great Qur'anic tradition must be mobilized by key Islamic leaders to stave this off.

Think of the humiliation of Islamic nations following World War I. Their Ottoman empire had plunged to defeat along with Germany. Before the guns had cooled, British colonialism had partitioned Palestine, and had sparked the formation of a Jewish state. Along with genuine sentiment for justice for the Jews of the Diaspora was heard the most blatant jingoism: A people without a land for a land without a people.

Except there were people there, the Palestinians. Stuck in the bowels of the surrounding Islamic nations was a foreign body, a Jewish state, and a largely European one at that. Moreover, it was finally to be backed by American might. As we have repeatedly noted, the greatest threat to a culture's reality, its very sanity, is an intrusive foreign body carrying its own way of constructing a world-experienced.

As I write, Israelis and Palestinians commit acts of terror against each other. There is little doubt that if Israel believes its very existence is at stake, because it is being attacked on a national scale, that it will use the ultimate weapon to defend itself: atomic arms. No great stretch of the imagination limns this scenario: atomic weapons that have fallen into the hands of Islamic terrorists are used in response (or initially). And then what? The major powers weigh in atomically, not really sure that they will not be attacked, and the Earth is incinerated.

There are now about two hundred thousand Israeli settlers in what is called the Palestinian-held West Bank. They are supported and protected at the cost to Israel and the United States of about a billion dollars a year. They live in strategically positioned armed camps. How could a cohesive Palestinian state ever be formed now? (As I write, a huge fence is being constructed by Israel that further dices up what might have been a Palestinian state.) Add to this the eminently understandable Israeli demand that its borders be defensible.

What if justice is never done to the Palestinians? Wouldn't this be the greatest occasion for revenge by Muslims, the most exciting incitement to get even? So much depends on the willingness of thoughtful Muslims in positions of power to be thrown back on their own tradition of refusing revenge (at least after their victories, after imposition of their vision of universal social justice—but now the greatest creativity, compassion, and courage is required of thoughtful Muslims).

The great Islamic philosopher Averroes maintained, following Aristotle at his best, that reason transcends merely cultural and personal positions and interests. This long before Christians could tolerate the pagan Aristotle. In Islam's first golden age, Baghdad and Cordoba, Spain, saw the founding of what can be called the world's first international centers for research. This is stunning historical fact.[6]

Today we must encourage a creative use of reasoning the likes of which the world has never seen. What happens when we follow out the integration of viewpoints that allows us to think, barely, the "unthinkable": I mean now, of course, the probable genocide of the world's peoples?

But perhaps I am thoughtlessly taking liberties with the concept or essence of genocide? As I have developed this idea, it has covered the attempt to harm or incapacitate another group as such, just because it is that group (and is considered evil or subhuman). We have never before faced a situation in which immediate and obvious harm could not be limited to a particular group, but would probably involve the whole planet. What are we to say of Muslims who commit acts of terror that may probably lead to atomic exchanges that would mean the death of humanity? There is a certain incitement here to the terrorist mind enthralled by the belief in a supermaterial paradise. For if humanity vanishes, then all the infidels vanish too. Isn't this genocide of a novel sort?

The boundaries for applying the concept or essence of genocide are greatly blurred, and are now uniquely so. We grope to know what we mean, or what we should mean if we would keep in touch with reality.

We seek to clarify, to turn over in our minds, this strangely turbulent and opaque experimental essence with its greatly floating spheres of application—genocide. Certainly, no mere deduction of instructions from within some theological system, as if it were a formal system such as geometry, will do. This is what Osama bin Laden does, enclosed as he is within his Wahhabist fundamentalist theology.

We must reason closely, compassionately, patiently, and thoughtful Muslims have a tradition that can empower them and us. We must look steadily at the new fact, that we can incinerate the planet. We can look around—can't we?—look closely, and we can think and feel and say, "We just don't want that, can't want that, to happen." No matter how grand and inspirational the call to self-sacrifice and martyrdom sounds to many meaning-hungry people here and there, the incineration of the planet must be utterly irrational. So it must appear, at least, to most secularized Western peoples. And we must act responsibly, as we understand responsibility.

*   *   *

The Qur'an and other holy books of Islam present a grand vision that assembles and integrates a multitude of viewpoints. It is a brimming legacy not only of Hebraism and Christianity, but, it seems to me, of aspects of Hinduism and Taoism as well. In the hands of a philosopher such as S. H. Nasr, we see it include indigenous viewpoints also—for example, North American (Sources, 36, 239-40, indexed under Native American). To put it in openly phenomenological terms, we might say that the Islamic holy books have worked out a set of free variations of viewpoints on the theme of human existence: a concrete essence with shifting and never strictly boundable scope.

Presented to our sight is no formal system that might imagine itself to be closed and complete! The awesome "concrete" and "experimental" vision so bedazzles that it hides numerous grave difficulties for actually applying it in our tortured twenty-first century. Glimpsing these difficulties tends to daunt. Interwoven deeply through the Islamic vision is a ferocious patriarchal bias that runs counter to the inclusion, toleration, and integration that is manifestly evident in the Qur'an. The twenty-first century calls for the encouragement and broadcasting of distinctively women's sensibilities and points of view.

Can this be done without losing the total bodily involvement of daily and seasonal Islamic ritual conducted by Islamic men? I don't know. Can Muslims, carefully instructed by their scholars, separate perennial truths of their religion from elements of it that are historically incidental, or so it seems to us? As an example of the latter: elements of ancient Arabian tribal and warrior cultures within which Islamic peoples grew up and, being human and finite, could only partially free themselves? I don't know. Is any doubt too much, as all fundamentalists maintain? I think we must try at least to apply the great vision in the present and actual world spread around us today.

Crown Prince Abdullah of Saudi Arabia may be trying to achieve a new inclusion and integration—of women, for a chief example. If so, he faces tremendous difficulties within his own camp. In October of 2002 the Saudi intelligence agency produced a confidential poll of men between twenty-five and forty-one. 95 percent said they approved of Osama bin Laden's cause. As one high-ranking Saudi said, "fortunately this is not a democracy" (*Newsweek*, 7-22-02, 37).

If Prince Abdullah can lead his people cannily, lovingly, resourcefully, he might be a candidate for prophethood. (In the Sunni version of Islam regnant in Saudi Arabia, this would not, strictly speaking, be possible. Though it would be in the Shi'ite or Shi'i version, dominant, say, in Iran).

*   *   *

Never before has the fate of the whole planet been in human hands. This is the new fact. Beginning to congeal around it, I believe, is a new corporate individual: Those from all quarters who will put the planet and all life, as we know them, first. Now, one can say that there have always been mystics of all conceivable ethnic and geographical extractions who have thought in terms of one humanity and one earth and heaven. Also there have been philosophers such as Plotinus and John Scotus Erigina who speak of the salvific power of the One. But I mean not only these, but persons with just a gut sense that we must all pull together now, and fast.

Doubtless, most members of the three great Western religions will remain rooted in literal images of the transcendent Deity as their own special protector. So there remains the ever-present possibility of an Armageddon clash between helmeted heads and their hordes. The subtle ideas of God's transcendence formulated by the philosopher Nasr, say, will elude them. I mean his idea that Nature directly reflects aspects of the Deity, and yet the aspects we enumerate can never add up to the mysterious whole.

Still, the planet endangered seems to be generating a planetary consciousness that can be found nearly everywhere, like scattered shoots of a springtime life on an earth just thawing (See Mazis, 2002, Sources). The more improbable it all sounds, the more the possibility of success—the possibility only—takes on a numinous life of its own. We are no longer so sure that we know what the actual world is, and that actuality precedes and limits possibility. For instance, we are no longer so sure that we know what the human faculty of reason actually is. Because the possibility dawns that we have not pushed to discover what reason in all its possible functions might be. The possibility dawns, now under duress, that possibility is prior in human life to actuality, and that we big-brained creatures can create possibility.

Properly attuned and primed, we can detect evidences of the new awareness on every hand. More than anarchists are involved in protests against the new tyranny of global trade. More than pretty movements were made by Isadora Duncan's dancers, for they tracked us on the earth under the sky—our participation in the Whole showing in its sacredness. More than academic exercise is revealed in the contemporary philosopher Calvin Schrag, for example. For him reasoning is transversal, not hierarchical and architectonic. That is, it explores and navigates across domains that are no longer integrated within themselves or between each other. He goads us to acknowledge the cultural fragmentation within which we live. He prompts us to look for a gift that derives from a source that we cannot specify within Being or reality. It belongs somehow with what Heidegger calls the silent power of possibility, but it is not possibility as one of the polarized pair, possibility/actuality. (See Schrag, Sources, also my essay on genocide in *Calvin O. Schrag and the Task of Philosophy after Postmodernity.*)

* * *

In the next and final chapter I explore the power of reason to provoke laughter. For when reason shipwrecks, as Karl Jaspers puts it, reason in some form must remain to laugh at its own limits, and must remain within the task of reconstituting itself on ever new bases. Knowing that catastrophe is probable gives life to possibility as never before. The cost of the probable—incineration—is so incalculably great that the improbable becomes necessary.

Laughter is the short-lived convulsion that occurs in relatively safe situations when the expectations of reason are abruptly disappointed. That I should cast my last attempt to grasp genocide in a variation on it that is humor may strike some as itself a joke. My last attempt at an integration and concretization of viewpoints may appear to explode, to fly to pieces, to lose the phenomenon of genocide itself.

Some of my inspiration comes from Dostoyevsky. In his astonishing *The Possessed* (or *Demons*), the most serious matters become funny. In fact, their funniness deepens their seriousness. How can this be? For example, he gives these lines to Kirillov:

> Man is unhappy because he doesn't know he's happy; only because of that. It's everything, everything! Whoever learns will at once immediately become happy, that same moment . . . I pray to everything. See, there's a spider crawling on the wall. I look and am thankful to it for crawling. (Sources, 237-38)

Asking, Could he possibly be serious? may open our minds to possibilities of seriousness that we would never have imagined otherwise. For isn't it true that if we awakened from the everyday constriction of consciousness, from the technological trance and various illusions, we would celebrate life? More, that we would fall to our knees just because we had avoided for one more minute the alternative to it, death? Humor can stretch and exercise consciousness and reason.

Will humor work on Muslim extremists planning terror? What they plan and do may seem morbidly funny to us. That is, they take steps that may lead to the incineration of the planet, this palpable if imperfect paradise, because they believe that they will inherit a perfect superearthly one. How could they possibly trade a certain if imperfect paradise on the chance of a perfect one? Incinerate the world and get paradise! The expectations of our reason are probably disappointed, and we may laugh.

But most of us have lost the grip of faith. We no longer feel, say, St. Paul's conviction expressed in his second letter to the church at Corinth. "While we look not at the things which are seen, but at the things which are not seen: for the things which are seen are temporal; but the things which are not seen are eternal" (4:18).

To think that our question, You can't be serious? will expand the domain of terrorists' reason, pump in free air, and loosen their commitment, strikes me as an exercise in self-deception. Maybe it will work with certain thoughtful Muslims in powerful places—which is no small matter—but not with the masses of extremists. They are deadly serious. Reason for them is in no condition to extend and reconstitute itself through humor or by any other means.

But how can we further work on ourselves, now that all the world's peoples are threatened with a novel sort of genocide? Humor is related to games in at least one key respect: What matters so much at the moment, matters so much that we are thrown into convulsions or paroxysms, typically ceases to matter much when the joke or the game has ended and life goes on. I suggest that we try a game, but a very peculiar one, because if we lose, life will not go on.

I suggest that we call the game Faith against Faith. Our faith against theirs—but, we believe, for the common good. I will adapt what Sören Kierkegaard says about the leap of faith. For him it is the leap to Christianity. He describes this faith as the passion of the infinite: "An objective uncertainty held fast in an appropriation process of the most passionate inwardness." "Objective uncertainty" is an understatement, for what the leap of faith must propel itself over to achieve the most passionate inwardness is a grotesque absurdity to reason: that in the Incarnation, in Jesus Christ, the Eternal entered time. The passion of the infinite is this uncanny burst and leap of faith.

I appropriate this as follows. Though it is probable that the human race will destroy itself, it is possible that we will not. To lose this contest is so incredibly horrifying for most of us, the sheer nullity of it so beyond our comprehension, that for us reason must leap to a domain beyond all conventional calculation or reckoning.

Possibility becomes numinous. The intrinsic value of palpable existence becomes numinous. Learning from Karl Jaspers in the next chapter, I propose that we leap so passionately, so "unreasonably," that a wave of "passionate reasoning" may be unleashed across the globe. Insofar as the expectations of conventional forms of reasoning will be frustrated, there will be a role for humor in this contest.

*　*　*

The book hastens to summing up and denouement. The whole point is to grasp our experienced world as failing to be coextensive with the world itself. The experienced world is not a dream world, but it is finite, incomplete. There are other ways of experiencing things that we in our culture cannot imagine. The shock comes when we grasp our finitude, and we see that we are left with choices: (1) We can sneer at otherness and try to suppress it ("Let them clean our toilets, pump our gas, and pick our lettuce"). (2) We can use our disturbance over their "weird" world-experienced and our terror to try to genocide them. (3) We can try humor and the game of Faith against Faith.

I opt for the last alternative.

NOTES

1. These passages are drawn from *Nausea*, trans. by Lloyd Alexander, New York: New Directions Paperback, 1959 [1938], 29, 172, 180-1. A similar idea occurs in G. Deleuze and F. Guattari, *Anti-Oedipus: Capitalism and Schizophrenia*, trans. by Hurley, Seem, and Lane, Minneapolis: U. of Minn. Press, 1983 [1972], 36: "Each associative flow must be seen as an ideal thing, an endless flux, flowing from something not unlike the immense thigh of a pig. The term *hyle* in fact designates the pure continuity that any one sort of matter ideally possesses." But *hyle*, pure matter, depends for its meaning on intelligible form (*morphe*): it is potentiality *for* form. But the whole idea of form—defining or essential characteristics as the key to rational explanation—must be rethought in the face of the phenomenon of genocide. I prefer William James's idea of the actual as the voluminous, the overflowing. "Every reality has an infinity of aspects or properties." (See his chapter "Reasoning" in vol. II of his *The Principles of Psychology*.) "My thinking is first and last and always for the sake of my doing, and I can only do one thing at a time." Likewise consult his idea of "vicious intellectualism": What is not explicitly included in the definition of something is excluded from that thing (in his *A Pluralistic Universe*). We do and must sort things out according to our interests at the moment, but things ooze into what intellectualistic logics say they are not. I prefer James, Peirce, and Dewey's experimental and piecemeal approach to reasoning and to phenomena (and certain existential-phenomenological approaches). They appeal to our free activity. Need we always be the imperiled body-soul that Sartre's character Roquentin seems to be, or merely hydraulic machines, as Deleuze and Guattari limn us? Seeking to grasp genocide through eternal essences—or through sheer opposition to them—is a losing proposition. Some progress can be made through piecemeal, particularistic, and, in a sense, experimental approaches.

2. Many issues arise that cannot be fully developed in this book. For example: the spontaneity of consciousness and the vexing issue of the freedom of the will. Attaching itself to the latter, is the whole issue of responsibility and culpability (suffice to say that if adults do evil deeds, and they are not out-and-out insane, I believe they are responsible). But I wish to think more about freedom and about eruptive acts, for it may help my cause in the next and last chapter. There I will try to appeal to peoples' selves as potential, to their being as potentiality—to what I would call their better selves. I believe that nobody has better written about this than has Dostoyevsky recounting some of his associates' behavior in prison. I quote again from *The House of the Dead*, but later in the book:

> The prison administrators are sometimes surprised that one convict or another can have lived quietly for several years, a model of good behavior . . . when suddenly for no apparent reason whatever—as if the devil had got into him—he starts to behave waywardly, to go on binges, get mixed up in brawls, and sometimes even takes the risk of committing a criminal offence. . . . The administrators view him with astonishment. But

all the while the cause of this sudden outburst in the man of whom one least expected it is nothing more than an anguished, convulsive manifestation of the man's personality, his instinctive anguish and anguished longing for himself, his desire to declare himself and his humiliated personality, a desire which appears suddenly and which sometimes ends in anger, in frenzied rage, in insanity, fits, convulsions. So perhaps a man who has been buried alive in his coffin and who has woken up in it hammers on its lid and struggles to throw it open, although of course his reason tells him that all his efforts will be in vain. But this is not a matter of reason; rather it is one of convulsions. (110)

The self as potentiality, once awakened, has its own tremendous potency. In his notion of impassioned reason, Karl Jaspers wants to appeal to it; so do I. But how to link it in any way to reason? And to what I implied above: to one's better self? What does "better" mean? In the convulsion, one may be awakened to martyrdom, to the tremendous suction of a fanatical dying for one's group, to what Dewey called learned ignorance and institutionalized paranoic systems. There are orders of complexity. When we move from natural science to distinctively human behavior, we move to a peculiar level of complexity—to what we might call metacomplexity. In the next and last chapter I try to imagine a passionate kind of humor in which we realize our finitude, both as individuals and as groups.

3. I have proposed an analogy between accounts of genocide that might emerge from conventional studies and Ptolemaic, earthcentric, accounts of the apparent movements of the planets (e.g., recessional movements at certain times of year). Once these movements were observed, Ptolemaic astronomy could account for them by adding epicycles to the planets' plotted orbits. Some of these movements could even be predicted. Likewise, conventional objectivizing scientific accounts— say, economical or historical—of genocide might very well account for genocidal eruptions, even predict some of them with some degree of probability, if that is possible at all.

But as observations of planets' movements increased in sensitivity and accuracy, more and more epicycles had to be added in the Ptolemaic theoretical model. Soon a welter of epicycles appeared, arousing the suspicion that something was going on theoretically that was out of keeping with the emerging conviction that Nature follows the line of least resistance, the simplest way.

Not only that. Previously unobserved movements could not be predicted by the Ptolemaic earth-centered model of the heavens. Finally, minute divergences in observed motion from that predicted could not be exploited by that model (for example, as occurred most famously later when Newtonian predictions about the reappearance of a planet emerging from behind the sun were not exactly borne out, but the reappearance could be quite exactly predicted by Einsteinian physics).

In sum, natural science working with its assemblage of measurable objects enabled Ptolemaic astronomy to be supplanted. Here the analogy to conventional accounts of genocide begins to break down. For no reasonable person would expect comparable exactitude in predicting a terrifically complex phenomenon such as genocide. So when exact prediction doesn't happen, nobody is much aroused. But there is an even stronger reason why the insufficiencies of conventional accounts would tend to go undetected. Though I have dreamed up two cases that meet a formal criterion of genocide but that do not conform to my X factor hypothesis, the actual and the most interesting cases of genocide simply don't occur between groups that share ideologies and worldviews (or world-constructions). If we can take this for granted, conventional factors alone might be the only ones that show up in whatever conventional predictions of genocide might conceivably emerge. The X factor would lie concealed, but still decisively at work.

4. Although John Maynard Keynes was one of the founders of "classical economics," the philosophical thrust of his later work carried him to fresh horizons. Note an article of 1937, "The General Theory of Employment":

> (We) have, as a rule, only vaguest idea of any but the most direct consequences of our acts. Sometimes we are not much concerned with their remoter consequences . . . But sometimes we are intensely concerned with them. . . . Now of all human activities which are affected by this remoter preoccupation, it happens that one of the most important is economic in character, namely, Wealth. The whole object of the accumulation of Wealth is to produce results, or potential results, at a comparatively distant, and sometimes at an indefinitely distant, date. Thus the fact that our knowledge of the future is fluctuating, vague, and uncertain, renders Wealth a peculiarly unsuitable subject for the methods of classical economic theory. (213)

This view of wealth lends itself to philosophical, religious, and existential generalization. One may "lay up one's treasure in heaven," and members of a corporate body may be cemented together by a shared ideal concerning an indefinitely distant future. Keynes glimpses an horizon that attracts beyond our abilities to calculate the attraction. (I am indebted to Stephen Marglin for this reference.)

5. Is addiction a disease? With respect to every parameter of the phenomenon— from the practical to the theoretical—this is the most vexing question. For some alcoholics, say, the thought that they are in some way guilty is more than they can bear, and they take refuge in more drinking. For still others, however, the thought that they are in some way guilty is a spur that, at some point, aids their resolution to recover and their ability to do so. On the theoretical level, we land in a vexing tangle of philosophical issues. As brain science rapidly develops, we see that brain correlates to addiction certainly exist (for example, with respect to morphines, ingestion seems to grow receptor sites in synapses of the brain: they remain "hungry"). But how to interpret this within a context sufficiently broad and deep to begin to account for human existence? Most people are unwitting Cartesians: they believe that mind and body are two separate "substances," so that what's true of one cannot be true of the other. Hence, if we have discovered a "truth about the body" (a truth about the brain, say), we have discovered "the causal basis" of the mind, so that the latter is merely an "epiphenomenon" of the former, utterly dependent upon it. So the person seems to be helpless in the face of this "physical reality." Critics of the Cartesian view derive largely from Spinoza: What we call physical states com-

prise merely a distinctive aspect of a whole system of energy exchanges, another aspect of which we call mental states. Within this critical model, talk of *the basis* of a phenomenon such as addiction is suspect: we must try to delineate the whole context of interdependent energy exchanges, the nature/culture/personal whole (and to be perfectly consistent, Whole). My thinking conforms more to the critical model. I do wish to distinguish between addictions in a simpler sense, and those in a more complex sense. If, for example, I contract malaria, after taking all reasonable precautions, it would seem to make no sense to make amends to others, even if they had been inconvenienced by my illness. Whereas if I am an alcoholic, say, it does seem at least to make some sense to offer amends (which is what Alcoholics Anonymous prescribes at a definite stage in one's recovery). What role does personal agency play? The human self is more complex and difficult to define, I believe, than we can at present even imagine. I, at least, cannot pretend to imagine it all.

6. The idea that reason and research transcend merely cultural differences implies as well that they transcend merely personal differences. This double transcendence implies, in turn, a public use of reason to resolve issues and to advance knowledge and civil behavior. We find here one of the deepest roots of pluralism and democracy. Amartya Sen expands our view of democracy by dilating our awareness beyond the importance of formal voting, balloting, to include other features of democracy (and to include contributions from non-North Atlantic sources).

> The great success of Arab civilization in the millennium following the emergence of Islam provides a marvelous example of indigenous creativity combined with openness to intellectual influences from elsewhere—often from people with very different religious beliefs and political systems. . . . Even though no formal system of democratic governance was involved in these achievements, the excellence of what was achieved . . . is a tribute . . . to the glory of open public reasoning. . . . The idea behind such openness was well articulated by Imam Ali bin abi Taleb in the early seventh century in his pronouncement that "no wealth can profit you more than the mind" and "no isolation can be more desolate than conceit." These and other such proclamations are quoted for their relevance to the contemporary world by the excellent "Arab Human Development Report 2002" of the United Nations. The thesis of European exceptionalism, by contrast, invites Arabs, like the rest of the non-Western world, to forget their own heritage of public reasoning. (Sources, 2003)

7

THINKING THE UNTHINKABLE?
A RELIGIOUS RETARDANT TO
GENOCIDE AND TERRORISM?

Reality is infinitely various when compared to the deductions of abstract thought, even those that are most cunning, and it will not tolerate rigid, hard-and-fast distinctions. Reality strives for diversification.

—F. M. Dostoyevsky

The tragic strategy for solving problems is to perceive them as warfare between polar oppositions. . . . The way of the tragic hero is to choose passionately one pole, then suffer from its opposite. Oedipus chooses moral purity and suffers from pollution, King Lear risks everything to gain the respect of his children and is destroyed by their scorn. Tragic dramas normally end with a funeral or its equivalent. . . . Comic stories most often end with a wedding or reconciliation. . . . There is no choice between opposites in comedy. . . . The comic way is not to get even but to get along.

—Joseph Meeker

I began this book emphasizing vulnerability and suffering. Then I moved to the illusions we create trying to protect ourselves. The most basic is the illusion of immortality: "I am not really an individual body that can suffer and will die. I am really a mind or soul that lives on and on."

Deeper than the illusion of personal immortality is the illusion of the group's, the corporate body's, immortality. Typically, conscious mind cannot penetrate these illusions, for it leans on, and is formed by, the relatively static meanings of the culture itself. Conscious mind continuously maintains the illusions, continuously curbs itself and prevents exploration.

Only great shocks can jolt us out of basic illusions. We easily underestimate how great the shocks must be. Many of the world's peoples are born into what Don Miguel Ruiz calls "the planetary dream of suffering" (Sources). The dream is constant and contrastless, hence seems normal and wakeful. Humans are so threatened by suffering that, awake or asleep, we see its potential sources everywhere. Terrible apprehension and then blame spread like wildfires, and we live choked in smoke.

The planetary dream of suffering is the world-as-experienced by and through the culture into which we bodily beings happen to have been born, and which is typically unquestionable—the way the world is. The dream is the particular form of intercorporeality and communal symbolization in which we support each other and our shared world-experienced against threats to our existence. "If we could just get rid of them, everything would be OK." Blame, projection, scapegoating, terrorism, madness.

Is there any escape from the planetary dream of suffering? That depends on whether we can come to terms with our vulnerable bodily being and our suffering in its actuality—not as dreamed. If we can, suffering will take its place within the whole picture. Its ever-present possibility will not color everything in a pulsing and menacing nightmare smear of "World!"

When we deny that our experiencing-bodies are ourselves, the body protests and takes its revenge. Attempting to protect itself, it spreads itself in a troubled smear through the world-experienced-by-it. As if it were screaming hysterically, Notice me, Notice me!

To break the dream of suffering, we have to wake up to the abounding Nature that formed us, and without which no cultures could be formed within and through Nature. For there is not only suffering. There can be exultation to be alive for another day. What Albert Einstein called the miracle of the existence of the universe comes to full fruition only in and through ourselves, only in and through our exulting, and our wonder and gratitude. There is not only the possibility of suffering, but also the possibility of celebrating the universe, its incredible creativity and variety, and our tiny but potentially vital contributions within it.

*   *   *

So habituated are most cultures and their members, so cemented into their own viewpoint and their own world-experienced, that they might be said to be buried alive. Everything feels fixed and changeless, including the amount of suffering that all are bound to endure. People who commit genocide feel perfectly justified because of the anxiety and suffering they have endured at the hands of those others ("There is no need to think through genocide, for it is obviously the good thing to do"). While those others who are genocide's victims think that genocide is so obviously evil, so obviously morally outrageous, that it is unthinkable (hence, for them there is also no need to think it through). Both victims and victimizers are cemented in their views, and in their suffering; both sides feel there is no reason to think this act through.

I have tried to break out of all cemented points of view, and to think "the unthinkable," think it through. I have tried to do this by assembling as many points of view on genocide as I can imagine gathering: historical and biological points of view; victims' and victimizers' points of view; artistic points of view; the points of view of the some of the Islamic holy books; and the use of metaphors that are free variations of viewpoints, because they place things in relationships that do not literally hold for them.

Metaphors have the added value of not turning us into objects, but of participating in the fantastical reality of our subjectivity and intersubjectivity—the whole experiencing-experienced reality-in-process that we live each instant. That is, the whole peculiar complexity, the shifting and curling metacomplexity of our lives. Now I attempt to round out these variations and integrations of viewpoints with humor.

We have been dealing with the grimmest subject matter. So it may not have occurred to us that our way of dealing with it contains an element of playfulness. We have pumped free air around things, have looked at genocide from this angle and that, in this way and that way. Only taking this route, I submit, can we begin to actually think "the unthinkable"; and only in this way can we begin to deliver ourselves from the illusion that there is a fixed amount of great suffering that must forever haunt our labile, vulnerable bodily selves and our tremulous experienced world.

You as readers and I as writer should try to comprehend what will probably seem to us to be a contradiction in terms: sacred play. For our cultures today take automatically a hierarchical, tragic, and patriarchal point of view in which oppositional dualisms and conflicts go unquestioned, particularly the opposition between serious and playful, and its many cognate oppositions—tragic/comic, sacred/profane, religious/secular, heaven/earth, human/animal, mind/body, and noble us/disgusting them. It must be one or the other, and if one, then not the other, either/or. I am proposing both-and.

Both sacred and playful, both animal and human, both serious and comic (my favorite genre is Eugene Ionesco's tragic farce), both us and them.

The ancient world knew of sacred games, as well as of a sacred geometry. This latter in fact has been knocking at the door throughout this book. We have been experimenting with human rights as rights to space; with violation as violation of these rights; with dread and aversion as a wrenching in our bodies when witnessing inappropriate movements in space; with up as up in power and authority, and with down as waste, disgrace, and collapse. We've begun playing with these polar oppositions, trying to dismantle them. This experimentation is a strange kind of serious play.

I am trying to formulate a religious attitude that holds that if deliverance is to happen, it must happen through this strange kind of serious play. "Nuke 'Em!" is far too eccentrically serious to be safe or wise. I think we best try to lure ourselves and our others into a kind of playfulness in which we begin to think "the unthinkable," and begin to conclude that we just do not want it to happen. We must find enough meaning in "the unthinkable" to know, viscerally know, that we don't want it to happen. Playfulness might be that passionate reasonableness that Jaspers thinks might yet save us from planetary catastrophe—though the probabilities are against us. People committed to play and to life will not dampen their enthusiasm just because they think they probably will lose. They will tend to play all the harder, won't they?

*   *   *

It is with this faith that I have ventured on this book. I believe that anyone not blinded by the greatest fear and fanaticism, anyone who has seriously-playfully pumped free air around things, can see that not only are the genocided terribly damaged, but that the genociders are terribly damaged as well. Because they gravely fall short of their full human potential to grow up and to patiently grapple with the difficulties that plague humanity. Can we call it sacred wrestling? If militant Muslims could think calmly for a moment, they would know that Islam cannot take us back to the Middle Ages, not even to the days of the Ottoman empire eighty-some years ago.

All mammals play. In a greatly serious sort of play, mammals bark and bluff and carry on to establish dominance/submission patterns without badly damaging or killing each other. Properly tuned to the comical-serious vein, we might learn from them. Joseph Meeker writes,

> Boundaries of all kinds are crossed during play. A stranger with an unknown language and culture will know how to respond if you smile and toss him a

ball. Play is one of the rare human languages that can cross all lines of culture, race, gender, status, or species. When your dog makes a mock pounce at you, it's clear that play time is at hand. Most species have clear behavioral signals to express invitations to play, and they use them with their own kind or with any other species that seems willing to play. (See Sources, *The Comedy of Survival*)

The fact is, there are more forms of otherness, and other forms of otherness, than anyone at any point can imagine. We have the capacity to dread ourselves to death. For all I know, this dread-death may be what the human race is trying, however fumblingly, to avoid with the spate of extraterrestrial monsters to which science fiction and electronic games are treating us. Are we trying to educate ourselves to tolerate otherness?

*   *   *

What is required, I think, is a new religious sense of the creative spontaneity, variety, and abundance of the universe. If we dare speak of the universe as one, or as the One, we can sense that any claim to exhaustively break it down into various sorts and their contraries, or others, is wildly presumptuous. How could we possibly know that our breakdown is exhaustive, or that an indefinite number of other inventories and contrasts weren't equally, or superiorly, applicable to reality? We can tap a sense of difference that we cannot say, that is preconceptual. (This I think is what Plato was getting at in "Parmenides," and perhaps what Jacques Derrida is suggesting with his *difference*.)

Now, how do we develop this new religious sense of the creative variety of the universe? First, the United States will have to catch itself (with a sardonic laugh?) in its brazen attempts to impose its viewpoint, its commercial and military will, its political ideology, on the rest of the world. "Globalization and free markets" must not mean open season for raping the world's populations and their environments by United States—and multinational—capitalist interests. (See Sources: Apffel-Marglin, Chua, Sachs, Hertz, Grim, Marglin, Stiglitz, Daly, Posey, Sahlins, Sharma, Aristede, Parajuli, Rosenberg, Cobb, Rasmussen, McCuen.) It must not mean that we always know what's best for others. It must not mean that the CEO of Nike, for example, can pile up billions of dollars on the backs of sweated workers in Indonesia—those with minimal or no protections.

Many of these workers are ones who have been forced into the cities by the inability of their indigenous farming practices and cottage industries to compete with worldwide agribusiness and with electronically hyped and economically overwhelming capitalist-commercial ventures. An elementary religious sense of the creative abundance of the universe will respect the local roots and forms of the world's peoples, insofar as these remain at all. I mean, all the rites and celebrations of living and dying supplied by a culture that authorize a life and give it meaning. Free trade and globalization must not mean the right to destroy cultures that have intimately and intricately attuned individuals to their environments over many, many generations. "People who connect with a place look after it; those who are rootless do not" (see Sources, Rasmussen). "Globalization is creating a world of powerless places at the mercy of placeless powers" (Wackernagel and Rees, Sources).

Take, for instance, the total life forms that give life meaning for those in the Andes, for example (See Frédèrique Apffel-Marglin, Sources). The 2000+ species of potato, for example, grown over 10,000 years, species far more numerous than could be wiped out by any foreseeable number of natural plagues (though not by atomic radiation). These are species bred, introduced, and cultivated in the most sedulous and intricate cooperation with altitude, climate, texture—even taste—of soil, patterns of sun, moon, and stars, and the traditional preferences and diets of the people of that locale over countless generations. We cannot mindlessly tear to shreds the forms of labor, play, and life that give indigenous persons life and meaning, that is, that give their lives and selves substance, heart, and the ecstasy of contributing.

Nor can anyone with any sense of humans' roots in Nature and of their total needs think that even another few billion dollars will crown the CEO of Nike with a blessed, meaningful life. When all we know is power-over, power for more power for more power, there is never enough of it. It is the restless hell of rapacity and addiction. It is the feeling of never being loved and cared for. Let us call it the Enron complex that has spread over our country and our system like a cancer.

But if we are playing, then the point is just to keep on playing. Though we know, in the back of our minds, that this may be the only possible way to survive.

As the monopolists and robber barons of the 1890s in the United States needed to have strong regulations and restraints placed upon them if they were not to keep creating misery for multitudes of people, so their kin in the first years of the twenty-first century need such restraints on the world scene.

Strong regulations should be built somehow into all global agreements on trade. If "third world" governments want the munificent revenues accruing from world trade, they must agree to regulations that protect their people and their environments from exploitation, from devastation. Particularly they must protect the indigenous populations and their cultures and environments—which includes the protection of nonhuman life. (See John Grim, Sources. Also Amy Chua on lack of international regulations and enforcements, and on how a few corporate outsiders collude with a few local government officials—through kickbacks—to control the wealth of a nation and to keep the mass of indigenous workers impoverished: a tinderbox for revenge, uprisings, genocides.)

* * *

All effective play involves play-within-limits, involves the secure sense that we cannot go too far. This can keep us constantly prepared for life. For to become aware of our limits in life is to become aware of an ultimate boundary, an horizon, in the actual world. Take the visual horizon as the one most accessible to inspection. Located and described just as it presents itself, the horizon points inward to everything it encloses, including ourselves. It also points outward, that is, away from ourselves and toward everything else in the universe.

We cannot know—and upon reflection know we cannot know—all the sorts of things that might be going on in the universe. We may dimly sense that we fail to comprehend how all these things might be experienceable by us. Since the meaning of things is a matter of how they are experienceable by us, we can sense that these things don't possess meaning, at least not in any of the usual senses of the term meaning.

But we do get a strange, ponderous, and awesome meaning: the mysterious. What we imagine to be real, but yet not experienceable by us as having any definite characteristics, we experience to be mysterious. When we can imagine only that something is, but not what it is, we imagine the mysterious.

Moreover, we can suspect that mysterious matters are not just out there, beyond us. But that in a universe that circulates back regeneratively through every node of itself, there are mysterious processes going on around and through us all the time. So mysterious that we cannot imagine to look for them and to investigate them? But we might just accept that they are? This would be an ecstatically expansive moment of meaning-making, substance-making for selves. Without the mysterious *that* of things held close to the chest, there is no ultimate support for us, no way to retain our poise in the midst of unpredictable dangers to our incredibly vulnerable bodily selves.

What is emerging here is a religious view of reality. To feel at home in such a world is to begin to liberate ourselves from illusion and fear. Knowing there is more to be known than any group will ever know, deflates the pretension that our world-experienced is the only one, the last word on everything. Deflated as well is the belief that a single head knows and controls all that is happening. (Deflated may be a sufficiently cautious word. The hold that the belief in a single head exerts on the patriarchal group must not be underestimated. Thus, for example, it was Francisco Pizarro's evil genius to see that if he publicly tortured and murdered all the Incas' chiefs, the people would have to have another head, and the only head that remained would be himself.)

*   *   *

Poised, more supple, we might even entertain the possibility of a genuine—not an illusory—immortality. Our bodily life as we live it each instant radiates ever into the world around us, far beyond our ability to comprehend its repercussions. The world picks up, prehends, each of our vibratory, rhythmic, tonic signatures, and perhaps keeps holding them in some kind of coherence we can't now imagine. It picks up our crying and our laughter in ways we can't imagine. Perhaps our personal identity is held in a coherence that endures beyond the death of the organism that had previously been essential to our identity. If true, this wouldn't spring from the *illusion* of immortality.

We live in a mysterious universe. Nobody knows why it exists. Why is there this universe rather than nothing? Nobody knows, but of course the very lack of knowledge prompts faiths fanatical in their assurance.

Yet it might also prompt an ultimate playfulness. The unknown ground from which springs the universe we see all around us, and which flows through us, may allow for personal immortality beyond our wildest dreams. It may! I'm not putting my life on hold, waiting for what I believe must certainly happen after the death of my organism. Nor am I deathly afraid that another group's view on immortality will cross-cut and undermine my own. For I know that nobody knows.

When I'm locked in the illusion of immortality's stupefying grip, I tend not to really live. Or like suicidal Muslim terrorists do, I too might commit dastardly acts by taking innocent people with me in death. When locked in the illusion of immortality, I tend not to live ecstatically in the unknown, freely reveling in its chanciness, and in its countless and nameless variety.

Persons in the grip of illusions that the world makes sense only for their group, cannot begin to think through the nature of genocide, even if they wanted to do so. They cannot think it through the many viewpoints that can be assembled on it, as we tried to do in the last chapter. They can make no headway at all on the path of passionate reason. They revel in a frenzy of fear and anger. But as I mentioned in the last chapter, mature adherents of each religion might be able to divert their fundamentalist colleagues with sops, or find some way to stifle them. Maybe by gently laughing at their plans for world domination?

I am trying to discover a new sense of rational, a new sense of the religious life, a new seriousness in comedy. We can and should think "the unthinkable," at least to the extent of our abilities. We can recognize that genocide is the destruction of humanity and personhood—the destruction of truly human variety and richness, and the destruction of traits of character like patience. Genocide is momentary excitement, then deadness and vacuity.

Enclosing ourselves tightly in our home group, we tend to think we are saving ourselves. This is part of the illusion of group immortality. As Primo Levi put it, we do nothing, we refuse to listen to cries from the others. In letting cries of terror and pitiful cries for help go unanswered, we are disconnecting our distinctive human selves from the ever-regenerating and sustaining universe—despite what our theologies may tell us. In dissociating ourselves from other humans, our humanity withers, or becomes grossly eccentric and murderous. For example, to ignore Mayans in visible and audible agony today is for each of us to wither in our central inner life, in our souls. (See Montejo, Sources)

Earlier in the book I quoted from Tolstoy's *War and Peace*: the scene in which Count Rostov wishes to die for the Czar, or at least to die heroically in battle so the Czar can see him go down, or at the very least hear about it. Later in Tolstoy's novel, Rostov is no longer so entranced by the corporate body's gleaming head. He captures a French soldier. He is about to kill him, when he looks deeply into that sad, frightened, young face. He identifies with the Frenchman. He sees himself in him. He recognizes viscerally that beyond their cultural differences, and beyond their corporate bodies locked in struggle, there lies their bond, their common humanity as vulnerable individuals created by Nature. He spares the French soldier. With this Tolstoy opens the door to what he calls divine love: that love of our enemies through which we might yet save ourselves.

The ripples from Christ and Tolstoy reached Mohandas Gandhi, and the ripples from them all reached Martin Luther King. Are these four, and the rest of us who have been touched by them, a match for the three great Western religions now at each other's throats, thanks to their fundamentalist members? With both Muslims in Pakistan and Hindus in India now atomically armed? Does any version of playful and passionate reason have a chance to mollify troubled human breasts and stomachs? To be playful-serious is not to believe the odds. It is to play against them.

*   *   *

I would like to grow up. I'd like to consider the three great Western religions' idea that the ultimate ground and order of reality—God, if you will—is mysterious. For Hebrew, Christian, and Islamic ultraorthodox religionists assert that, and then pretend to know exactly who God is and what He wants from us (He?). And the other groups claim exact knowledge as well, and then, of course, they can't agree, and hysterically try to extrude or displace each other.

Childish religion demands immediate closure and gratification. It supposes a crude parallelism between individual and corporate human bodies, on the one hand, and God's on the other. God's physiognomy—supposing such a thing—may be unimaginably different from ours. Such a being may not have a head in any of our senses at all. It may be just a mysterious nourishing ground in which each thing resonates, as only it can, with everything else, for as long as it can. On the level of the deepest nisus and tendency, everything is enriched interactively by everything else, and beyond our comprehension.

In the appropriate playful frame of mind, we see that we must have metaphors. So why not play with the ultimate ground as female? God as a She? The ultimate ground as the dark womb of creation and sustenance? From which abundance emerges unimaginably other forms of otherness? What harm would there be in trying this way of modeling the universe? It is hard to imagine that we could do worse than what we've already done throughout history since patriarchy and agriculture. Why not look in prehistory, in the Old Stone Age, for female models and metaphors? (See Donna Wilshire, Sources)

We give up rigid assurance when we play with metaphors. We may miss deep, maniacal, hysterically exciting, self-sacrificial urges. But we might gain a suppleness, humility, and powerful ease and centeredness that are well worth the price. At least I think it is possible, as I try to make sense of things.

*   *   *

Will the human race survive? Will we grow up, cease being terrified of differences and of the dark? Will we cease being afraid of—or contemptuous of—our own partially known and appreciated bodily-communal and potentially ecstatic reality? That is, afraid of the miracle of matter?

As I have suggested, we might return to our Paleolithic forebears for guidance. This sounds counterintuitive because we have long assumed that they were primitive and backward. But they are the ones who proved that their way of living was sustainable for many tens of thousands of years. We moderns have not survived long enough to prove that we are viable forms of humanity.

Taking the long-term view, our eruptive modern revolutions have occurred in the blink of an eye. We have simply not established that our ways of living are sustainable. Our big brains have created many marvels (take the Hubble telescope and the new astrophysics for starters). But our brains are now in a runaway state. The very tools, the marvelous technological tools and understandings that our brainy bodies have created, keep spurring us to ever-faster and frantic blind plunging in our daily living. Not to mention again that our marvelous technologies, when they become tools in terrorists' hands, can create hell right here.

Why? Because we have staggering abilities to create words and symbols and electronic tools such as computers, and projectiles that shrink experienced time and space, and that create destruction so massive that we cannot really comprehend it. We have created marvelous and wondrous sciences and technologies, but we also live in the technological trance, bastard faiths unaware of themselves.

We have distracted ourselves from our ancient, habituatable whole bodies immediately involved every moment in the mysterious and chancy universe. Too many of us are caught in rigid, frightened, hierarchically and patriarchally ordered bodies—both personal and corporate—that dread being violated by other such bodies. Too many are on edge most of the time—not relaxed enough to really laugh. Our capacities for play have been gravely limited.

We in "the West," as we like to locate ourselves, have acquired the habit of disregarding the fertile background of space and time and the dark womb of ancient cultures out of which we grew. (Jesus Christ, after all, was an Asiatic.) As corporate bodies, we no longer welcome kinship with other living things. We think nonsense (but not the laugh-making kind). Such as that we can live well without ritual attunement in the world that birthed us, that we can live without sacred play. Many endure day by day, but without a visceral sense of the wholeness of things enveloping, holding, and nurturing us every moment, live without the holy and the sacred. Many of my students have never seen the black velvet sky carpeted with stars. So of course they haven't learned to identify the stars by their Arabic names, Altair (al-Ta'ir: the flyer or bird), or Aldebaran (al-Debaran: the one that follows the Pleiades), etc. We can go to a good dictionary and dig out these names' roots, but many never imagine going there. We just huddle together stupefied, or rush around in SUVs. The loss of the consciously and deliberately ritualized and contemplative life is a loss beyond estimation.

* * *

As the world more and more embraces contemporary North Atlantic values and becomes a monoculture, it loses variety and invigorating novelty; it becomes flat and insidiously boring. Many can only feel the sporadic excitement of greed—or of drugs. Our bodies feel this boredom and begin to rebel, wither, and to create dull, miasmic menace in our world-experienced.

As I've suggested a number of times, often the reactive counteraction to the withering is feverish addictive and addictive-like activities. But these are just other ways of withering. We may think we can dominate the planet as if we were the male God atop the pyramid of our cleverness and power. But we can't, and our bodies dimly but profoundly sense this. Both indigenous and other premodern peoples fall into despair at what we are doing, despair in the face of the alienation that we in North Atlantic culture are creating. We don't create this maliciously, probably, just unwittingly, which is harder for us to detect and to change.

I take Paul Shepard's last book, *Coming Home to the Pleistocene*, Robert Neville's *Recovery of the Measure*, James Hillman's *The Soul's Code*, and David Ehrenfeld's essay "Forgetting" very seriously. We can try to relearn where we came from and what formed us. There are archetypes, ways of perceiving, feeling, and remembering deeply embedded in our muscles and nervous systems. They beg to be let out and play.

These archetypes are primal gifts. We belong to them before anything can belong to us. To mention again the meditation in movement, T'ai Chi, which derives from ancient Chinese Nature religion. It is a way of experiencing a universe that harmonizes itself, and a way of experiencing ourselves vitally at home in it. The Native American daily ceremony of the seven directions has deep sources as well. It harmonizes, orients, and roots us. Our bodies might perceive and dream and act it into themselves.

Let's look at Native Americans for a moment, those who struggle to survive with us on this continent. In the ceremony of the seven directions we see variations, liberations from encrusted monoviewpoints; we see sacred play. The four cardinal directions—East, South, West, North—and the typical gifts from each, are acknowledged sequentially in the appropriate posture, gesture, and ambience of a flowing giving of thanks. Then the upper world where our kin, the birds, see everything connected is thanked. Then the lower world of fertile darkness, the womb of the Great Mother. Finally, the seventh direction, our own thinking and feeling hearts, where all the nurturance and knowledge from the six directions can be gathered, planted, replanted. (See the cover of my *The Primal Roots of American Philosophy*: the Mandan Indian offering the buffalo skull in thanksgiving to the dawn.)

As experienced, space and time are indissolubly connected; moreover, they are indissolubly connected with our breathing. All meditations in movement discipline the breathing, for breathing goes deep: it bridges the voluntary and involuntary nervous systems (See my *Wild Hunger: The Primal Roots of Modern Addiction*, Sources, 209–10). Moreover, breathing in these various traditions is disciplined in similar ways. It is to become as seamless and smooth as the regenerative cycles, the inhalations and exhalations, of Nature herself. In heavy sighs the air is let out quickly. The rest or quietus that follows has no vitality. In quietus with vitality, there is no exertion, but always something in reserve, something potential. It is the brimming sense of gifts that will come unbidden on the next inhalation, the next inspiration. It is poise, readiness, gratitude. It is the real readiness to laugh, if that is appropriate. (See again, Schrag, 2002)

Meditations in movement worldwide exhibit a startling universality. We really shouldn't be surprised, for the human organism took shape over many millennia in hunter-gatherer and wilderness environments in which similarities of circumstances were more fundamental than were the differences. Alertness, curiosity, poise, flexibility, endurance, the ability to hope—these were always fundamental for survival. Retrieval of these aspects of hunter-gatherer societies might help us combat the obsessive nationalism and corporate egoism of today's world, and the panicked overreaction to cultural differences.

As with all the great meditations and meditations in movement that humans have discovered worldwide, we might yet find centeredness, poise: the power of the potential. It is possible. Aligned with the axis of the world, we are in the best company. Poised, we would be less apt to shrivel in panic when encountering otherness. We would be less apt to look up to whatever charismatic head happens to appear and who promises salvation. Less likely to look up as if we were frightened children awaiting instructions. Evidently, there are thousands of brainwashed Muslim children that have been turned into jihad machines. On our own streets we see idle, unenlisted, dangerously alienated and disoriented young people. On what great wheel could they press their shoulders and be confirmed in their vitality and worth? In what sacred contest or game could they find themselves laughing, challenged, contented?

We descendents of the three great Western religions might drill ourselves every day in ancient Chinese and Native American rituals (those cultures at some of their best). If, in our chaotic and driven lives, we fail to do this, all is not lost. The simple ritual of saying grace before each of the three meals a day is much better than nothing. This may be a family holding hands for a moment before the meal and looking into each others' eyes. How infinitely better than throwing ourselves onto our food like hungry animals as the TV spreads its heedless chatter and caringless images through the room. This is a form of germ warfare turned on ourselves that we might detect if we could pump free air around things and see ourselves through certain other groups' eyes. Habitually watched commercial TV is only a transient diversion—death in life.

Or, is washing one's teeth a ritual? Isn't it merely mechanical motion? Not necessarily. It can become a ritual of caring in which we bodily beings establish for ourselves and for others that we care about ourselves, for others, and for the vulnerable preciousness and miraculousness of overabounding life itself.

*   *   *

An essential condition for a fresh start is to allow others who care for us to jolt us awake. Or to allow others who don't care for us to jolt us awake. This would be minimal alertness and integrity.

We must transform ourselves. If we have roots in traditional religions, might we become strong enough not to need everyone to agree with us if we are to experience our faith as real? We just might learn to feel at home in the unknown. The human condition in a mysterious world places us ultimately beyond consensus.

Actually, I should say that some of us can be placed beyond consensus in the usual sense of that term: as consensus on a particular matter in the world. On the matter, say, that eels swim improperly (though acknowledging that others with still-vital roots in Judaism, as in this example, can hold to their laws while encouraging other groups to hold to theirs).

But with respect to consensus on the world as world, on the Whole, we might possibly achieve a super- or a metaconsensus. That is, dynamic groups in all cultures might come to see that the world exceeds any possible inventory of the sorts of things and events that might be going on in it.

The World is not the super object, the colossal container, and it exceeds our comprehension. It is mysterious. Some will call this natural piety, some will call it who cares what?

Might we playfully vary perspectives on the idea of goodness? So that we see it not just as onerous duty, or not just as that which makes us feel strangely good when we do it? But also as that which may be necessary for our survival? Because in a world of shrunken experienced space and time, in which weapons of fearsome powers are widely available, if peoples feel unjustly treated, and throb with desire for revenge, our very survival may be at stake. This should move us—if we have not lost entirely the will to live.

Is the playfulness that might come to greet us in times of dire peril the Divinity itself, the Creating Ground itself? If this sounds too overstuffed and grandparently to transmit playfulness, we can try out the American Indian tradition of Coyote, the Trickster. (See Glen Mazis, *Trickster, Magician, Grieving Man*, Sources).

*   *   *

In the end, can we think "the unthinkable"? Yes, barely—far from perfectly. I am attempting now to think it within a religious sketch of the human condition, though I have not included religious institutions in the sketch. I don't know if this sketchy religion is institutionally formulable, and that's an important point. Because we are so much creatures of our situations, and the world is so contingent and chancy, our emotions and attentions so labile and eruptive, that we can lose the thread of our identity if we lose our institutions. New religious institutions may be essential for us to weave our identities day by day.

In any case, we must go on. Immanuel Kant thought that one of the fundamental questions is, What can I hope? I imagine that without an elemental and playful hopefulness we won't generate the poise needed to glance over the edge into the abyss of genocide: the out-of-this-world gulf into which it is ever possible to fall. Without hope I imagine that we will keep finding frightened excuses for not trying to really look, to think, to act daily.

Calvin Schrag writes, "Kierkegaard elucidates (in *Works of Love*) the internal connection of love with hope. 'But love, which is greater than faith and hope, also takes upon itself the work of hope . . . ' To love is to hope, to be projected into the future, to exist as possibility." (Sources, *God as Otherwise Than Being*, 136)

In our context, the work of hope is also a superlative playing. For at stake is survival, and we avow only the possibility, not the probability, of success. Possibility can become enchanting, numinous.

Bruno Bettelheim, like Primo Levi and Jean Amery also a survivor of Auschwitz, describes that murder machine in psychiatric terms, for example, neurotic. Levi scoffs at this. He thinks it is born of minds safely ensconced in the "normal" world of the clinical Western university.

If we wake up, we may be chastened and humbled in the face of the immeasurable unknown. Not humiliated, for we will not have fallen from perches of sleepy pretension and pretending. We may be both humbled and exhilarated to have gotten even a little way in thinking "the unthinkable." Won't we be elated over what before might have seemed so little: that we can marvel at the existence of a universe we can't explain, and at ourselves as tiny but potentially vital parts of it. That above all: delighted and grateful that we live for another day, and that we have been spared the tormented world or nonworld of genocide, if indeed we have been spared it.

If through a kind of focused play we were to be loosened from dumbly taking life for granted, wouldn't we see each dawn as a new chance to participate in creation? Wouldn't we know that every instant of life is a loan from an unknown source that can be called in any moment? Whatever the source might be, it must be awesome beyond imagination.

At times I feel surrounded and sustained by a kind of effulgence. It is a feeling of total health. It is more suggested and divined than comprehended. It is always and everywhere, except where I'm looking. It is the answer to everything, except to the question I am asking. It is background that never becomes foreground. It besets me, before and behind. It stays me.

Is it enough to go on? Is this strange buoyancy and childlike wonder enough to go on, to grope with?

Ah, reader, what do you think?

BIBLIOGRAPHY

Abram, David, *The Spell of the Sensuous*, New York: Pantheon, 1996.
———, "The Ecology of Magic," *Orion*, Summer, 1991.
Adelman, Howard, and Astri Suhrke, *The Path of Genocide: The Rwanda Crisis from Uganda to Zaire*, London: Transaction Publishers, 1999.
Adorno, T. W., et al., *The Authoritarian Personality*, New York: Harper and Bros., 1950.
al Baladhuri, Abu-l Abbas Ahmad, *Origins of the Islamic State*, trans. Hitti, New York: Columbia Univ. Press, 1916
al Ghazali, Abu Hamid, *The Precious Pearl*, trans. from the Arabic by Jane I. Smith, Cambridge: Harvard Univ. Press (CSWR Publications), 1979.
Alexander, J. C., "Towards a Theory of Cultural Trauma," in *The Meanings of Social Life: A Cultural Sociology*, New York: Oxford Univ. Press, 2003. Trauma enters into "the core of the collectivity's sense of its own identity."
Ali, Maulana Muhammad, See *Qur'an, The Holy*, below
Ali, Tariq, *The Clash of Fundamentalisms: Crusades, Jihads and Modernity*, London and New York: Verso Press, 2002.
Améry, Jean, *At the Mind's Limits: Contemplations by a Survivor on Auschwitz and Its Realities*, Bloomington, Ind.: Indiana Univ. Press, 1977 [1966].
Amin, Yousreay, et al., "Mass Hysteria in an Arab Culture," *International Journal of Social Psychiatry*, vol. 43 (4), winter 1997, 303–6, England: Avenue Publishing Co.
Andric, Ivo, *The Bridge on the Drina*, trans. L. F. Edwards, Chicago: The University Press, 1977 [1942].

Anzulovic, Branimir, *Heavenly Serbia: From Myth to Genocide*, New York: NYU Press, 1999.

Apffel-Marglin, Frédèrique, *The Spirit of Regeneration: Andean Culture Confronting Western Notions of Development*, London: Zed Books, 1998 (distributed by St. Martin's Press).

———, and Loyda Sanchez, "Developmentalist Feminism and Neocolonialism in Andean Communities," *Femminist Post-Development Thought: Rethinking Modernity, Post-Colonialism, and Representation*, ed. K. Saunders, London and New York: Zed Books, 2002.

Arendt, Hannah, *Totalitarianism*, Part III of *The Origins of Totalitarianism*, New York: Harcourt, Brace and World, 1968 [1951].

Aristede, Jean-Bertrand, *Eyes of the Heart: Seeking a Path for the Poor in the Age of Globalization*, Monroe, Maine: Common Courage Press, 2000.

Armstrong, Karen, *Islam: A Short History*, New York: Modern Library, 2002.

Atwood, George E., Donna M. Orange, Robert E. Stolorow, "Shattered Worlds/Psychotic States: A Post-Cartesian View of the Experience of Personal Annihilation," *Psychoanalytic Psychology*, vol. 19, 2, 281–306, 2002.

Bacon, Roger, *Opus Majus*, trans. Burke, Philadelphia: Univ. of Penn. Press, 1928.

Balakian, Peter, *The Burning Tigris: The Armenian Genocide and America's Response*, New York: Harper-Collins, 2004.

———, *Black Dog of Fate: A Memoir*, New York: Broadway Books, 1998.

Ball, Howard, *Prosecuting War Crimes and Genocide: The 20th Century Experience*, Lawrence: University of Kansas Press, 1999.

Barber, Benjamin, *Jihad vs. McWorld: How Globalism and Tribalism Are Reshaping the World*, New York: Ballantine, 1995.

———, *Fear's Empire: War, Terrorism, and Democracy in an Age of Interdependency*, New York: Norton, 2003.

Bartholomew, Robert E., *Little Green Men, Meowing Nuns, and Head Hunting Panics: A Study of Mass Psychogenic Illness and Social Delusion*, Jefferson, N.C.: McFarland and Co., 2001.

Benjamin, Daniel and Stephen Simon, *The Age of Sacred Terror*, N.Y.: Random House, 2002.

Bercuson, David J. and Holger H. Herwig, *The Destruction of the Bismarck*, Woodstock and New York: The Overlook Press, 2003 [2001].

Berger, Pamela, The *Goddess Obscured: Transformation of the Grain Protectress from Goddess to Saint*, Boston: Beacon Press, 1985.

Berger, Peter L. and Thomas Luckman, *The Social Construction of Reality: A Treatise on the Sociology of Knowledge*, Garden City, N.Y.: Doubleday, 1966.

Berman, Paul, *Terror and Liberalism*, New York: W. W. Norton, 2003.

Berry, Thomas, *The Dream of the Earth*, San Francisco: Sierra Club Books, 1988.

Berry, Wendell, *The Unsettling of America: Culture and Agriculture*, San Francisco: Sierra Club Books, 1977.

Birdwhistle, Ray, *Kinesics and Context: Essays on Body Motion Communication*, Philadelphia: Univ. of Penn. Press, 1970.

Bradley, Raymond T., *Charisma and Social Structure: A Study of Love and Power, Wholeness and Transformation*, New York: Paragon House, 1987.

Bradshaw, Isabel Gay, "Not by Bread Alone: Symbolic Loss, Trauma, and Recovery in Elephant Communities," in *Society and Animals*, vol. 12(2) 2004.

Browning, Christopher, *Ordinary Men: Police Battalion 101 and the Final Solution in Poland*, New York: Harper-Collins, 1993.

Cameron, Sharon, *Writing Nature: Henry Thoreau's Journal*, Chicago: The Univ. Press, 1985. The quote from Thoreau is on 31–32.

Canetti, Elias, *Crowds and Power*, trans. by C. Stewart, New York: Continuum, 1978 [1960].

Capaldi, Nicholas, *The Enlightenment Project in the Analytic Conversation*, Dordrecht and Boston: Kluwer Academic Publishers, 1998 (Crucial for grasping analytic philosophy).

Casey, Edward S., *Getting Back Into Place: Toward a Renewed Understanding of the Place-World*, Bloomington and Indianapolis: Indiana Univ. Press, 1993.

———. *Representing Place*, Minneapolis: Univ. of Minnesota Press, 2002.

Cassirer, Ernst, *The Philosophy of Symbolic Forms*, Vol. 2: *Mythical Thought*, New Haven: Yale U. Press, 1955.

Cesarani, David, *Genocide and Rescue: The Holocaust in Hungary, 1944*, New York: Oxford Univ. Press, 1997.

Chandler, David P., *Brother Number One: A Political Biography of Pol Pot*, revised ed., Boulder, Colo.: Westview Press, 1999.

Chase, Kenneth R., et al., eds., *Must Christianity Be Violent?*, Ada, Mich.: Brazos, 2003.

Chorbajian, Levon, and George Shinnian, *Studies in Comparative Genocide*, New York: St. Martin's Press, 1999.

Chua, Amy, *World on Fire: How Exporting Free Market Breeds Ethnic Hatred and Global Instability*, N.Y.: Doubleday, 2003.

Churchill, Ward, *Fantasies of the Master Race: Literature, Cinema, and the Colonization of American Indians*, San Francisco: City Lights Books, 1998.

Cixous, Hélène, *The Terrible but Unfinished Story of Norodom Sihanouk, King of Cambodia*, trans. by MacCannell, Pike, and Groth, Lincoln: Univ. of Nebraska Press, 1994 [1985].

Clark, Mary, *In Search of Human Nature*, London and New York: Routledge, 2002.

Cobb, John B., Jr., *The Earthist Challenge to Economism: A Theological Criticism of the World Bank*, New York: Palgrave Macmillan, 1998.

Cobb, John B., Jr. and Herman E. Daly, *For the Common Good: Redirecting the Economy Towards Community, the Environment, and a Sustainable Future*, Boston: Beacon Press, 1989.

Cole, Juan, "The Iraqi Shiites: On the history of America's would-be allies," *The Boston Review*, vol. 28, (5) Oct./Nov. 2003.

Connor, John W., "From Ghost Dance to Death Camps: Nazi Germany as a Crisis Cult," *Ethos*, vol. 17 (3), Sept. 1989, 259–88.

"Convention on the Prevention and Punishment of the Crime of Genocide," 78 U.N.T.S. 277, *Resolution 260 (III)A of the General Assembly of the United Nations*, Dec. 9, 1948.

Corlette, J. Angelo, *Race, Racism, and Reparations*, Ithaca: Cornell University Press, 2003.

———, *Terrorism: A Philosophical Analysis*, Dordrecht, Holland: Kluwer, 2004.

Croq, L., "Collective Panics and Age-Old Fears" [French], *Psycholgie Medicale*, vol. 24 (Special Issue 4, 1992).

Dadrian, Vahakn, *The History of the Armenian Genocide*, Providence, R.I.: Berghahn Books, 1995.

Daly, Herman E., "Sustainable Development: Definitions, Principles, Policies," Invited Address, World Bank, April 30, 2002, Washington, DC. (hd22@umail.umd.edu)

Deleuze, Gilles and Felix Guattari, *Anti-Oedipus: Capitalism and Schizophrenia*, trans. by Hurley, Seem, and Lane, Minneapolis: Univ. of Minnesota Press, 1983 [1972].

Deloria, Vine, Jr., *God is Red*, second ed., Golden, Colo.: Fulcrum Pub. Co., 1994.

Dewey, John, *Essays on School and Society*, Carbondale, IL: So. Illinois Univ. Press, 1976 [1899].

———. *Human Nature and Conduct*, New York: The Modern Library, 1930 [1922].

———. *Experience and Nature*, New York: Dover Books, 1958 [1929].

———. *Art as Experience*, New York: G. P. Putnam's Sons, 1980 [1934].

Dobkowski, Michael and Isodor Wallman, *The Coming Age of Scarcity: Preventing Mass Death in the 21st Century*, Syracuse: Syracuse Univ. Press, 1998.

Dostoyevsky, F. M., *The House of the Dead*, trans. by D. McDuff, New York and London: Penguin Books, 1985 [1860].

———. *Demons* (or *The Possessed*), trans. by R. Pevear and L. Volokhonsky, New York: Vintage Books, 1995 [1874].

Douglas, Mary, *Purity and Danger: An Analysis of the Concepts of Pollution and Taboo*, London: Routledge, 1966.

Duerr, Hans Peter, *Dreamtime: Concerning the Boundary Between Wilderness and Civilization*, trans. F. Goodman, New York: Basil Blackwell, 1985 [1978].

Ehrenfeld, David, *The Arrogance of Humanism*, New York: Oxford Univ. Press, 1978.

———. "Forgetting," in *Beginning Again: People and Nature in the New Millennium*, New York: Oxford Univ. Press, 1993.

———. *Swimming Lessons: Staying Afloat in the Age of Technologies*, New York: Oxford Univ. Press, 2002.

Elder, Bruce, *Blood on the Wattle: Massacres and Maltreatment of Aboriginal Australians*, Australia: New Holland Pub. Co., 1988 (reprints 1999, 2000).

Elias, Norbert, *The Civilizing Process: The History of Manners*, trans. E. Jephcott, New York: Urizen Books, 1978 [1939].

———. *The Germans: Power Struggles and the Development of Habitus in the 19th and 20th Centuries*, ed. M. Schroter, trans. E. Dunning and S. Mennell, Cambridge, Eng.: Polity Press, 1996.

Ellis, Marc H., *Unholy Alliance: Religion and Atrocity in Our Time*, Minneapolis: Fortress Press, 1997

Emerson, Ralph Waldo, *R. W. Emerson: Selected Essays*, ed. Ziff, New York: Penguin, 1982. My quotation from "Circles" is from its last lines.

Epstein, Joshua M., John D. Steinbruner, and Miles T. Parker, "Modeling Civil Violence: An Agent Based Computational Approach," Center on Social Change and Economic Dynamics, Working Paper No. 20 (in association with the Brookings Institution), Jan. 2001.

Esposito, John L., *Unholy War: Terror in the Name of Islam*, New York: Oxford Univ. Press, 2002.

Feitlowitz, Marguerite, *A Lexicon of Terror: Argentina and the Legacies of Torture*, New York: Oxford University Press, 1998.

Feldman, Y., "The Problem of Intrauterine Anxiety: Its Consequences and Resolution," *Modern Psychoanalysis*, 6: 183–85, 1981.

Finkielkraut, Alain, *The Future of a Negation: Reflections on the Question of Negation*, trans. M. Kelly, Lincoln: Univ. of Nebraska Press, 1998.

Fletcher, George P., *Romantics at War: Glory and Guilt in the Age of Terrorism*, Princeton: The University Press, 2002.

Förster, Eckart, *Kant's Final Synthesis: An Essay on the Opus Postumum*, Cambridge: Harvard Univ. Press, 2000.

Freud, Sigmund, *Group Psychology and the Analysis of the Ego*, trans. J. Strachey, New York: W. W. Norton, 1959 [1922].

Friedrichsmeyer, Sara, and Susan Zantop, *The Imperialist Imagination: German Colonialism and its Legacy*, Ann Arbor: Univ. of Michigan Press, 1998.

Fromkin, David, *The Peace to End all Peace: The Fall of the Ottoman Empire and the Creation of the Modern Middle East*, New York: Morrow/Avon, 1990. Western imperialist states chop up the Middle East after World War I.

Gallately, Robert, and Ben Kiernan, eds., *The Spectre of Genocide: Mass Murder in Historical Perspective*, Cambridge: University Press, 2003.

Gebser, Jean, *The Ever Present Origin*, trans. Barstad and Mikunas, Athens: Ohio Univ. Press, 1985 [1949].

Gendlin, Eugene, *Experiencing and the Creation of Meaning: A Philosophical and Psychological Approach to the Subjective*, Evanston: Northwestern Univ. Press, 1997 [1962]. A classic.

Ghiglieri, Michael, *The Dark Side of Man: Tracing the Origins of Male Violence*, Reading, Mass.: Perseus Books, 1999.

Goldhagen, Daniel, *Hitler's Willing Executioners: Ordinary Germans and the Holocaust*, New York: Knopf, 1996.

Goodman, Felicitas, *How About Demons?* Bloomington: Indiana Univ. Press, 1988.

Gorsline, Jerry and Freeman House, "Future Primitive," North Pacific Rim Alive. *Planet Drum*, Box 31251, San Francisco, Calif.

Gourevitch, Philip, *We Wish to Inform You that Tomorrow We Will be Killed with our Families: Stories from Rwanda*, New York: Farrar, Straus and Giroux, 1998.

Grant, Ulysses S., *Personal Memoirs*, New York: Dover Books, 1995, numerous reprintings since its publication (Lincoln's and Grant's commitment to preserving the Union at all costs epitomizes the mythic-actual power of the corporate body).

Grim, John A., ed., *Indigenous Traditions and Ecology: The Interbeing of Cosmology and Community*, Cambridge: Harvard Univ. Press, 2001.

Gulden, Tim, "Spatial and Temporal Patterns in Civil Violence: Guatemala 1977–1986," The Brookings Institution Center on Social and Economic Dynamics, Working Paper No. 26, Feb. 2002.

Hall, Edward, *The Silent Language*, Garden City, N.Y.: Doubleday and Co., 1959.

Hanke, Lewis, *Aristotle and the American Indians*, Bloomington: Indiana Univ. Press, 1959.

Haraway, Donna, *Primate Visions: Gender, Race, Nature in the World of Modern Science*, New York: Routledge, 1989.

Heidegger, *Being and Time*, trans. by Macquarrie and Robinson, Oxford: Basil Blackwell, 1967 [1926].

Hertz, Noreena, *The Silent Take Over: Global Capitalism and the Death of Democracy*, New York: The Free Press, 2001.

Hillman, James, *The Soul's Code*, New York: Random House, 1996.

———. *Revisioning Psychology*, New York: Harper and Row, 1977.

Hinton, A. L., *Annihilating Difference: The Anthropology of Genocide*, Berkeley: The Univ. of California Press, 2002.

Ho, Mae-Won, *Genetic Engineering: Dream or Nightmare?*, New York: Continuum Pub. Co., 2000, revised ed. [1998].

Honig, Jay Willem, and Norbert Both, *Srebrenica: Record of a War Crime*, New York: Penguin Books, 1997.

Horowitz, Irving Lewis, *Taking Lives: Genocide and State Power*, 5th ed. revised, New Brunswick N.J.: Transaction Publishers, 2002.

Jacobs, Don T. (Four Arrows), *Primal Awareness: A True Story of Survival, Awakening, and Transformation with the Raramuri Shamans of Mexico*, Rochester, Vt.: Inner Traditions, 1998.

James, William, *The Essential Writings*, ed. B. Wilshire, Albany: SUNY Press, 1984 [1971].

Jardine, Mathew, *East Timor, Genocide in Paradise*, Monroe, Maine: Odion Press, 1999.

Jaspers, Karl, *The Idea of the University*, trans. by Reiche and Vanderschmidt, Boston: Beacon Press, 1959 [1946].

———. *The Atom Bomb and the Future of Man*, trans. E. B. Ashton, Chicago: The Univ. Press, 1961 [1958].

Judson, Katherine B., *Myths and Legends of California and the Old Southwest*, Lincoln: Univ. of Nebraska Press, 1994 [1912].

Jurgensmeyer, Mark, *Terror in the Mind of God: The Global Rise of Religious Violence*, Berkeley: Univ. of California Press, 2003 [2000].

Kamber, Richard, "Historical Sociology and the Reconstruction of the Holocaust," *Social Interaction*, ed. H. Robboy and R. Priest, New York: Worth, 2004.

———, "Goldhagen and Sartre on Eliminationist Antisemitism: False Beliefs and Moral Blame," *Genocide and Holocaust Studies*, Vol. 13, (2) 1999.

Kamm, Henry, *Cambodia: Report from a Stricken Land*, New York: Arcade Publishers, 1998.

Keller, Catherine, *From a Broken Web: Separation, Sexism, and Self*, Boston: Beacon Press, 1986. Also see Whitehead, below.

Keynes, John Maynard, "The General Theory of Employment," *The Quarterly Journal of Economics*, Vol. 51, (2), Feb. 1937, 209–23.

Khalidi, Rashid, *Resurrecting Empire*, Boston: Beacon, 2004.

Kiernan, Ben, *The Pol Pot Regime: Race, Power, and Genocide Under the Khmer Rouge, 1975–79*, New Haven: Yale Univ. Press, 1996.

Kinzer, Stephen, *All the Shaw's Men: An American Coup and the Roots of Middle Eastern Terror*, New York: John Wiley and Son, 2003.

Kirsch, Jonathan, *The Woman Who Laughed at God: The Untold History of the Jewish People*, N.Y.: Penguin Compass, 2001.

Kressel, Neil J., *Mass Hate: The Global Rise of Genocide and Terror*, New York: Plenum Books, 1996.

Kroeber, Alfred L., *Handbook of the Indians of California*, New York: Dover Publications, 1976 [1925].

Kroeber, Theodora, *Ishi in Two Worlds: A Biography of the Last Wild Indian in North America*, Berkeley: Univ. of California Press, 1961.

LaChappelle, Dolores, *Sacred Land, Sacred Sex, Rapture of the Deep*, Silverton, Colo.: Finn Hill Arts, 1988.

———. *D. H. Lawrence: Future Primitive*, Denton, Tex.: Univ. of North Texas Press, 1996.

La Guardia, Anton, *War Without End: Israelis, Palestinians, and the Struggle for a Promised Land*, New York: Thomas Dunne Books, St. Martin's Press, 2002 (American edition) [2001].

Lachs, John, In *Love with Life: Reflections on the Joy of Living and Why We Hate to Die*, Nashville: Vanderbilt Univ. Press, 1998.

Lang, Berel, *Act and the Idea in the Nazi Genocide*, Chicago: Univ. of Chicago Press, 1990.

———. *The Future of the Holocaust*, Ithaca: Cornell Univ. Press, 1999.

Langer, Lawrence L., *Art from the Ashes: A Holocaust Anthology*, New York: Oxford University Press, 1995.

Langer, Susanne, *Mind: An Essay on Human Feeling*, Vol. III, Baltimore: Johns Hopkins Univ. Press, 1982.

Layton, Deborah, *Seductive Poison: A Jonestown Survivor's Story of Life and Death in The People's Temple*, New York: Anchor Books, 1998.

LeDoux, Joseph E., *Synaptic Self: How Our Brains Become Who We Are*, New York: Viking Press, 2002.

Leghausen, Muhammad, *Islam and Religious Pluralism*, London: Al-Hoda, 1999.

Levi, Primo, *Survival in Auschwitz*, New York: Simon and Schuster, 1995 [1958].

———. *The Drowned and the Saved*, New York: Random House, 1989 [1986].

Levinas, Emmanuel, *Collected Philosophical Papers*, Amsterdam: Kluwer Academic Publishers, 1993.

Levine, Mark, and Penny Roberts, *The Massacre in History*, New York: Oxford U. Press, 1999.

Lewis, Bernard, ed., *Islam and the Arab World*, New York: Alfred Knopf, 1976.

———. *What Went Wrong?: Western Impact and Middle Eastern Response*, New York: Oxford Univ. Press, 2002.

———. *The Crisis of Islam: Holy War and Unholy Terror*, New York: Modern Library, 2003. See particularly, "The Marriage of Saudi Power and Wahhabi Teaching."

Lifton, Robert Jay, *The Nazi Doctors: Medical Killing and the Psychology of Genocide*, New York: Basic Books, 1986

Lindqvist, Sven, *Exterminate All the Brutes: One Man's Odyssey into the Heart of Darkness and the Origins of European Genocide*, trans. by J. Tate, New York: The New Press, 1996 [1992].

Linke, Uli, *German Bodies: Race and Representation After Hitler*, New York: Routledge, 1999.

Loewen, James W., *Lies across America: What our Historic Sites get Wrong*, New York: New Press, distributed by Norton, 1999.

Lomborg, Bjorn, *The Skeptical Environmentalist: Measuring the Real State of the World*, Cambridge: University Press, 2001 [1998]. The case for science and technology.

Maimonides (Moses ben Maimon), *The Guide of the Perplexed*, trans. by S. Pines, Chicago: The Univ. Press, 1963.

Mamdani, Mahmood, *When Victims Become Killers*, Princeton: Princeton Univ. Press, 2001. Particularly good on the political-cultural background of Rwandan genocide.

Manning, Richard, *Against the Grain: How Agriculture Has Hijacked Civilization*, New York: Northpoint Press, 2004.

Marglin, Stephen A., *Perdiendo el Contacto: Hacia la Descolonizacion de la Economia*, PRATEC: Lima, Peru, 2000.

Margolis, Joseph, "Terrorism and the New Forms of War," *Metaphilosophy*, Vol. 34, 4, July 2003.

———, "Collective Entities and the Rules of War," read to the International Conference on War and Violence, Kean College, Union, N.J., April 1974.

Marshack, Alexander, *The Roots of Civilization: The Cognitive Beginnings of Man's First Art, Symbol and Notation*, New York: McGraw-Hill, 1972.

Marty, Martin and R. Scott Appleby, *Fundamentalisms Observed*, Chicago: The University Press, 1994 [1991].

Mazis, Glen, A., *Trickster, Magician, and Grieving Man: Reconnecting Men with Earth*, Rochester, VT: Bear and Co., 1994.

————. *Earthbodies: Rediscovering our Planetary Senses*, Albany: SUNY Press, 2002

McCuen, Gary E., *Ecocide and Genocide in the Vanishing Forest: The Rainforests and Native People*, Hudson, Wisconsin: G. E. McCuen Publications, 1993.

McCumber, John, *Time in a Ditch: American Philosophy in the McCarthy Era*, Evanston: Northwestern Univ. Press, 2001.

McDermott, John J., *The Culture of Experience: Philosophical Essays in the American Grain*, New York: N.Y.U. Press, 1976.

————, The Writings of William James: A Comprehensive Edition, New York: 1968. Excellent commentary and James bibliography.

McGary, Howard, and Bill Lawson, *Between Slavery and Freedom: Philosophy and American Slavery*, Bloomington: Indiana Univ. Press, 1992.

Meeker, Joseph W., *The Comedy of Survival: Literary Ecology and the Play Ethic*, 3rd ed., Tucson: The Univ. of Arizona Press, 1997.

————. "Comedy and a Play Ethic," *Whole Terrain*, Antioch New England Graduate School, 2000.

Melville, Herman, "Bartleby," in *Billy Budd and Other Tales*, New York: New American Library, 1961

Menocal, Maria Rosa, *The Ornament of the World: How Muslims, Jews, and Christians Created a Culture of Tolerance in Medieval Spain,* Boston: Little, Brown, & Co., 2002.

Midgley, Mary, *Beast and Man: The Roots of Human Nature*, Ithaca, N.Y.: Cornell Univ. Press, 1978.

Milgram, Stanley, *Obedience to Authority: An Experimental View*, New York: Harper and Row, 1974.

Mitscherlich, A., and Mitscherlich, M., *The Inability to Mourn: Principles of Collective Behavior*, New York: Grove Press, 1975.

Moeller, Susan, *Compassion Fatigue: How the Media Sell Disease, Famine, Death, and War*, New York: Routledge, 1999.

Montejo, Victor, *Testimony: Death of a Guatemalan Village*, trans. V. Perera, Willimantic, Conn.: Curbstone Press, 1987.

Morris, Virginia, and Michael Scharf, *The International Criminal Tribunal for Rwanda*, Irvington-on-Hudson, New York: Transnational Publishers, 1998.

————. *Voices from Exile: Violence and Survival in Modern Maya History*, Norman: Univ. of Oklahoma Press, 1999.

Montmarquet, James A., "Culpable Ignorance and Excuses," *Philosophical Studies* 80 (1995).

Morganthau, Henry, *Ambassador Morganthau's Story* (Armenia), Plandome, N.Y.: New Age Publishers, 1975 [1919].

Nafisi, Azar, *Reading Lolita in Tehran: A Memoir in Books*, New York: Random House, 2004.

Nandi, D. N., et. al., "Contagious Hysteria in a West Bengal Village," *American Journal of Psychotherapy*, vol. 39 (2), April, 1985, 247–52.

Nasr, Seyyed Hossein, *Religion and the Order of Nature*, New York: Oxford Univ. Press, 1996.

———. *The Philosophy of Seyyed Hussein Nasr*, The Library of Living Philosophers, vol. xxvii, ed. by Hahn, Auxier, and Stone, Chicago: Open Court Pub., 2001.

Nath, Vann, trans. M. Nariddh, *A Cambodian Prison Portrait: One Year in the Khmer Rouge's S-21*, Bangkok: White Lotus Press, 1998.

Neske, Donald E., "The Law of the Jungle: The Philosophy of Primo Levi," Rutgers University, Honors Thesis, 1996.

Neville, Robert Cummings, *Recovery of the Measure*, Albany: State Univ. of New York Press, 1989.

Nobakov, Peter, *Native American Testimony: A Chronicle of Indian-White Relations from Prophecy to the Present*, New York: Penguin, 1992 [1991].

Norretranders, Tor, *The User Illusion: Cutting Consciousness Down to Size*, trans. J. Sydenham, New York: Viking, 1998 [1991].

Oliver, Kelly, *Witnessing: Beyond Recognition*, Minneapolis: Univ. of Minnesota Press, 2001.

Parajuli, Pramod, "Ecological Ethnicity in the Making: Developmentalist Hegemonies and Emergent Identities in India," *Identities*, vol. 3, (1–2) 1996.

Perle, Richard and David Frum, *An End to Evil: Strategies for Victory in the War on Terror*, New York: Random House, Dec. 2003. Dazzling simplification.

Petropoulos, Jonathan, *The Faustian Bargain: The Art World in Nazi Germany*, Oxford: The University Press, 2000.

Piaget, Jean, *Play, Dreams, and Imitation in Childhood*, New York: W. W. Norton, 1962.

Posey, Darrell Addison, "Intellectual Property Rights and the Sacred Balance: Some Spiritual Consequences from the Commercialization of Traditional Resources," in Grim, above.

Possuelo, Sydney, quoted in "Hidden Tribes of the Amazon," *National Geographic*, Aug., 2003

Power, Samantha, *"A Probem from Hell": America and the Age of Genocide*, Boulder, CO: Basic Books, 2002.

Pribram, Karl, *Brain and Perception: Holonomy and Structure in Figural Processing*, Hillsdale, N.J.: Lawrence Earlbaum, 1991.

Proctor, Robert N., *Racial Hygiene: Medicine Under the Nazis*, Cambridge: Harvard Univ. Press, 1988. Fig. 34 shows a medical microscope and beside it the view seen through it: among the germs are numerous Stars of David.

Prunier, Gerard, *Rwanda in Zaire: From Genocide to Continental War*, Cambridge, Mass.: Hurst and Co., 2000.

Putnam, Hillary, *Ethics without Ontology*, Cambridge, Mass.: Harvard, 2004.

———, *Renewing Philosophy*, Cambridge: Harvard Univ. Press, 1992.

———. *The Many Faces of Realism*, LaSalle, Ill.: Open Court, 1987.

Qtub, Seyyid, *Islam: the Religion of the Future*, Chicago: Kazi Publishers, 1996.

———. *Social Justice in Islam*, Cambridge, U.K.: Amana Books, 1993.

———. *Milestones*, Indianapolis: American Trust Publications, 1991.

———. *In the Shade of the Qur'on*, Falls Church, Va.: ongoing translation of a commentary on the Qur'on in 30 volumes.

Qur'an, The Holy, Arabic Text with English Translation and Commentary by Maulana Muhammad Ali, Lahore: Ahmadiyya Anjuman Isha'at Islam, 2002 (new edition with fine index).

Rahman, Fazlur, *Islam*, 2nd ed., Chicago: The University Press, 1979 [1966].

———. *Islam and Modernity: Transformation of an Intellectual Tradition*, Chicago: The University Press, 1982.

Ramsland, Katherine, *Engaging the Immediate: Applying Kierkegaard's Theory of Indirect Communication to the Practice of Psychotherapy*, Lewisburg, PA: Bucknell Univ. Press, 1989.

Rasmussen, Derek, "Dissolving Inuit Society Through Education and Money: the Myth of Educating Inuit Out of 'Primitive Childhood' and into Economic Adulthood," *Interculture*, Issue No. 139, Oct. 2000.

Roberts, David, *A Newer World: Kit Carson, John C. Fremont and the Claiming of the American West*, New York: Simon and Schuster, 2000.

Rosenberg, Tina, "The Free Trade Fix," *The New York Times Magazine*, Aug. 18, 2002.

Royce, Josiah, *California: From the Conquest in 1846 to the Second Vigilance Committee in San Francisco*, Santa Barbara and Salt Lake City: The Peregrine Press, 1970 [1886].

Rummel, Rudolph J., *Statistics of Democide: Genocide and Mass Murder Since 1900*, Piscataway, N.J.: Transaction Books, 1998.

Sachs, Wolfgang, ed., *Development Dictionary*, London: Zed Books, 1992.

Sahlins, Marshall, *Stone Age Economics*, Chicago: The Univ. Press, 1972.

Said, Edward, *Humanism and Democratic Criticism*, New York: Columbia, 2004.

———, *Orientalism*, New York: Vintage Books, 1979.

Sartre, Jean-Paul, *Anti-Semite and Jew*, trans. G. Becker, New York: Schocken Books, 1948 [1946].

———. *Nausea*, trans. by L. Alexander, New York: New Directions, 1959.

Schelling, Thomas, *Micromotives and Macrobehavior*, New York: W. W. Norton, 1978.

Schrag, Calvin O., *The Self After Postmodernity*, New Haven and London: Yale University Press, 1997.

———. *God as Otherwise than Being: Toward a Semantics of the Gift*, Evanston: Northwestern Univ. Press, 2002.

Schwartz, Regina, *The Curse of Cain: The Violent Legacy of Monotheism*, Chicago: The University Press, 1997.

Schwartz, Stephen, *The Two Faces of Islam: The House of Sa'ud From Tradition to Terror*, N.Y.: Doubleday, Nov. 2002.

Scott, Stanley J., *Frontiers of Consciousness: Interdisciplinary Studies in American Philosophy and Poetry*, New York: Fordham Univ. Press, 1991. See especially chap. 3 on metaphors for consciousness and the Conclusion.

Sells, Michael A., *The Bridge Betrayed: Religion and Genocide in Bosnia*, Berkeley: University of California Press, 1996.

Sen, Amartya, "Democracy and Its Global Roots: Why Democratization is not the same as Westernization," *The New Republic*, Oct. 6, 2003.

Sereny, Gitta, *Albert Speer: His Battle with Truth*, New York: Vintage Books, 1996 [1995].

Sharma, B. D., *Globalization: The Tribal Encounter*, New Delhi: Har-Ananda Publications, 1996.

Sheldrick, Daphne, "Saving Olly—Now Named Madiba," *The David Sheldrick Trust Newsletter*, Jan. 2004.

Sheldrick, David, "Elephant Emotion," www.sheldrickwildlifetrust.org/html/elephant_emotion.html, 1991.

Shepard, Paul, *The Others: How Animals Made Us Human*, Covelo, CA: Island Press, 1996.

———. *Coming Home to the Pleistocene*, ed. by Florence Shepard, Covelo, Calif.: Island Press, 1998.

Sibomana, Andre, *Hope for Rwanda: Conversations with Laure Guilbert and Herve Deguini*, trans. A. Des Forges, London: Mikukina Nyota Publishers, 1999.

Skaggs, Merrill Maguire, *After the World Broke in Two: The Later Novels of Willa Cather*, Charlottesville and London: Univ. of Virginia Press, 1990.

Small, Gary, et al., "Mass Hysteria Among Student Performers: Social Relationship as Symptom Predictors," *American Journal of Psychiatry*, vol. 148 (9), Sept. 1991, 1200–1205.

Smith, Holly, "Culpable Ignorance," *The Philosophical Review*, 92 (1983).

Smith, Quentin, *The Felt Meanings of the World: A Metaphysics of Feeling*, W. Lafayette, Ind.: Purdue Univ. Press, 1986.

Smith, Roger, E. Markusen, R. J. Lifton, "Professional Ethics and the Denial of the Armenian Genocide," *Journal of Holocaust and Genocide Studies*, Vol. 9, 1, Spring, 1995.

Sophocles, *Oedipus Rex*, in many editions and translations.

Staub, Ervin, *The Roots of Evil: The Origins of Genocide and Other Group Violence*, New York: Cambridge University Press, 1989

Stern, Jessica, *Terror in the Name of God: Why Religious Militants Kill*, New York: ECCO, an imprint of HarperCollins, 2003.

Stiglitz, Joseph E., *Globalization and Its Discontents*, N.Y.: W. W. Norton, 2002.

Theweleit, Klaus, *Male Fantasies: Women, Floods, Bodies, History*, Vol. 1, Minneapolis: University of Minnesota Press, 1987 [1977]

Tinker, George E., *Missionary Conquest: The Gospel and Native American Cultural Genocide*, Minneapolis: Fortress Press, 1993.

Todes, Samuel, *The Body as the Material Subject of the World*, New York: Garland Publishing Co., 1989.

Todorev, Tzvetan, *The Conquest of America*, Cambridge: Harvard U. Press, 1984,

Tolstoy, Leo, *War and Peace*, trans. by L. and A. Maude, New York: Oxford Univ. Press, 1998 [1864].

Toynbee, Arnold J., *Armenian Atrocities: The Murder of a Nation*, New York: Tankian Publishing, 1975 [1917].

Trotsky, Leon, *The Defense of Terrorism*, London: Labor Publishing Co and Allen and Unwin, 1921.

Ulman, R. B., et al.,"The Group Psychology of Mass Madness: Jonestown," *Political Psychology*, vol. 4 (4), Dec. 1983, 637–61.

Vico, Giambattista, *The New Science*, trans. by Bergin and Fisch, Ithaca: Cornell Univ. Press, second revised edition, 1968 [1948]. A great anti-Cartesian and transdisciplinary treatise. [1725, 1730, 1744]

Vidal, Gore, *Burr*, New York: Bantam Books, 1973.

Weine, S. M., *When History is a Nightmare: Lives and Memories of Ethnic Cleansing in Bosnia-Herzegovina*, New Brunswick, N.J.: Rutgers Univ. Press, 1999.

Weldes, Jutta, et. al., *Cultures of Insecurity: States, Communities, and the Production of Danger*, Minneapolis: Univ. of Minn. Press, 1999.

Whitehead, A. N., *Process and Reality: An Essay in Cosmology*, Corrected edition, New York: Free Press, 1978 [1929].

Wiesel, Elie, *The Night Trilogy: Night; Dawn; The Accident*, New York: Farrar, Straus, and Giroux (Noonday Books), 1987.

Williams, Bernard, *Ethics and the Limits of Philosophy*, Cambridge, MA: Harvard Univ. Press, 1986.

Wilshire, Bruce, *Role Playing and Identity: The Limits of Theatre as Metaphor*, Bloomington: Indiana Univ. Press, 1991 [1982].

———. *The Moral Collapse of the University: Professionalism, Purity, Alienation*, Albany: State Univ. of N.Y. Press, 1990.

———. *Wild Hunger: The Primal Roots of Modern Addiction*, Lanham, Md.: Rowman & Littlefield, 1998.

———. *The Primal Roots of American Philosophy: Pragmatism, Phenomenology, Native American Thought*, Univ. Park, PA: Penn State Univ. Press, 2000.

———. *Fashionable Nihilism: A Critique of Analytic Philosophy*, Albany: State Univ. of N.Y. Press, 2002.

———. "Decentered Subjectivity, Transversal Rationality, and Genocide," in *Calvin O. Schrag amd the Task of Philosophy after Postmodernity*, Evanston, Ill.: Northwestern Univ. Press, 2001.

———. "But Where Are the Metaphysics?" review of L. Menand's *The Metaphysical Club*, London: *Times Literary Supplement*, July 26, 2002.

———, "On the Very Idea of a World-View and of Alternative World-Views," in *Indigenous World-Views: First Nation Scholars Challenge Anti-Indian Hegemony*, ed. Don T. Jacobs, Four Arrows, Austin: University of Texas, forthcoming.

———, "Sidney Hook: Teacher and Public Philosopher," in a forthcoming book on Hook, Buffalo: Prometheus Books.

———. "Ways of Knowing," in a volume ed. by David Scott, New York: Peter Lang, forthcoming.

Wilshire, Donna, *Virgin Mother Crone: Myths and Mysteries of the Triple Goddess*, Rochester, Vt.: Inner Traditions, 1994.

———. "The Uses of Image, Myth, and the Female Body, in Re-Visioning Knowledge," in *Gender, Body, Knowledge: Femininst Reconstructions of Knowing and Being*, ed. by A. Jaggar and S. Bordo, New Brunswick, N.J.: Rutgers U. Press, 1989.

Wilshire, Leland Edward, "The Servant City: A New Interpretation of the 'Servant of the Lord' in the Servant Songs of Deutero-Isaiah," *Journal of Biblical Literature*, 94, 1975.

———. "Jerusalem as the 'Servant City' . . . Reflections in the Light of Further Study . . ." in *The Bible in the Light of Cuneiform Literature*, Lewiston, ME: Edwin Mellon, 1990. Studies of corporate individuation in a Biblical context.

Wittgenstein, Ludwig, *Philosophical Investigations*, 3rd ed., ed. Anscombe, Oxford, 2001 [1953].

Zbarsky, Ilya, and Samuel Hutchinson, *Lenin's Embalmers*, trans. by B. Bray, London: The Harvill Press, 1997.

INDEX

ABOUT THE AUTHOR

Bruce Wilshire is Senior Professor of Philosophy at Rutgers University. From 1973 to 1977 he was Executive Secretary of the Society for Phenomenology and Existential Philosophy and in 2002 was given a Herbert Schneider Award for lifetime achievement by the Society for the Advancement of American Philosophy. He has lectured in Australia, South America, and Europe. His dissertation at New York University was written under the direction of William Barrett (with stimulating comments by Sidney Hook) and was published as *William James and Phenomenology: A Study of "The Principles of Psychology,"* a work that illuminated the linkage of American classical philosophies and the phenomenologies of the Continent. He has also published *Role Playing and Identity: The Limits of Theatre as Metaphor* and *The Moral Collapse of the University: Professionalism, Purity, Alienation*. More recently, he has published *Wild Hunger: The Primal Roots of Modern Addiction* and *The Primal Roots of American Philosophy: Pragmatism, Phenomenology, and Native American Thought*. John McDermott, revered elder of American Philosophy, referred to the latter as an "incandescent work" and to the former as a "startling, creative" book. In 2002, Wilshire published *Fashionable Nihilism: A Critique of Analytic Philosophy*, which Library Journal called "Wilshire's headlong assault on establishment formulation of what is to be called philosophy." See also www.brucewilshire.com.